AESTHETICS OF CHANGE

THE GUILFORD FAMILY THERAPY SERIES

ALAN S. GURMAN, EDITOR

AESTHETICS OF CHANGE
Bradford P. Keeney

FAMILY THERAPY IN SCHIZOPHRENIA
William R. McFarlane, Editor

MASTERING RESISTANCE: A PRACTICAL GUIDE TO FAMILY
THERAPY
Carol M. Anderson and Susan Stewart

FAMILY THERAPY AND FAMILY MEDICINE: TOWARD THE
PRIMARY CARE OF FAMILIES
William J. Doherty and Macaran A. Baird

ETHNICITY AND FAMILY THERAPY
Monica McGoldrick, John K. Pearce, and Joseph Giordano, Editors

PATTERNS OF BRIEF FAMILY THERAPY: AN ECOSYSTEMIC
APPROACH
Steve de Shazer

THE FAMILY THERAPY OF DRUG ABUSE AND ADDICTION
M. Duncan Stanton, Thomas C. Todd, and Associates

FROM PSYCHE TO SYSTEM: THE EVOLVING THERAPY OF
CARL WHITAKER
John R. Neill and David P. Kniskern, Editors

NORMAL FAMILY PROCESSES
Froma Walsh, Editor

HELPING COUPLES CHANGE: A SOCIAL LEARNING APPROACH
TO MARITAL THERAPY
Richard B. Stuart

AESTHETICS
OF
CHANGE

BRADFORD P. KEENEY

Foreword by Heinz von Foerster

THE GUILFORD PRESS
New York   London

© 1983 The Guilford Press

A Division of Guilford Publications, Inc.

200 Park Avenue South, New York, N.Y. 10003

Printed in the United States of America

LIBRARY OF CONGRESS CATALOGING IN PUBLICATION DATA

Keeney, Bradford P.
  Aesthetics of change.

  (The Guilford family therapy series)
  Bibliography: p.
  Includes index.
  1. Family psychotherapy.   2. Social systems — Thera-
peutic use.   3. Bateson, Gregory.   I. Title.   II. Series.
[DNLM: 1. Cybernetics.   2. Family therapy.   WM 430.5.F2 K26a]
RC488.5.K43   1983   616.89 '156 '01   82-15720
ISBN 0-89862-043-0

TO GREGORY BATESON

I leave to the various futures (not to all) my garden of forking paths. —*Jorge Luis Borges*

Always the more beautiful answer who asks the more difficult question. —*e.e. cummings*

FOREWORD

One of the least understood things is understanding. Bradford Keeney, as family therapist and cybernetician, understands this, and his enlightening book *Aesthetics of Change* is a tour de force to remedy this deficiency. *Understanding Understanding* could also have been the title for this book whose first business it is to set down an appropriate epistemology, that is, one that includes the observer into his observations, the scientist into his science and, of course, the family therapist into the therapeutic process. Unorthodox? Of course! Otherwise change not only would be undesirable, it also could not be explained. In other words, *Aesthetics of Change* lays the foundation for a change of aesthetics. For this monumental task Keeney assembles lucidly and perceptively one of the most powerful conceptual machinery of today, the latest notions of self-referential logic, circular causality, recursive function theory, and others that are integral to today's version of a cybernetics that can be applied to itself: a cybernetics of cybernetics. Keeney correctly refers to his book as a "handbook of cybernetic ideas relevant to the clinician." He devotes it to his mentor Gregory Bateson. Could Bateson have seen it, I am convinced, the progenitor would delight in his offspring.

Heinz von Foerster

PREFACE

This work probably began when I set out to build a bioelectric ampli-
fier in an eighth-grade science room in the farm town of Smithville,
Missouri. The following year that apparatus was connected to a series
of relays, a mechanical arm, and other paraphernalia in an effort to
create a "myoelectric control prosthetic device." Although these investigations technically failed, they brought me to the world of cybernetics. At that time I was introduced to the work of Wiener, Ashby,
and Pask.

My latter years in high school were characterized by moving from
bioelectric to physiological control devices. Thanks to funding of my
research by a local hospital, I constructed a perfusion apparatus for
studying whole organs of mammals *in vitro*. Investigations in this territory led me to an international science fair, research at Roswell Park
Memorial Institute in Buffalo, and finally to undergraduate work at
the Massachusetts Institute of Technology.

These early experiences were the beginnings of my involvement
with cybernetic thinking and science. I am therefore most grateful to
all those who provided a context for that work to develop — my family,
science teachers, and friends.

I eventually took a leave of absence from science and explored
the world of music and the arts. Subsequently, I experienced the oscillations of what I perceived as a dialectic between art and science. I am
grateful for all those who helped (and endured) me through those tur-
bulent years.

My explorations became directed toward more rewarding expression when I discovered the ideas and person of Gregory Bateson.
It was Bateson who provided the integrative metaphor. This work
would not be possible without his teachings, encouragement, and
friendship.

The field of family therapy has provided a context for cybernetic ideas to germinate and grow. My involvement with that professional community with respect to this work deserves particular notes of appreciation. To my colleagues at the Ackerman Institute for Family Therapy, the Menninger Foundation, the Philadelphia Child Guidance Clinic, and Purdue University, I am especially thankful for all the discussions that helped shape these ideas.

This book was closely associated with the development of the Project for Human Cybernetics with its commitment to the study and application of contemporary cybernetics to psychotherapy and the social sciences. I would like to thank all of those who have supported and contributed to its operation, particularly its cofounder, my colleague Jeffrey Ross.

The task of transforming a collection of ideas into a book was ably assisted by the staff of The Guilford Press. My special thanks go to Seymour Weingarten for his graceful management and to Jean Ford and Jim Blight for their innumerable suggestions that proved invaluable.

I would like to express my deepest appreciation to my companion, Melissa, who served as first critic and advisor. Her ever present involvement inspired this work. And finally, we would like to thank our beast, Mandy, who shared the journey with us.

CONTENTS

AESTHETICS OF CHANGE

1

INTRODUCTION

Everyone writes fiction to some extent, but most
write it without having the slightest idea that they
are doing so. —*Joyce Carol Oates*

In the early 1970's, the anthropologist Carlos Castaneda presented an
experiential account of his journey as an apprentice to a Mexican Indian sorcerer. In *The Teachings of don Juan: A Yaqui Way of Knowledge* (1968), *A Separate Reality: Further Conversations with don
Juan* (1971), *Journey to Ixtlan: The Lessons of don Juan* (1972), and
other volumes, Castaneda recorded how his teacher, don Juan,
helped him completely dismantle and reorganize his sensory experience. As a sorcerer, Castaneda claimed to encounter a world in which
the most basic units of conventional "reality" were irrelevant, a world
where he could fly like a crow, appear at several places at once, talk to
coyotes, and catch spirits.

The stories of Carlos Castaneda were among the most analyzed
cultural events of contemporary times. In addition to being featured
on the cover of *Time* magazine, Castaneda became the focal point of
intellectual circles composed of anthropologists, literary critics, phi-
losophers, psychologists, physicists, and theologians. These scholars
questioned whether Castaneda's works were factual accounts or literary inventions.

During this time I taught a course in a small midwestern college
on Carlos Castaneda. My first lecture presented material that "proved"
the authenticity of Castaneda's anthropological work. I reminded the
class that Castaneda had received an MA and PhD from the Depart-
ment of Anthropology at UCLA for his field research. All skeptical
questions from the students were met with "convincing evidence"
drawn from several books about the Castaneda phenomena (de Mille,

1

1976, 1980; Noel, 1976). The class session ended and stunned faces left the room wondering what it would mean to accept the proposition that such an alternative world of experience could be encountered.

The second session began with an apology: I asked the students to forgive me for playing a trick on them. I announced that the Castaneda books were a hoax and that my aim in the previous session had been to show the class how easily they could be persuaded by "authoritative" statements to accept an irrational story. Other evidence that I now introduced clearly "proved" the falseness of Castaneda's account and suggested that he had borrowed ideas for his invented account from the psilocybic visions of the botanist Robert Gordon Wasson. I added that Castaneda had on numerous occasions admitted making up the whole thing. The class then discussed how they had been tricked into believing in the authenticity of the stories.

A week later I apologized again. This time I confessed to having previously deceived them by presenting a one-sided argument against Castaneda's work in the same way I had earlier argued for its authenticity. I explained that it was necessary to set them up as I had so that we could reach a point where more profound questions could be articulated. Several problematic issues were now apparent: What criteria for distinguishing fact from fiction are inherent in particular contexts? Does the fiction–nonfiction dichotomy itself arise from a particular world view? How real is real?

The value of Castaneda's work is that it challenges any assumption of naive realism we may hold about our world. Consequently, we may be shaken up enough to begin examining how we participate in constructing a world of experience. The idea that we construct an experiential reality is exemplified by an account from Puharich (1962). He gathered a group of scholars and took them to India to observe a fakir. They all watched the fakir throw a rope into the air and climb it—the Indian rope trick. All of the scholars testified to seeing this take place. However, when the film of that event was viewed it was obvious that the fakir had thrown a rope into the air, the rope had fallen to the ground, and they had all stood there in silence. The individuals had constructed a world of experience that the film could not record.

The episode suggests that there is no direct correspondence between an event occurring "outside" of us and our inner experience of it. Indeed, we may further propose that the world as each one of us knows it is entirely constructed by ourselves. I hold that this position of "naive solipsism" is as limited as the view that there is a real world out there which our senses internally model. A more encompassing view is to see each perspective — naive solipsism and naive realism — as only partial glimpses of the whole picture.

Similarly, it is periodically fashionable for a scholar to claim that he has cornered truth. When the academic climate changes, he may then piously argue that there is no such thing as truth. I maintain that any position, perspective, conceptual frame of reference, or idea is a partial embodiment of a whole we can never completely grasp. The truth may snare us at times, but we can never snare truth.

Therefore, I begin this book with a disclaimer: I do not believe that anyone *fully* knows or can *ever* fully know the processes that account for personal and social change inside or outside of therapy. Rather, I see social science's attempts to understand change as providing innumerable partial models of therapeutic process. More often than not, these partial models are sorted into either/or dualities in which only one side of a distinction is held to be true, correct, or more useful. Battles between individual and family orientations toward treatment, experiential and strategic interventions, lineal and recursive epistemologies, theory and practice, aesthetic and pragmatic perspectives, and so on, arise from this manner of drawing distinctions. My intention is to demonstrate that many of the distinctions therapists argue about are actually the two sides of a complementary relationship. In the most general sense, my purpose is to uncover patterns that connect both sides of these distinctions. The thread that weaves my ideas together is one that attempts to bridge dichotomies too long considered opposites.

I began this book with the example of Carlos Castaneda as a timely reminder of how easy it is to get caught in an either/or trap. We need not limit ourselves to asking "Do we make it all up?" or "Are our descriptions of experience real?" The more fascinating and comprehensive question is "How do we converge different perspectives, whether they be fact and fiction, formal understanding and practical action, or problem and cure?"

It is interesting to note that at the same time Castaneda's stories were being published, another figure was becoming more familiar and respected in the world of psychotherapy. This therapist happened to live in the same geographical territory where Castenada met his mentor, a coincidence that tempted some clinicians to jest that don Juan was actually this master therapist—Milton H. Erickson. An example of Erickson's style follows:

> Milton was working with an alcoholic. The guy was an ace in World War I and he comes in with an album of photographs of himself, newspaper clippings, and he's a lush. He wants to be cured of being a lush. He shows this book to Milton. Milton picks it up and throws it in the wastepaper basket. "It's nothing to do with you, that." Then after various exchanges, Milton asks him how he always starts on a binge. "Well, I set up two boiler-makers, and I drink one and wash it down with a beer, and I drink the other and I wash it down with a beer, and then I'm off." "Okay," says Milton, "you will leave this office, you will proceed to the nearest bar, you will order two boiler-makers, you will finish one off and as you do so you will say, 'Here's to that bastard Milton Erickson, may he choke on his own spit.' When you pick up the other one you will say, 'Here's to that bastard Milton Erickson, may he rot in hell.' Good night." (cited in Bateson & Brown, 1975, p. 33)

What stands out in Milton Erickson's work is the uncanny way he was able to enter the experiential world of his client and alter that world in a way that evaporated symptomology and helped the client access his own resources. In the example cited, Erickson placed the man's drinking within the contextual frame of a "bastard" who took his album and threw it in a wastepaper basket. The man could not take a drink without getting angry at "that bastard Milton Erickson." This anger gave the man a new resource to help manage his problematic behavior.

Like Carlos Castaneda, Milton Erickson has also helped jar many therapists from any assumption of naive realism. His work indicates that therapists can play an active part in the reconstruction of a client's world of experience. As don Juan helped to alter Castaneda's reality, Milton Erickson has altered innumerable therapeutic realities. The fact that the popularity of Carlos Castaneda and Milton Erickson appeared at roughly the same time may be no accident. Throughout the sciences and humanities a quiet revolution has been taking place that promises to transform the way we think about human experience.

In the mental health professions, family therapy has often been closely associated with this zeitgeist of ideas and action. The term "family therapy," however, may be somewhat misleading since it refers to such a diverse body of therapeutic methods and theories. What

I mean by "family therapy" are those approaches to human dilemmas that are most directly connected to a formal consideration of human relationship systems. While this orientation is often described as being theoretically rooted in cybernetics, ecology, and systems theory, the figures of don Juan and Milton Erickson are examples of its expression in strategic action.

Although the works of Castaneda and Erickson suggest that our world of experience is socially constructed, or at least partially so, neither provides a formal map or language for clearly articulating this position. Gregory Bateson's ideas provide direction toward such a frame of reference and language. His work attempts to formally capture a perspective exemplified by the work and writings of Castaneda, Erickson, and many family therapists, among others.

Bateson was an unusual man for our time. Rollo May (1976) described him thus:

> Gregory Bateson reminds me of the classical philosophers . . . in Bateson we see an example of the classical breadth along with extraordinary penetration . . . Gregory Bateson stands at midpoint between the truths elucidated by American science and those which spring from the wisdom of the East. (pp. 49–50)

Bateson's greatest talent was his possession of keen observational skills. R. D. Laing (cited in Evans, 1976) claimed that Gregory Bateson

> had the most distinctive perceptual capacities of anyone I've met, and to see someone like him observing other human beings, to be with someone who is taking in more than usual and putting out more than usual, to get the feel of just what they're picking up and seeing, and the edge they have on even the quickest of their contemporaries . . . was a great consolation about life. (p. 75)

Bateson would sometimes admit he was pleased he had an "outstanding nose." What he meant was that he could readily distinguish nonsense from brilliance, a skill too often absent in the human sciences. The value of Bateson's "nose" was that it uncovered and connected a wide variety of ideas and observations that provide a foundation for an alternative human science. Stephen Toulmin (cited in Wilder-Mott & Weakland, 1981), Professor of Social Thought and Philosophy at The University of Chicago, states that "what makes Gregory Bateson's work so significant is the fact that he has acted as a prophet of 'postmodern' science" who "saw the first step toward the necessary philosophical reorientation of the human sciences as calling for a new epistemology" (p. 365).

A careful reading[1] of Bateson's work clearly indicates that he considered *cybernetics* to be the appropriate epistemological foundation and language for talking about personal and social change. Thus, understanding Bateson requires understanding cybernetics, an often difficult task since social science (including family therapy) is corrupted with many misinterpretations of this discipline. Cybernetics, most simply defined, is part of a general science of pattern and organization. To adopt a cybernetic view is to enter a radically different world of description. To enter that world, a clinician needs a systematic delineation of cybernetic thinking. This book represents an effort to clarify cybernetic concepts and facilitate their application to therapy. It is my hope that given this handbook of cybernetic ideas relevant to clinicians, the field of family therapy may become reconnected to a more illuminating epistemological tradition.

A word of caution: This book is not a manual on how to do therapy. What follows has more to do with developing an epistemology and formal language for family therapy. Its purpose is to improve the clinician's understanding of the context in which he is a participating member. At the same time, it is important to realize that an understanding of cybernetic epistemology may completely alter one's habits of action—inside and outside therapy.

Therapists are often akin to a chef whose interests are more connected with cookbooks than theories of food science. Extending this analogy, although a chef may argue that formal theories of food science are irrelevant to his cooking, his choice of recipe and culinary action reflect particular premises regarding nutrition as well as rules governing cookery. In this sense practical action always embodies formal ideas.

A clinician who fails to explicitly recognize the premises underlying his work may be less effective because of his deficiency in understanding. More significantly, a clinician may blindly strip a theoretical map to its pragmatic implications, focusing on its applicability but ignoring its broader explanatory value. Bateson (1978) warns of this exploitation:

1. Bateson is sometimes regarded as difficult to read. The obstacle is one of form rather than content. The misconception that his works are flights into abstraction or ungrounded speculation arise from his use of alternative forms of description.

Theory is becoming available to action-oriented people, whose first impulse is . . . "Take it to the wards and try it. Don't waste years trying to understand the theory. Just use whatever hunches seem to follow from it." Such people are likely to be frustrated and their patients hurt. . . . Theory is not just another gadget which can be used without understanding. (p. 237)

Ideally, clinicians should move beyond the traditional dichotomy between clinical theory and practice and come to grips with both realms of therapy. To develop a perspective that encompasses these apparent opposites requires that we attend to epistemology. Following Bateson, I use the term epistemology to indicate the basic premises underlying action and cognition. Examination of our epistemological assumptions will enable us to more fully understand how a clinician perceives, thinks, and acts in the course of therapy.

Furthermore, the deepest order of change that human beings are capable of demonstrating is epistemological change. A change in epistemology means transforming one's way of experiencing the world. Don Juan speaks of "stopping the internal dialogue" as a prerequisite for experiencing an alternative epistemology:

The first act of a teacher is to introduce the idea that the world we think we see is only a view, a description of the world. Every effort of a teacher is geared to prove this point to his apprentice. But accepting it seems to be one of the hardest things one can do; we are complacently caught in our particular view of the world, which compels us to feel and act as if we know everything about the world. A teacher, from the very first act he performs, aims at stopping that view. Sorcerers call it stopping the internal dialogue, and they are convinced that it is the single most important technique that an apprentice can learn. (Castaneda, 1974, p. 231)

The dilemma of master and pupil as well as therapist and client is that these orders of learning or change can seldom be accomplished in a straightforward way. Although many schools of therapy maintain that conscious insight, understanding, and direct logical persuasion are required tools of change, Bateson, don Juan, and Erickson often proceeded differently. Their methods of inducing change involved such techniques as encouraging problem behavior, amplifying deviations, suggesting a relapse, emphasizing the positive aspects of a symptom, and introducing confusion.

Don Juan (Castaneda, 1974) points out that "sorcerers are convinced that all of us are a bunch of nincompoops" who "can never relinquish our crummy control voluntarily, thus we have to be tricked" (p. 234). He adds that "tricking" is "meant to distract your attention, or to trap it as the case required" (p. 234). For example, don Juan would instruct Castaneda to stalk toward a mountain in a prescribed manner: He was told to curl his fingers, draw attention to his arms, and then focus his eyes on the horizon in order to experience being a warrior. Don Juan later explained that the specific instructions were actually irrelevant and simply served to distract Castaneda's reason and habitual routines. In a similar fashion, Milton Erickson would often give a client elaborate assignments that only served to disrupt the organization of his symptomatic context.

Both don Juan and Erickson also made use of introducing confusion to bring about change. Castaneda (1974) suggests that the jump from one world of experience to another requires an ample supply of illogical and confusing experience—don Juan's "tricking." Erickson explains that confusion is a way of distracting a client's consciousness so that his unconscious may be allowed to encounter a solution.

Cybernetics can be described as a formal way of discussing these processes and methods of change. This perspective views a symptom as part of the organizational logic of its ecology. Therapists who adopt such a view choose to speak the language of a client's particular form of symptomatic communication. The important point, sometimes obscured, is that symptomatic communication always provides the direction for therapeutic change. In a sense, all a therapist does is provide a context in which a client can utilize his own resources to achieve the necessary change(s). As Milton Erickson put it (cited in Zieg, 1980), "I don't think the therapist does anything except provide the opportunity to think about your problem in a favorable climate."

One aim of this book is to demonstrate how cybernetics provides an aesthetic understanding of change, a type of respect, wonder, and appreciation of natural systems often overlooked by the various fields of psychotherapy, in Bateson's view. He objected to clinicians who implemented new techniques and methods without regard to aesthetics.

My position is to avoid any type of either/or dichotomy between aesthetics and pragmatics; I prefer to view aesthetics as a contextual frame for practical action. A singular emphasis upon pragmatics potentially leads to an ecological decontextualization of therapy where one's bag of tricks, cures, and problem-solving procedures is too easily disconnected from the more encompassing aesthetic patterns of ecology. Similarly, an aesthetics of therapy without appropriate regard for pragmatic technique may lead to free-associative nonsense.

Therefore, the task of this book is to present a more comprehensive framework for understanding change, where the aesthetics of change can be seen as a way of recontextualizing the pragmatics of therapy. Throughout the text illustrations will be drawn from Carlos Castaneda as well as Milton Erickson, Carl Whitaker, and other family therapists. In a more historical sense, my work is rooted in the contemporary revolution in formal thinking embodied by the field of cybernetics. What I propose stands on the ancestral shoulders of Ashby, Bateson, McCulloch, and Wiener, among others, and is connected to the recent contributions of Maturana, Varela, and von Foerster.

To enter the world of cybernetic thought it is first necessary to more clearly understand what is meant by "epistemology." Without an adequate understanding of this term, it is too easy to make the mistake of interpreting cybernetics as simply another theoretical map rather than a radically different world view. Chapter 2 provides a sketch of the fundamentals of epistemology.

Chapter 3 defines "cybernetic epistemology." The main principles of cybernetic thought are presented and their historical development discussed. This chapter demonstrates how many of the major insights of cybernetics arose from biology and the human sciences and explains why cybernetics is the appropriate science for studying mental and living process. In addition, the chapter will show how cybernetics, as an evolving, self-corrective science, has altered some of its early reductionistic trends and advanced its capacity to explain complex phenomena. This latter consideration will lead to an examination of what is called cybernetics of cybernetics.

Chapters 2 and 3 provide the epistemological tools necessary to think cybernetically about family therapy and change. These chapters may be the most difficult and should be approached as though they were an introduction to a foreign language. An adequate understanding of these chapters will enable one to deal with therapy as a cybernetician.

The remaining chapters use these ideas to indicate how cybernetic patterns in family therapy may be identified. Chapter 4 provides a general cybernetic framing of the major distinctions of therapy including system, pathology, health, therapist, and ecology. These examples illustrate how to construct a cybernetic description.

Change, the central issue of family therapy, is the subject of Chapter 5. It is here that cybernetics is revealed as a way of conceptualizing the organization of change and stability: Cybernetics provides a complementary view of change and stability in which it is impossible to consider one without the other. The discussion of change in this chapter will also begin to unravel what actually goes on in the course of therapy.

The final chapter, entitled "An Aesthetic Base for Family Therapy," demonstrates an aesthetic approach to contextualizing our thinking about action in therapy. The pathologies of conscious purpose and manipulation unaided by aesthetic principles are illuminated and the relation of technique, practice, and art are discussed.

The reader may discover that each chapter is in fact a different way of saying the same thing. Each road leads to an epistemology appropriate for the aesthetics of change. By comparing the chapters and integrating them, the landscape of cybernetic epistemology may be re-cognized.

If what follows helps the reader understand how cybernetic epistemology is radically different from our habitual ways of knowing, then it is more probable that the world of therapy will be transformed. Readers with that insight may proceed to see cybernetic epistemology as a way of (re)discovering the biological nature of ourselves, our interpersonal relations, and our planet. Such an understanding is absolutely critical for the time and place in which we now find ourselves: Armaments continue to be stockpiled, populations still rival territory, man-made poisons reside in our offspring, and education frequently breeds trivial knowledge. The aesthetic wisdom necessary to save ourselves and our planet is too often discarded for pragmatic solutions engendered by greed and biological misunderstanding. This situation leads to one conclusion: Much of the culture in which we live is insane. Some of us even agree with Bateson (1972) that, at best, "perhaps we have an even chance of getting through the next 20 years with no disaster more serious than the mere destruction of a nation or group of nations" (p. 487).

Yet hope still remains. The poets remind us that what is required is an understanding of our own nature. Cybernetic epistemology provides such a path. In T. S. Eliot's words, this awareness requires

> A condition of complete simplicity
> (Costing not less than everything)
> And all shall be well. . . . (1943/1973, p. 59)

Being a therapist requires nothing less.

2

FUNDAMENTALS OF EPISTEMOLOGY

We draw the boundaries, *we* shuffle the cards, *we* make the distinctions. —*James Keys*

ALTERNATIVE EPISTEMOLOGIES

It may be a mistake to consider the history of psychotherapy as embodying numerous autonomous paradigms such as psychoanalysis, behaviorism, and humanistic psychology. Gregory Bateson argued that since humanistic psychology is "materialistic," it does not differ from the basic premises of behaviorism and psychoanalysis. This is another way of saying that all these various approaches to psychology belong to the same world view, that is, one postulating a material world of physical objects obeying the laws of force and energy. The implication of this criticism has been acknowledged by Rollo May (1976):

> Bateson is obviously talking on a deeper level than we generally consider. He holds that we tend unconsciously to assume that material is all there is, which is shown in our use of the term "third force." This force, like energy, is a term that is applicable to mechanics and engineering but is not applicable to human beings. . . . Bateson says this is what makes us so defensive with respect to behaviorists. In the use of terms like "force" we are resurrecting an old battle, a struggle which dates back to the 17th century. Our continuing this old struggle makes us actually the conservatives. (p. 47)

The level at which Bateson critized psychology is the fundamental one he termed "epistemology." More basic than any particular theory, epistemology is concerned with the rules of operation that govern cognition. Epistemology, by definition, attempts to specify "how particular organisms or aggregates of organisms *know, think* and *decide*" (Bateson, 1979a, p. 228).

In the context of philosophy, epistemology traditionally refers to a set of analytical and critical techniques that defines boundaries for the processes of knowing. Outside the philosopher's den, one of the places epistemology can be found is in the experimental discipline of biology, in the work of contemporary scientists such as McCulloch, Lettvin, Maturana, Varela, and von Foerster. The role of this work, called "experimental epistemology"[1] by McCulloch (1965), in providing discoveries basic to an understanding of cybernetic epistemology will be discussed later.

Beyond the neurophysiologist's lab, epistemological concerns are present in the broader contexts of natural history. In the sociocultural domain, epistemology becomes a study of how people or systems of people know things and how they think they know things. From this perspective, "anthropology becomes a critical study of epistemology" (Bateson, 1976d). The study of epistemology, in more general terms, becomes a way of recognizing how people come to construct and maintain their habits of cognition.

It is impossible for one to not have an epistemology. Bateson (1977) elaborates this point: "You cannot claim to have no epistemology. Those who so claim have nothing but a bad epistemology" (p. 147). I would add, however, that the claim to have no epistemology is "bad" only if the individual uses such a claim to avoid responsibility for his ideas, perceptions, and decisions. Having no conscious awareness of one's epistemology is not necessarily bad, although such unawareness may be risky. I would prefer to say that the claim to have no epistemology reveals an epistemology that does not include a conscious awareness of itself.

1. McCulloch (1965) has placed experimental epistemology in the history of science as follows: "Just as chemistry got off to a bad start in the rigid doctrine of alchemy and was saved only by the 'puffers,' so psychology was hindered by doctrinaire epistemology and saved only by the biologists. To make psychology into experimental epistemology is to attempt to understand the embodiment of mind" (p. 389). (A "puffer" is an operator of a small steam engine, often used in small cargo ships or for hauling mine cars.) McCulloch's point is that the development of psychology into a science requires that we study systems of formal relations that can be said to embody mind. As we will later discover, mind is embodied by a wide diversity of phenomena including brains, conversations, families, and entire ecosystems.

Further, epistemological premises may be critically examined with regard to their particular ecological consequences. Pathology, for example, is presently characterized by some premises implicit in man's[2] relationship with his environment. The premise that "more is better," for instance, has often led to ecological chaos in a wide variety of geophysical, biological, and economic domains. It is critical (even to the extent of survival) that the epistemological bases underlying patterns of action and perception be made explicit and understood. Auerswald (1973), in addressing family therapy (and, implicitly, mankind), conveys a sense of urgency when he suggests that "we seem hell-bent on a course of self-destruction" and that "what is called for is a whole new epistemology" (p. 696).

Previous discussions of epistemology in the context of family therapy have sometimes made the distinction between lineal[3] and nonlineal (also called systemic, ecological, ecosystemic, circular, recursive, or cybernetic) forms of epistemology. Traditional lineal epistemology is exemplified by psychiatric nomenclature and the classical medical model of psychopathology. It is atomistic, reductionistic, and anticontextual and follows an analytical logic concerned with combinations of discrete elements. Therapists who view their work as an attempt to correct, dissect, or exorcise bad, sick, or mad elements of their clients operate within a lineal epistemology. Biochemical, surgical, and electrical approaches to therapy most dramatically illustrate this approach.

Nonlineal epistemology emphasizes ecology, relationship, and whole systems. In contrast to lineal epistemology, it is attuned to interrelation, complexity, and context. This alternative epistemology is manifested by therapists who view their relationship with clients as part of the process of change, learning, and evolution.

Therapists sometimes claim to be following an alternative, nonlineal epistemology because they are treating whole families, using "therapeutic paradox," working as a "systemic team," thinking in terms of "ecological metaphors," or following an "interactional view."

2. Throughout this work, "man" should be regarded as a category of animal that includes both sexes, female and male.

3. Following Bateson (1979a), I will use the term "lineal" rather than "linear" to refer to a sequence of ideas or propositions that does not circle back to a starting point. The latter term, "linear," is reserved for discussions of geometry.

These actions alone, however, are not necessarily connected to an alternative, nonlineal epistemology. Epistemology is more fundamental than the action and ideas most clinicians describe. One simply cannot clearly describe an alternative epistemology in conventional terms any more than a sorcerer can describe an alternative world of experience to an uninitiated outsider.

The roadblock for the reader is that no school of therapy, sequence of action, or collection of metaphors can be provided to concretely illustrate an alternative epistemology. What one sees will always be shaped by the world in which one is presently operating. To view an alternative world requires being in that world. Thus, the most this text can do is prescribe various paths for encountering an alternative epistemology and then warn of the possibility that each of these paths may be twisted and disorted by the world view of which one is already part.

Thus, a therapist can choose to operate within the framework of a lineal or nonlineal epistemology.[4] This choice leads to the construction, maintenance, and experience of a particular world view (or paradigm). Following Auerswald (1973), we can categorize family therapists into three classes according to their epistemological points of view: (1) those who follow a traditional lineal epistemology, (2) those who follow a nonlineal epistemology, and (3) those who are in transition from the former to the latter.

Insofar as lineal and nonlineal therapists experience different worlds, the "world of transition" is a fuzzy one. Being in transition from one epistemology to another means moving toward seeing a world that, by definition, is impossible to grasp in the world to which one is traditionally accustomed. For example, although astronomers have proven that the earth rotates, we continue to perceive "sunset" and "sunrise." Moving from conceptual understanding to habitual, common sense perception of a rotating planet represents a paradigmatic transition. Seeing a family organism rather than a collection of individuals is comparable.

---

4. I will later demonstrate that this distinction should not be taken as an either/or dichotomy, but as a complementary pattern. It is impossible to be either lineal or nonlineal — we embody both. The more relevant issue is how we operate with this yin-yang distinction. Drawing a distinction here in order to understand each half of it will facilitate understanding of the total pattern later.

It is unlikely that anyone has fully realized a nonlineal epistemology. Bateson (1972) has admitted the difficulty of this nevertheless imperative task:

> If I am right, the whole of our thinking about what we are and what other people are has got to be restructured. This is not funny, and I do not know how long we have to do it. If we continue to operate on the premises that were fashionable in the precybernetic era, and which were especially underlined and strengthened during the Industrial Revolution, which seemed to validate the Darwinian unit of survival, we may have twenty or thirty years before the logical reductio ad absurdum of our old positions destroys us. . . . The most important task today is, perhaps, to learn to think in the new way. Let me say that *I* don't know how to think that way. Intellectually, I can stand here and give you a reasoned exposition of this matter; but if I am cutting down a tree, I still think "Gregory Bateson" is cutting down the tree. *I* am cutting down the tree. "Myself" is still to me an excessively concrete object. (p. 462)

We are, therefore, caught in a state of transition. The sense of being caught between two "realities" is evoked by lines from Matthew Arnold's "Stanzas from the Grande Chartreuse":

> Wandering between two worlds, one dead,
> The other powerless to be born. (1855/1973, p. 608)

There is even confusion over the appropriate name of the alternative paradigm. "Ecological epistemology" (Auerswald, 1973), "general systems paradigm" (Bloch, 1980), and "ecosystemic epistemology" (Keeney, 1979a)[5] have all been suggested as names in the field of family therapy. I now propose that "cybernetic epistemology" be adopted as the appropriate name. This term connects us to the intellectual tradition including Ashby, Bateson, McCulloch, Maturana, Varela, von Foerster, and Wiener, among others. Bateson (1972) maintained: "Cybernetics is the biggest bite out of the fruit of the Tree of Knowledge that mankind has taken in the last 2000 years" (p. 476). The field of cybernetics has become the major context for studying epistemological issues. In particular, the Biological Computer

---

5. Ecosystemic epistemology was defined as the epistemological framework representing cybernetics, ecology, and system theory. The term itself was first proposed by the communication theorists Wilden and Wilson (1976) and then used in the field of family therapy by Keeney (1979a).

Laboratory, founded by Heinz von Foerster,[6] has been a refuge and resource center for the development of many of the major innovations in contemporary cybernetic epistemology.

Since what we think, say, and do is determined by our particular epistemology, to understand cybernetic epistemology one must speak and hear its language. Castaneda (1968) makes a similar point:

> To any beginner, Indian or non-Indian, the knowledge of sorcery was rendered incomprehensible by the outlandish characteristics of the phenomena he experienced. Personally, as a Western man, I found these characteristics so bizarre that it was virtually impossible to explain them in terms of my own everyday life, and I was forced to the conclusion that any attempt to classify my field data in my own terms would be futile.
>
> Thus it became obvious to me that don Juan's knowledge had to be examined in terms of how he himself understood it; only in such terms could it be made evident and convincing. (pp. 8–9)

For Castaneda to explain don Juan's way of knowing in any symbolic system other than a sorcerer's language would be to engage in futility. Similarly, to know cybernetics requires using cybernetic forms of description. The challenge here is to specify the basic premises of cybernetic epistemology. Before doing so, a discussion of some fundamentals of epistemology is necessary in order to construct a context for articulating cybernetic epistemology.

It should be pointed out that we have been using the term epistemology in a double sense — to indicate *how* one thinks, perceives, and decides, and *what* one thinks, perceives, and decides. We will now begin to see that *how* one knows is inseparable from *what* one knows. In addition we will discover that all individuals share the fundamental epistemological operation of drawing distinctions. However, although all human beings begin with the same epistemological operation, we

6. Heinz von Foerster, who is related to the Wittgenstein family, was formally trained as a physicist, and has long been fascinated with the relation between the observer and the observed. With the encouragement of Viktor Frankl he published a quantum mechanical theory of physiological memory. After studying with McCulloch and Rosenblueth he established the Biological Computer Laboratory (BCL) at the University of Illinois at Urbana–Champaign, which has focused on the "study of computational principles in living organisms" (von Foerster, 1964, p. 330). The BCL has been the major terminal for cyberneticians ever since its founding, with its residents having included Ashby, Günther, Löfgren, Maturana, Pask, and Varela, among others.

may still develop different epistemologies. For instance, the distinction between lineal and cybernetic epistemology does not in itself necessarily circumscribe alternative world views. How we handle this distinction, however, begins to disclose a different order of difference.

LAWS OF FORM

The most basic act of epistemology is the creation of a difference. It is only by distinguishing one pattern from another that we are able to know our world. The distinctions between therapist and client, intervention and symptom, solution and problem, for example, enable us to discern the clinical world. Although this idea may seem intuitively obvious, it was only recently formalized in logic and mathematics, an effort largely begun by G. Spencer-Brown and acknowledged as a major foundation for cybernetic thinking.

Draw a Distinction!

In the beginning G. Spencer-Brown wrote: "Draw a distinction!" This basic command, whether obeyed consciously or unconsciously, is the starting point for any action, decision, perception, thought, description, theory, and epistemology. In his classic book, *Laws of Form,*[7] Spencer-Brown (1973) states "that a universe comes into being when a space is severed or taken apart" and that "the boundaries can be drawn anywhere we please" (p. v); thus, an infinitude of universes are possible from the primordial creative act of drawing distinctions.

Consider the illustration of a man hitting a baseball with a bat.

---

7. The enthusiasm surrounding *Laws of Form* has been monumental. In the setting of philosophy, Watts (cited in Spencer-Brown, 1973) called it "the most wonderful contribution to Western philosophy since Wittgenstein's *Tractatus.*" When Stewart Brand of *The Whole Earth Catalog* asked John Lilly to review the book, Lilly (Lilly & Lilly, 1976) suggested that he "knew only one person in the U.S., possibly the world, who was capable of reviewing this book justly and in depth" (p. 177). That person was Heinz von Foerster. Von Foerster saw Spencer-Brown as similar to Ludwig Wittgenstein and Carlos Castaneda's teacher, don Juan, in that all three shared "a state of melancholy that befalls those who know that they know" (cited in Lilly & Lilly, 1976, p. 179).

Part of the intrigue surrounding Spencer-Brown is that he has created a mysterious ambience for himself. For example, he is also James Keys (1972), the novelist,

The conventional way of understanding that scenario is to see a separate creature called a "man" using a clearly demarcated physical object called a "bat" to unilaterally hit another separate chunk of matter called a "ball." If we see the man–bat–ball scenario as a product of our drawing distinctions, then we are free to order the sequence of events in any way we choose. We might even argue that balls cause bats to be hit. The point is that a world can be discerned in an infinitude of ways depending on the distinctions one establishes.

Drawing a circle through the man, bat, and ball reveals a different pattern of organization. From this perspective, seeing the ball as causing the bat to move the man's arms is as logical as the typical occidental sequencing in which a man hits a ball with a bat. Yet neither of these views is complete: A focus on the circular or recursive organization of these events, rather than on any particular lineal sequence, is the more complete view of cybernetics.

Like the man, bat, and ball a therapist, intervention, and client can also be shuffled, epistemologically speaking. The traditional view is that a therapist treats a client through a given intervention. However, it may be useful for a therapist to imagine a client's behavior as an intervention. His interventions, so to speak, attempt to provoke the therapist to come up with a useful directive or solution. In this "reverse view" the therapist's behavior is problematic when he fails to help the client. Treatment is successful when the client provokes the therapist to say or prescribe the appropriate action.

Both of these perspectives are lineal and, hence, incomplete. One could view the therapeutic situation as being more complexly organized: The behaviors of client and therapist could be seen as "interventions" that attempt to alter, modify, transform, or change the

---

whose ideas include a mystical view on "the five levels of eternity." In addition, he and his "brother" have patents in the British Patent Office, and in *Laws of Form* he mentions how work with his "brother" led to the new calculus. Is there a brother outside of G. Spencer-Brown's imagination?

Spencer-Brown manages to keep his territory obscure, as the following story by Bateson (cited in Keeney, 1977) demonstrates:

> I talked to von Foerster the morning before I met Brown to see if I was getting it right. I said these upside down L-shaped symbols of this fellow are some sort of negative. . . . He said, "Yes, you've got it Gregory." At that moment Brown came into the room and Heinz turned to Brown and said, "Gregory has got it — those things are sort of negatives." And Brown said, "They are not!" (p. 14)

behavior of the other individual in a way that will solve his problem. In other words, clients are treating therapists at the same time therapists treat clients. This framing of therapy is an example of cybernetics, which views the behavior of both client and therapist as circularly or recursively connected. In such an organization of events, any behavior is simultaneously a cause and effect (or intervention and problem) in relation to all other behaviors in that context. The next chapter will provide a more detailed definition of this cybernetic pattern.

There is no end to the variety of distinctions within therapy that one can draw. Drawing distinctions, Varela (1979) points out, enables us to create "physical boundaries, functional groupings, conceptual categorization, and so on, in an infinitely variegated museum of possible distinctions" (p. 107). Thus, the epistemological knife of discrimination, called an "operator" in Spencer-Brown's system (and a "Spencer-Brown transistorized power razor" by von Foerster) is a way of constructing and knowing a world of experience. The historic contribution of family therapy can now be seen as having provided a different way of prescribing distinctions: drawing the boundary of a symptom around a family rather than an individual. This distinction led to a multitude of alternative therapeutic styles and practices.

One way of understanding Spencer-Brown's concept of drawing distinctions is to look at cookery and music. Here we may observe that the written records associated with them (the recipes and transcribed notes, respectively) are actually a chain of commands which if obeyed result in a re-creation of the originator's experience. By following a recipe, for example, you may end up with the multisensory experience of encountering a soufflé. Spencer-Brown (1973) extends this understanding to suggest that mathematics and *all* forms of experience arise from sets of commands. The implication here is that description is secondary to the act of having obeyed a command, injunction, or prescription for drawing a distinction. Thus a description always follows an act of demarcation by a describer. Although this may be apparent in the case of the culinary and musical arts, a larger leap of understanding is required to recognize that all experience arises as a consequence of particular "programs, rules, plans, scripts, recipes, agenda, dramas, sequences, relations, recursive systems, careers, structures, grammars, 'schticks,' and so forth" (Rabkin, 1978, p. 487).

The observer first distinguishes and then describes. A question, by proposing a distinction, constructs its answer, or as Pearce (1974) might phrase it, "passionate questions" generate answers.[8] Similarly, Laing (cited in Spencer-Brown, 1973) suggests "that what in empirical science are called *data,* being in a real sense *arbitrarily* chosen by the nature of the hypothesis already formed, could more honestly be called *capta*" (pp. vx–vxi).[9]

This implies, for a therapist, that the method by which "data" are "captured" (diagnosis) is one of the ways in which the therapeutic context is constructed and maintained. In other words, the therapist's questions and hypotheses help create the "reality" of the problem being treated. Therapists join their clients in constructing a shared reality through the epistemological distinctions they establish.

For example, the manner of identifying the intervening therapist prescribes a way of performing as well as understanding therapy. Placing clinicians behind a mirror and indicating them as involved in the intervention process marks a different way of operating than traditional models of supervisory observation. The work of so-called "systemic teams," among others, makes this difference very apparent.

Spencer-Brown's work is significant for family therapy because it provides a way of specifying the recursive connection of description and prescription, diagnosis and intervention. Describing who is the therapist or client always prescribes a way of intervening.

Knowing about Knowing

To understand any realm of phenomena, we should begin by noting how it was constructed, that is, what distinctions underlie its creation. As Spencer-Brown (1973) suggests, "Our understanding of such a universe comes not from discovering its present appearance, but in remembering what we originally did to bring it about" (p. 104). Whitehead (1925/1967) makes a similar point when he claims that in criticizing a body of ideas such as a "learned book of applied mathematics, or a memoir, one's whole trouble is with the first chapter, or even with

8. A "passionate question" is one to which the questioner passionately wants an answer and with which he is obsessively concerned. Pearce essentially argued that holding on to such a question for a significant period of time, like an incubation period, leads to hatching an answer.

9. It is this view which supports von Foerster's (1976c) suggestion to speak of perception as "closer to an act of creation, as in *con*-ception, than to a passive state of affairs as in *re*-ception" (pp. 2–3).

the first page" (pp. 23–24). In the beginning, one's epistemological slip is always showing. Whitehead continues:

> The trouble is not with what the author does say, but with what he does not say. Also it is not with what he knows he has assumed, but with what he has unconsciously assumed. We do not doubt the author's honesty. It is his perspicacity which we are criticizing. Each generation criticizes the unconscious assumptions made by its parents. . . . (pp. 23–24)

Epistemologically speaking, we are led to finding the primitive distinctions that specify the author's or any other individual's knowing. The task of an epistemologist therefore becomes identifying the way a particular system (whether it is an organism, family, group of therapists, or scientific community) specifies and maintains forms of demarcation. This task also includes acknowledging how the epistemologist comes to know about another system's knowing. Such a self-referential component generates recursive epistemologies. For instance, suppose we begin with the question "How do we know effective therapy?" We may proceed by asking another question, "How do we know that we know effective therapy?" And subsequently, "How do we know that we know that we know?" In this process, each item of knowing becomes subject to a higher order of inquiry. Thus, our epistemological probes become the very subject of their own investigation.

In the epistemologist's laboratory, epistemologies will confront higher order epistemologies that will confront even higher order epistemologies, and so on, ad infinitum. This again suggests that epistemologies are recursive processes, in that any attempt to "fixate" an epistemology on one's screen of consciousness is to inevitably invite subsequent investigation and modification. In the field of psychology, Bugental (1967) was aware of this consequence:

> Indeed, we must recognize that the very process of describing the human experience changes that experience and that the more such a description approaches completeness, the more it is apt to be a basis for change in the very experience it describes. This is probably true for all science, but it is particularly true for the sciences that deal with man. Man's awareness about himself acts as a constantly "recycling" agency to produce changes in himself. (p. 7)

Bateson (1951/1968) also remarked on the recursive epistemology inherent in the relationship between theory and clinical practice: "The theorist can only build his theories about what the practitioner was doing yesterday. Tomorrow the practitioner will be doing something different because of these theories" (p. 272). In other words, one's knowing about therapy changes one's therapy, which subsequently changes one's knowing about therapy.

In general terms we may say that drawing any distinction necessarily leaves us with an altered, expanded universe for subsequent investigation. As Spencer-Brown (1973) notes, "The universe *must* expand to escape the telescopes through which we, who are it, are trying to capture it, which is us" (p. 106). The dog chases its tail, the explanation is in the explained, the descriptor in the description, the observer in the observed, the therapist in the therapy, the reader in what is read.

Outside of formal logic, Pearce (1974) has outlined how properties of the observer shape what is observed. He is particularly interested in "the formation of answers to passionate questions, or the filling of empty categories by creative imagination" (p. xiii). His contention is that "passionate questions" and "empty categories"[10] alter the world and provide the opportunity for self-verifying responses:

> The empty category proposed by a scientist, for instance, brings about its own fulfillment in the same way, and for the same reasons, that a popular disease is entertained, promoted by publicity, feared by all, and watched for in the contemporary form of physician–priest and patient–supplicant, until it fulfills itself on a statistically predictable and self-verifying basis. (p. xiii)

The implication for the mental health field is that it can easily fall prey to perpetuating the very problems it seeks to cure. Any effort to "discover" pathology will contribute to the creation of that pathology. Increasing distinctions of psychiatric nomenclature mobilizes the construction and discovery of those "disorders." Similarly, the invention of new problem-solving techniques and cures will ultimately be part of a more general process that will produce a population of clients with problems perfectly designed for the new cure.

---

10. An "empty category" is exemplified by the periodic table of elements. An undiscovered element is proposed by an empty category, which in turn helps lead to its discovery. More specifically, the formal relations prescribed by an empty category of the periodic table orient a scientist to draw the distinctions necessary to discover the element.

Let us pause for a moment and remind ourselves who it is that draws distinctions. Although the answer is obvious, it is amazingly profound. It is, of course, an observer who draws a distinction. *Any distinction drawn is drawn by an observer.* We should not forget, however, that an observer draws a distinction *for* another observer who may be himself. Knowing a world therefore always implies a social context of at least two observing systems. Now, why does an observer draw a distinction? *An observer observes by drawing distinctions.* In other words, what we perceive always follows from an act of making a distinction. As Heinz von Foerster (1973b) has put it, "If you desire to see, learn to act" (p. 45).

The starting point of epistemology is therefore an observer drawing distinctions in order to observe. What an observer observes can be described. Here an interesting situation arises — namely, descriptions are themselves the drawing of distinctions upon what we observe. A recursion thus enters: We draw distinctions in order to observe and subsequently, we draw distinctions in order to describe what we observe. The recursive operation of drawing distinctions upon distinctions again points toward the world of cybernetics where action and perception, prescription and description, and construction and representation are intertwined.

PUNCTUATION

Basic to understanding epistemology is the idea that what one perceives and knows is largely due to the distinctions one draws. Bateson (1972) commented on how we organize our experience into a coherent pattern:

> "What circumstances determine that a given scientist will punctuate the stream of events so as to conclude that all is predetermined, while another will see the stream of events as so regular as to be susceptible of control?" . . . "What circumstances promote that specific habitual phrasing of the universe which we call 'free will' and those others which we call 'responsibility,' 'constructiveness,' 'energy,' 'passivity,' 'dominance,' and the rest?" For all these abstract qualities . . . can be seen as various habits of punctuating the stream of experience so that it takes on one or another sort of coherence and sense. (p. 163)

This idea, identified as "the punctuation of the sequence of events" by Watzlawick, Beavin, and Jackson (1967, p. 54), is analogous to Spencer-Brown's concept of indication. When an observer draws a distinction he concomitantly makes an indication, that is, he marks one of the two distinguished sides as being primary (e.g., "this," "I," "us"). As Goguen and Varela (1979) note, "It is the very purpose of the distinction to create this indication" (p. 32). The use of distinction to create indication is a way of defining "punctuation."

As the general semanticists (e.g., Korzybski, 1973) have demonstrated, language is a tool for imposing distinctions upon our world. Given a language system, we make choices regarding the patterns we discern. Thus a therapist can choose to indicate or punctuate his unit of treatment as an individual or a family organization or to see it from a perspective that makes the individual–family distinction irrelevant.

The formal study of the ways people punctuate their experience becomes a method for identifying their epistemology. Their habitual patterns of punctuation presuppose epistemological premises for making distinctions as the following illustrations reveal.

Reframing Frames of Reference

Watzlawick *et al.* (1967) suggested that "disagreement about how to punctuate the sequence of events is at the root of countless relationship struggles" (p. 56). They provide the well-worn example of a marital fight consisting of an exchange of the messages "I withdraw because you nag" and "I nag because you withdraw." The couple's dilemma arises from the epistemological assumption, shared by each interactant, that his or her behavior is a response to the other's antecedent stimulus. The task for the therapist is to reshuffle the punctuated segments of this interactive system so that an alternative frame of reference may emerge. For example, the couple's bickering may be relabeled an indication of how much concern each spouse has for the other. Watzlawick and his colleagues have provided the field with fascinating maps and techniques to help accomplish such a task, which they call "reframing."

Watzlawick (1976) has stated that "ordering sequences in one way or another creates what, without undue exaggeration, may be called different realities" (p. 62). This idea will be staggering to a traditional social scientist or therapist bred on naive assumptions about "objectivity."

In the case of stimulus–response psychology, Bateson and Jackson (cited in Watzlawick *et al.*, 1967) have noted that the "reality" of what is called "stimulus" and "response" is "only of the same order as the reality of a bat on a Rorschach card—a more or less over-determined creation of the perceptive process" (p. 55). From this perspective, they suggest that an act of punctuation determines whether the rat or the experimenter is seen as being trained.

An interesting example of a situation where an experimenter's punctuation of a laboratory setting did not hold for the "experimental subject" is given by Bateson (cited in Keeney, 1979b):

> A graduate student at Yale in the days when they were all running rats in mazes said, "Why do we run rats? Why don't we get an animal which lives in mazes? Like a ferret." A ferret is a small pole cat, a weasel type which is a parasite on rabbits. It lives underground most of the time in rabbit quarters which are mazes. And it bites like hell! So he got himself a couple of ferrets, some gloves and a sack. And he built what seemed to him a suitable maze for ferrets. He put a piece of rabbit in the reward chamber and started the ferret off from the entrance. The ferret systematically went down every blind alley until he got to the reward chamber where he ate the rabbit. He was put back to the beginning and the experimenter put another piece of rabbit in the reward chamber. The ferret systematically went down every blind alley until he came to the one going to the reward chamber which he did not go down, because he had eaten that rabbit. The experiment was never published. It was seen as a failure. (pp. 23–24)

This illustration suggests that the ferret rejected the way in which the experimenter attempted to punctuate the context, that is, he rejected the experimenter's paradigm of instrumental learning. Perhaps if the investigator had continued experimenting with ferrets, he might have changed his theory regarding learning. One could then contend that the ferret had "taught" (or conditioned) the investigator.

Another example from experimental psychology is provided by Konorski (1962), who replicated Pavlov's conditioning experiment with one modification—he removed the bell's clapper so it could not make a sound. Those accustomed to punctuating the laboratory context in a "classical" fashion might be surprised to discover that Konorski's dogs would salivate whether or not the bell produced sound. In reviewing this study, von Foerster (1976c) concludes "that this shows that the sound of the bell was a stimulus for Pavlov, and not for the dogs" (p. 14).

In line with these restructurings of the experimental context, therapy can be defined as a context wherein social premises (usually unconscious) regarding punctuation may be altered. Montalvo (1976) defines therapy as an "interpersonal agreement to abrogate the usual rules that structure reality, in order to reshape reality" (p. 333). For example, from studying amnesic events during the therapeutic hour, Montalvo (1976) proposes the following:

> Clinicians just like patients "vanish" by the ways in which they structure and unstructure their contribution to interpersonal sequences. This allows them to influence whether they are remembered or not — and allows them to dodge, as well as place blame, determining whether they are remembered in negative or positive terms. (p. 334)

Montalvo's work clearly suggests that all members of the social context called "therapy" participate in punctuating the interactional flow and thereby shape one another's experience.

Clinical Epistemology

The therapist can understand an individual's experience only by observing how his social context is punctuated. Since an individual or family enters a therapist's office with established habits of punctuation, the therapist must have a way of punctuating their punctuation (or an epistemology about their epistemology). Bateson's (1976c) anthropological work provides guidelines applicable to therapy. The first step is to remember that an observed culture (or family) may categorize its experience in an entirely different way than the observer (or therapist). As Bateson comments, "They've got their way of slicing it," so "if you want to think about their categories you have to have an epistemology which is more abstract than the categories into which they divide life." In other words, you must have an epistemology about how they punctuate their life into categories.

Rabkin's (1977) proposal for a new specialty of therapy, which he would call "clinical epistemology," partly exemplifies what Bateson had in mind. This discipline would investigate how clients acquire their particular ways of knowing the world: for example, how a paranoid establishes right from wrong or how a depressive comes to view events through a darkly colored lens. This kind of understanding requires a higher order epistemology—that is, an epistemology about how others come to punctuate and know their world.

Bateson's anthropological work suggests what such an epistemological stance would be. In an epilogue to *Naven*, Bateson (1958b) describes his project as a "weaving of three levels of abstraction" (p. 281): the first, a concrete level of ethnographic data; the second, more abstract level, the arrangement of data to create "various pictures of the culture"; and the third, most abstract level, a "self-conscious discussion of the procedures by which the pieces of the jigsaw are put together." Teasing apart the levels inherent in one's attempt to understand a phenomenon constitutes an epistemological method applicable to the therapeutic setting.

What this means is that the therapist can identify three basic ways in which he draws distinctions. First of all, there is the drawing of primary distinctions which the therapist uses to discern what can be called his "raw data." Does the therapist, for example, choose to distinguish the key historical events in the family of the symptomatic individual's life? Or is the data drawn from a focus on interactional sequences as they appear within the therapeutic hour?

Given that first order of distinction, the therapist then jumps a level of abstraction and draws distinctions that organize his raw data. Here the therapist attempts to draw patterns that connect his data. He may look for historical themes or he may focus on identifying repetitive patterns in the organization of behavioral events that occur within more immediate time frames.

And finally, once the therapist has drawn distinctions that carve out his data and patterns that organize these data, he can step back and examine what he has done. In other words, he recalls that he, as an observer, has drawn these distinctions and that there are other ways of discerning data and patterns of organization.

These three ways of drawing distinctions again point to recursion: The therapist is drawing distinctions, distinctions upon distinctions, and distinctions upon distinctions upon distinctions. What the therapist does when he engages in drawing these distinctions is construct an epistemology—a way of knowing and a way of knowing about his knowing. In this process the therapist's knowledge can be constantly recycled and modified in order that he may know how to act.

ORDERS OF RECURSION

Whether one is speaking of language, description, explanation, theory, or epistemology, discussion of these topics is often structured in terms of levels, strata, order, or frames or reference. Having a theory about theories or a description of descriptions involves differences in logical frames of reference. To mark a distinction in space is to indicate two different levels—for example, an inside and outside. Similarly, distinguishing between a system and subsystem implies different orders of demarcation.

Logical Typing

Explicitly noting these differences in order is an important procedure in epistemology. Bateson did this by using "logical typing," a conceptual tool that emerged from Whitehead and Russell's (1910) *Principia Mathematica.* It is important to first look at how logical typing developed and then examine how Bateson modified it.

Logicians have noted that "paradox" can arise when a frame of reference is confused with the items within its frame. The classic example of the Cretan who announced that "All Cretans lie" demonstrates how a self-referential statement can oscillate between being a statement and a frame of reference about itself as a statement. The Cretan's audience is bewildered as to whether he is lying when he utters, "All Cretans lie." If he is lying, he tells the truth. If he is telling the truth, he lies. The early logicians did not like to admit such indeterminable oscillations, so paradoxes were banned from the philosopher's world of order. Russell's "Theory of Logical Types" (Whitehead & Russell, 1910) became a *rule* for logic specifying that paradoxes were to be avoided by always pointing out the logical typing of statements. In this way, different logical levels were not permitted to become confounded. For instance, the distinction between a book and the pages of a book points toward two logical levels analogous to a class and its members, respectively. Russell argued that specifying the logical level of a term, concept, or expression prevented it from being self-referential. In this way, the original use of logical typing was to prohibit expressions from oscillating between different logical levels. In the case of a book and its pages, this is natural: A page typically isn't viewed as a book nor a book as a page. The Cretan's utterance, however, can be seen as either a frame or item of reference. Attempts to avoid this self-reference imply that an observer must stipulate where on the hierarchy of logical levels he is observing the statement. The oversight of logical typing was that paradox arises precisely because an observer doesn't know which level to choose — it is this ambiguity that leads to an experience of paradox.

The acceptance of self-referential paradoxes into logic was sanctioned by Russell when Spencer-Brown invented/discovered laws of form. Spencer-Brown (1973) has described this event:

> Recalling Russell's connection with the Theory of Types, it was with some trepidation that I approached him in 1967 with the proof that it was unnecessary. To my relief he was delighted. The Theory was, he said, the most arbitrary thing he and Whitehead had ever had to do, not really a theory but a stopgap, and he was glad to have lived long enough to see the matter resolved. (pp. vii–ix)

Russell's point was that he and Whitehead did not know how to formally use paradox, so they swept it under the philosopher's rug.

The epistemology of Russell's Theory of Types has been challenged by von Foerster (1978), who objected to its use as an injunction against paradox, since an alternative way of dealing with paradox is possible. Self-referential paradoxes can be used as conceptual building blocks for an alternative view of the world. For example, we may begin as we have in this discussion by noting that an observer always participates in what he observes. Thus, all statements, being statements by observers, are self-referential and hence laden with paradox.

While agreeing with von Foerster's proposal, Bateson adopted logical typing as a descriptive tool for discerning the formal patterns of communication that underlie human experience and interaction. Watzlawick, Weakland, and Fisch (1974) also viewed the Theory of Types as descriptive rather than injunctive: They considered it "an attempt at exemplification through analogy" (p. 2). Logical typing can therefore be simply regarded as a way of drawing distinctions. From this perspective, logical typing can be used to disclose rather than conceal self-reference and paradox.

Although Bateson's use of logical types is distinct from its original conceptualization, his work has not clearly distinguished his own idiosyncratic use of the term. He typically referred to "Russell's types" and proposed that "insofar as behavioral scientists still ignore the problems of *Principia Mathematica,* they can claim approximately sixty years of obsolescence" (Bateson, 1972, p. 279). Nevertheless, Bateson (1979a) was aware that he was using Russell and Whitehead's construct in an extended way:

> Whether Russell and Whitehead had any idea when they were working on *Principia* that the matter of their interest was vital to the life of human beings and other organisms, I do not know. Whitehead certainly knew that human beings could be amused and humor generated by kidding around with the types. But I doubt whether he ever made the step from enjoying this game to seeing that the game was nontrivial and would cast light on the whole of biology. The more general insight was — perhaps unconsciously — avoided rather than contemplate the nature of the human dilemmas that the insight would propose. (p. 116)

To literally translate the Theory of Types to the behavioral sciences would mean that there would be a rule forbidding intentional mistyping of levels. However, Bateson (1972), Fry (1963), and Wynne (1976), among others, have shown that patterns of logical mistyping characterize poetry, humor, learning, and creativity. A successful elimination of logical mistyping would result in a flat and stagnant experiential world. On the other hand, the use of logical typing in a solely descriptive manner leads us to a fuller awareness and appreciation of our patterns of knowing.

Recursion

The use of logical typing sometimes suggests that our world of experience is hierarchically structured. For instance, we may distinguish a multivolume encyclopedia from a book and a book from a page. These distinctions, analogous to the logical typing of metaframe, frame, and member, do not refer to a situation of mutually exclusive items. A page, after all, is part of a book and a book may be part of an encyclopedia. Although we, as observers, may punctuate our experience in terms of a hierarchy of logical levels, we should not forget that this hierarchy is recursively structured. Therefore, our distinctions of the volumes and pages of an encyclopedia are always distinctions drawn on distinctions.

One way of thinking about recursiveness is to imagine the mythical creature Ouroborous, the snake that eats its own tail. Each time the creature swallows itself, we can speak of the creation of a different order of recursion. It is unnecessary to imagine the beast getting larger (or smaller) with each episode of infolding, but it is important to realize that we can indicate a difference whenever the circle travels through itself. Speaking of recursion enables us to point to the same snake, while indicating the order of recycling. Speaking of orders of recursion provides an alternative way of using logical typing in order to more fully encounter the nature of recursive process. Given the perspective of recursion, an epistemologist's basic task is to mark the orders of recursion invoked in any given description/explanation.

Thus, the Cretan who utters "All Cretans lie" issues a self-referential message — one that infolds upon itself. The oscillation between its truth and falsity arises from going around and through the recursive loop. As an observer of Cretans including himself as one of the group, he lies in order to tell the truth. As an observer of Cretans excluding himself from the group, he may be telling the truth in order to reveal a lie. Thus, we encounter a general self-referential paradox underlying all observing systems: The observer's observations may include his observing.

An interesting version of self-reference occurs when therapists propose the view that clients and therapists are always engaged in tactics of manipulation. These therapists regard all social interaction, including hypnosis, psychotherapy, and religion, as manipulative strategy. A dilemma arises when these therapists are asked whether their particular view is itself an example of a manipulative strategy. Is the set of ideas regarding power tactics, social manipulation, and the art of one-upmanship itself an example of what is being talked about?

This dilemma is most apparent during conversation with proponents of such a view. Their habit of punctuation will frame or reframe the other person's statements as examples of manipulation. For example, if you propose that you do not believe in the myth of social power, a proponent of it might respond by claiming that you are simply trying to go "one up" on him in order to gain power or control of the situation. Your view of what he is doing, however, may only self-verify the premise that he cannot see any statement or action outside of *his* frame of reference. With each social interchange, each of you verifies your particular view of what is going on.

The implication of this mutually self-verifying encounter is that there is no such thing as an objective demonstration of which side is correct. All encounters, social or otherwise, may only lead to further self-verification of a particular view. We can, however, choose *how* we will regard our views: We can see them as partial and open to correction or as complete and closed to correction. This reasoning, of course, can be applied to this particular view of views. Whatever we decide, we cannot escape the paradoxes of existence derived from the self-reference of being natural observing systems.

Dormitive Principles

If we examine traditional explanations of behavior through the lens of recursion, we will sometimes find what Bateson called "dormitive principles," a form of circular description. A "dormitive principle" is a more abstract repackaging of a description of the item you claim to be explaining.[11] To paraphrase Bateson (1979a), this occurs when the cause of a simple action is said to be an abstract word derived from the name for the action, as, for example, when aggression is explained as being caused by an "aggressive instinct" or psychotic symptomology is attributed to "madness."

To invent a dormitive principle, begin with simple descriptions of the phenomena to be explained. For example, a person may be described as unhappy and unwilling to work or eat. These descriptions can be classified as a category of symptomatic action such as "depression." The claim to then "explain" these particular descriptions as the result of "depression" is to invoke a dormitive principle. What one does, in that case, is to say that an item of simple action is caused by a class of action. This recycling of a term does not constitute formal explanation.

This practice often leads to unfortunate consequences. An individual easily becomes mystified by such pseudoexplanations, often perpetuating undesirable self-fulfilling prophecies. For example, a child's natural episode of unhappiness may be seen by his parents as a consequence of a "depression" (dormitive principle). This view would

11. "Molière, long ago, depicted an oral doctoral examination in which the learned doctors ask the candidate to state the 'cause and reason' why opium puts people to sleep. The candidate triumphantly answers in dog Latin, 'Because there is in it a dormitive principle (*virtus dormitiva*)'" (Bateson, 1972, p. xx).

lead the parents to problem-solving behavior which, as Watzlawick (1976) demonstrates, may serve to escalate a mere case of natural unhappiness into the experience of "clinical depression." This sort of event is an everyday occurrence in mental hospitals where the benevolent doctor may ask a patient who is napping under a tree, "Are you depressed today?" The recycling or reframing of a particular instance of action into a category of action, particularly when posed as a question by an authority figure, can result in a sort of hypnotic command that often induces, escalates, and maintains a problematic context.

The reverse situation, that is, treating categories of action as though they were items of action may be another important way in which symptomatic behavior and experience are generated and maintained. Such confusion is apparent in attempts to reform criminals by punishment. As Bateson (cited in Keeney, 1979b) framed it:

> You cannot stop crime by punishment. All you get is better criminals, because crime isn't an action. Crime is not the name of an action — crime is a category or context of action. The things which are categories of action do not obey the reinforcement rules the way action obeys the reinforcement rules. (p. 21)

Clinical epistemology examines how human dilemmas are created and perpetuated by these epistemological knots. The clinical epistemologist examines patterns within social contexts that organize the recursive, vicious cycles surrounding symptomatic experience. The previous examples show how knots of experience occur when individuals abuse the semanticist's axiom, "The name is not the thing named." In addition, individuals may forget that "the name of the name is not the name." For example, Lewis Carroll's Alice asks the White Knight the name of the song he's going to sing for her. He says the name is called "Haddock's Eyes." Alice thought that to be an odd name for a song and the Knight responded, "No, you don't understand. That's not the name of the song, that's what the name is called" (1865/1971, pp. 186–187). Identifying names, names of names, names of names of names, and so on, is a way of specifying different orders of recursion. Once these different orders are discerned, an epistemologist can note the ways in which these cascades of recursion are confounded, tied together, and generally shaped into patterns.

It is here that logical typing has its use, when it is defined as a way of indicating orders of recursion. From this perspective, the term "mistyping" signifies the confounding of different recursive orders. Using logical typing in this way enables us to detect patterns that organize any given system of knowing. Stopgaps in theoretical explanations and inconsistencies between data and theoretical prediction often become apparent when an observer's orders of recursion are made explicit.

For example, an examination of stimulus–response psychology reveals that most of the rules of reinforcement apply to that which is associated with a name of a simple action such as "lifting a paw" or "pushing a button." These rules, like the names of simple actions, do not apply to contexts of action.[12] Any attempt to induce an organism to acquire (or extinguish) "exploration," "curiosity," "dependency," and so forth, is to mistype the name of a context of action with the name of a simple action, that is, to confuse one with the other. Contexts of action are higher orders of recursion than simple actions and are not subject to lower order reinforcement rules. All contexts of action are punctuated by the organism itself (or the social interactions of which it is part). Changing an organism's way of punctuating its experience is a higher order of learning than is typically associated with stimulus–response psychology. Confusing these orders of learning is an instance of logical mistyping.

Bateson's reframe of a Pavlovian experiment provides an example. The experimental scenario for what Pavlov termed "experimental neurosis" is the following: A dog is first trained to distinguish between a circle and ellipse. After training, the circle and ellipse are gradually made to resemble one another, making the task more difficult for the dog. Finally, when it is impossible to make a discrimination, the dog begins to manifest psychotic symptoms ranging from manic biting to comatose behavior.

In analyzing this situation, Bateson (1979a) remarks:

> "What has the dog learned in his training that makes him unable to accept failure at the end?" And the answer to this question would seem to be: The dog has learned that this is a context for discrimination. That is, he "should" look for two stimuli and "should" look for the possibility of acting on a difference between them. For the dog, this is the "task" which has been set — the context in which success will be rewarded. . . .

12. Bateson (1979a) recently proposed using the phrase "categories of contextual organization of behavior" (p. 134) instead of "contexts of action."

> He now imposes this interpretation on a context that is not a context
> for discrimination. (pp. 119–120)

If the dog were to change his punctuation and assume that the laboratory situation had become a context for guessing, he might not attempt to discriminate between a circle and an ellipse. This punctuation, however, still fails to account for the experimenter's participation in structuring this context. The experimenter is not discriminating between two classes of context (when discrimination is appropriate and when it is not). Instead, the experimenter punctuates the situation as a context for discrimination, even when it is not possible to discriminate. Consequently, the dog and experimenter are placed in an impossible situation. If the dog attempts to discriminate, the experimenter observes that he cannot; if the dog does not discriminate, the experimenter proposes that the dog's "discrimination" has broken down.

The experimental psychologist's attribution of the dog's symptoms to a "breakdown in discrimination" reveals a mistyping. Saying that a dog discriminates due to his "discrimination" is to invoke a dormitive principle. As Bateson (1979a) teases this reasoning apart:

> In this jump, the scientist has moved from a statement about a particular incident or incident which can be *seen* to a generalization that is hooked up to an abstraction — "discrimination" — located *beyond vision* perhaps inside the dog. It is this jump in logical type that is the theorist's error. I can, in a sense, see the dog *discriminate,* but I cannot see his "discrimination." (p. 119)

This example illustrates a double bind pattern in which each participant is tightly bound in a relationship plagued by mutual logical mistyping. The dog's inappropriate punctuation leads to behavior that only verifies the experimenter's inappropriate punctuation, which in turn reinforces the dog's punctuation. The dog generates symptoms and the experimenter laments over the dog's failure to discriminate. Of course, it is conceivable that a relationship between dog and experimenter could emerge wherein the experimenter would grieve over his dog's "breakdown." The benevolent master then might attempt to help the dog by psychological or medical treatment. This would more than likely lead to that other contextual pattern called "therapy."

DOUBLE DESCRIPTION

When two people interact, each member punctuates the flow of interaction. If an observer combines the views of both individuals, a sense of the whole system will begin to emerge. There are several ways such a holistic description can be conceptualized. First, the punctuation generated by each person can be presented in sequential fashion, with the whole series seen as a representation of the dyadic system. For example, when the two descriptions "he nags, I withdraw" and "she withdraws, I nag" are collectively viewed, they provide a quick glimpse of the interactive system.[13] This glimpse is somewhat equivalent to taking a series of snapshots of each individual over time and then holding the pictures side by side.

Once an observer presents these different punctuations in a sequential fashion, he may then attempt to discern a pattern that connects them. One way of doing this is to assume that the punctuation pattern of person A interacts with the punctuation pattern of person B to create a moiré-like hybrid pattern. For the observer, this means that the simultaneous combination of their punctuations yields a glimpse of the whole relationship. Bateson (1979a) calls this latter view "double description" and compares it to binocular vision:

> It is correct (and a great improvement) to begin to think of the two parties to the interaction as two eyes, each giving a monocular view of what goes on and, together, giving a binocular view in depth. This double view *is* the relationship. (p. 133)

In the case of the "he nags, I withdraw—she withdraws, I nag" system, the binocular view would see what Bateson came to call a "complementary relationship."

Distinguishing Patterns of Relationship

Seeing relationship requires double description. If double descriptions of relationship are dissected and each part held to be something localized inside a person, a "dormitive principle" is created. To see a

13. This particular description is demonstrated by Watzlawick *et al.* (1967) who note that such an "oscillatory yes–no–yes–no–yes" interaction is analogous to what mathematicians call an "infinite, oscillating series" (pp. 56–58).

nagging husband without considering a withdrawing wife may lead to treating a "nagger" rather than a nagging-withdrawing relationship system. Similarly, to view "leadership" as something that resides in a person is to generate a dormitive principle. This would inspire such pseudoexplanations as "He leads because he possesses leadership qualities." Note, however, that we can always ask the observer who makes such a statement how he knows that the described person is a leader. His reply will necessarily make reference to another person's "follower" behavior, thus bringing us back to a relationship system. "Leadership," in other words, is an extracted half of the double description "leader-follower relationship." In general, all descriptions of personality characteristics consist of extracted halves of larger relationship patterns. Following Bateson's (1979a) advice, "Only if you hold on tight to the primacy and priority of relationship can you avoid dormitive explanations" (p. 133).

Since therapy occurs in the context of a therapist-client relationship, any attempt to identify traits of a successful therapist (or client) is to focus on an extracted half of the relationship. Such a view too easily leads to the search for dormitive principles. Clinicians then speak of what causes therapists to be successful or what causes clients to be sick, bad, or mad. The alternative view is to focus on the patterns of interaction taking place between therapist and client.

Fundamentally, double description is an epistemological tool that enables one to generate and discern different orders of pattern. Although language, through the limits of its particular terms and structure, constrains our knowing, double description provides a way of using language to direct us toward higher order description. By doing this, we can begin pulling ourselves up by our bootstraps to get out of the epistemological quagmire. As two eyes can derive depth, two descriptions can derive pattern and relationship.

The structure of Bateson's thinking (1958b, 1972, 1979a) provides an example of how to proceed. In his beginning distinctions, Bateson reflected on the relation of descriptions of simple action, categories of action, and categories of interaction. He found that these relations could be discussed in terms of logical typing, or what I prefer to call orders of recursion with respect to an observer's distinctions. As we've discussed, contexts of action (a higher order distinction) are logically distinct from descriptions of simple action (lower order distinction)[14]: "Play" is a higher order abstraction than "throwing a ball." When Bateson examined contexts of action, he noted that they determine how simple actions are linked in social organization, that is, the way in which the reactions of individuals to the reactions of other individuals are organized in time. This order of analysis demonstrated that "no action is an island." All actions are parts of organized interaction.

Bateson (1979a) proceeded to name two categories of interactive process—complementary and symmetrical relationship. These categories of interaction represent two types of "binocular view." He defined them as follows:

> I applied the term *symmetric* to all those forms of interaction that could be described in terms of competition, mutual emulation and so on (i.e., those in which A's action of a given kind would stimulate B to action of the same kind, which, in turn, would stimulate A to further similar actions . . .). In contrast, I applied the term *complementary* to interactional sequences in which the actions of A and B were different but mutually fitted each other (e.g., dominance-submission, exhibition-spectatorship, dependence-nurturance). (pp. 192-193)

It is important to note that a binocular view of relationship requires an appropriate vocabulary. For example, from the perspective of relationship, one does not speak of a series of nagging and withdrawing episodes between husband and wife; that would constitute a behavioral description of the whole system. Instead one makes reference to a complementary relationship. To achieve this higher order view, or binocular image, requires jumping an order of abstraction, from behavior to context, with a concomitant jump in descriptive expression. In this case, descriptions of action are fused to create a description of interaction.

When Bateson pondered how patterns of interaction may themselves be patterned, he found that unchecked symmetry or complementarity led to "schismogenesis," a term he coined to refer to a runaway or escalating process that, if unchecked, would inevitably lead to

---

14. An observer may first distinguish a simple action and then, subsequently, draw a higher order distinction to mark its context. This context of simple action, a distinction upon a distinction, is therefore a recursion of the distinction the observer drew to indicate simple action.

intolerable stress and dissolution of the relationship system. If, on the other hand, symmetrical and complementary interactions were mixed, a kind of balance might be achieved. Bateson (cited in Keeney, 1979b) provides an analogy:

> If the marriage becomes too complementary, you can put them on a tennis court and they'll feel better. Or if it becomes too symmetrical or rivalrous, you just wait for one of them to sprain an ankle and then they'll both feel better. (p. 18)

This suggests that the way symmetric and complementary patterns of interaction are patterned represents a kind of choreography for the participants. At this order of analysis, conversations, human sexuality, family dinners, and international conflicts are organized according to the rules of choreography that govern (i.e., pattern) their interactional themes. In family therapy, searches for "family rules" and "dances" sometimes characterize those dealing with this order of organization.[15]

Dialectic of Form and Process

In reviewing his life's work, Bateson (1979a) noted that his "procedures of inquiry were punctuated by an alternation between classification [of form] and the description of process" (p. 193). This "zigzag ladder between typology [form] on the one side and the study of process on the other" (p. 193) has been mapped in several ways in his book, *Mind and Nature*. A modified and more general chart of this analysis is presented in Fig. 1. The chart demonstrates a recursive approach to epistemology: Rather than spelling out lineal hierarchies of abstraction, it sets forth a "zigzag ladder of dialectic between form and process" (p. 194).

The right column of Fig. 1, called "description of process" refers to the unit being observed. These units of observation follow from how an observer punctuates a stream of events. Descriptions of process, in general, refer to an order of observation that can be called "sensory based experience." This is the closest one can come to en-

---

15. We will later see that there is an important recursion at this order of process. Here, the patterned interactions specify a system of choreography that specifies the patterned interactions. This recursion, as the next chapter will point out, indicates that the system is organizationally closed and self-referential at this order of process.

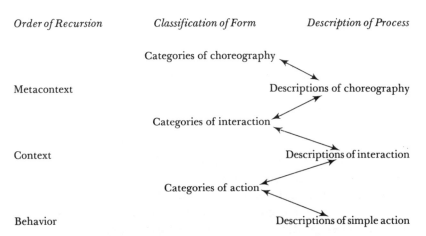

FIG. 1. ORDERS OF EPISTEMOLOGICAL ANALYSIS.

countering "raw data" and is a form of description empty, for all practical purposes, of lofty theoretical abstractions.

To move from one order of description to another within this system of analyzing experience requires an act of double description: That is, a view from each side of a relationship must be juxtaposed to generate a sense of the relationship as a whole. For example, interaction is discerned by fusing descriptions of each participant's simple action. At a higher order of analysis, an awareness of patterns of choreography is specified by the relations of interactive episodes: For example, "healthy" dyadic relationships may be characterized by patterns of alternation between complementary and symmetric themes. Once again, views from each side of the relationship, this time involving descriptions of patterns of interaction, must be combined to form a picture of the choreography.

The middle column of Fig. 1, which is also the left side of the "zigzag ladder" of analysis, is called "classification of form." It refers to the names given to the patterns that organize simple action, interaction, and choreography. A classification of form is an abstraction that "organizes" each order of description by connecting its elements together in a meaningful way. A step-by-step examination of the ladder will reveal how form and process are intertwined.

Descriptions of simple action refer to observations of singular, isolated units of simple action, including facial expressions; body position; breathing patterns; eye fixation patterns; voice tonality and volume; speech tempo; uttered words, phrases, and sentences; and so on. In the case of analyzing the simple actions of a dance, for example, this order of analysis would involve attending to the immediately perceivable events characterizing each individual step. For instance, the right foot of a dancer may move forward while the shoulders lean back and the head turns to the right.

When items of simple action are classified as belonging to a particular *category of action,* one swings to the other side of analysis, that of form. Classifying 5 minutes of action as "dance" or "play" becomes a way of naming a category of action. This act of categorization, what the left side of the ladder refers to as "classification of form," is a way of identifying and naming the pattern that organizes the observed order of process. Categories of action, such as play, exploration, combat, crime, schizophrenia, and therapy are names we ascribe to the way simple actions are patterned. It is important to realize that any particular simple action may be found across diverse categories. "Lifting an arm," for example, may be part of a dance, military ritual, classroom performance, or sport. The naming of a category of action simply indicates that we see simple actions as meaningfully organized in a particular context.

Moving across the ladder to the next order of process, we find that it does not focus on isolated bits of action, but on chains or sequences of action that are exhibited by interacting individuals or groups. *Descriptions of interaction,* however, are still given in terms of sensory based language. What differentiates this order of process from descriptions of simple action is that it attends to how bits of simple action among participants are connected. In analyzing the dance of a couple, this description would give a serial ordering of the flow of dance steps. For example, step M might be followed by step N, then step O, step N, step O, and so on. At this perspective, any description of a simple action must be accompanied by a description of the actions of another person that precede and follow it. Here, the ordering of streams of action is more important than the individual actions themselves.

When one attempts to classify descriptions of interaction, this classification of form consists of naming patterns of relationship rather than patterns of action. *Categories of interaction* refer to patterns that characterize the relationship of different participants' actions. For example, any dance step of one member of a dancing couple will be preceded and followed by steps from the other member. The pattern of each interactive episode can be classified as either symmetrical or complementary. Each consequent step will again be preceded and followed by other steps, and each new interactive pattern can then be classified.

Note that although the relationship is between the action of two individuals (or groups, parts of groups, or parts of individuals), to classify these relations requires a view of at least three bits of simple action. As Bateson and Jackson (cited in Sluzki & Beavin, 1977) proposed, a relationship is complementary or symmetrical depending on how a "piece of behavior is related to preceding and subsequent behaviors of the vis-à-vis" (p. 77).

Swinging back to the description of process side of the ladder, the next order of analysis views these patterns of interaction as parts of an even larger organizational fabric. *Descriptions of choreography* therefore specify how the previously identified interactional patterns (symmetric and complementary themes) are themselves patterned, that is, connected or sequenced. Ballet, jazz, and ballroom dancing, for instance, specify different ways of organizing simple action and categories of action. These higher order organizational patterns can consequently be named *categories of choreography* in a classification of form.

These different ways of punctuating a stream of events and naming the emergent patterns correspond to particular orders of recursion with respect to the distinctions drawn by an observer (the far left column of Fig. 1). Let us look at the nagging husband—withdrawing wife scenario as an example. We can begin by describing and classifying simple actions. A husband's speech behavior with its accompanying body orchestration may be classified as "nagging," while a wife's silence and yawning may be classified as "withdrawing." The order of distinction involved is that of behavior. The identification of the categories of action leads us to an analysis of context, the next order of recursion. Here interaction, rather than simple action, becomes the unit of analysis serially organizing particular bits of action. For example, the alternation of nagging and withdrawing (a description of interaction) may be named as a complementary relationship (a classification of form). These contexts, or sequences, of interaction are themselves subject to higher order organization. Metacontexts—the highest order of recursion in this system—refers to how interactions are patterned as parts of a whole system of choreography. At this order of analysis, the married couple's escalating complementary interaction may itself be subject to higher order constraints, such as receiving a complaining call from a neighbor, the husband having an asthma attack, or a child becoming disobedient. Given this description of choreography, it is logical that we should proceed to name a category of choreography. Unfortunately, we have little, if any, language for this order of categorization. Even the term "schismogenesis" is not a name for a patterned set of interactions, but refers to the *process* whereby repetitive, that is, unchecked interactions lead to intolerable stress and dissolution. With regard to the term "double bind," perhaps we could propose that it is the name of a category of choreographed interaction. This is in accord with Bateson's (1972) later acknowledgment that double bind is the name of a pattern of "transcontextual process" (p. 272).

The broader organizational view demonstrates that action and sequences of action are always part of a more encompassing ecological system. It is this comprehensive view that has captured the attention of therapists sensitive to the dramas enacted by families and social networks.

CONSTRUCTING A REALITY

"Description of process" (the right column of Fig. 1) refers to what Bateson (1979a) described as an "analogue of the aggregate of phenomena to be explained" (p. 191). That is, the items in this column are closest to what we may regard as "sensory data." We have identified the orders of description as bits of action, interactional episodes, and choreography. Although we can really have no direct experience of any of these, we can still differentiate between a description of our sensory experience and a typology or categorization of that description (classification of form).

For example, a therapist may report a client's facial expressions, breathing patterns, and leg movements. These descriptions can then be categorized or typologized as a class of action such as "fright" or "enthusiasm." However, when a therapist claims to see "fright" or "enthusiasm" he is speaking nonsense. These terms are classifications of descriptions of sensory experience and cannot be directly perceived.

The difference between a "description of process," based on sensory experience, and "classification of form," a higher order abstraction, is not trivial. Bandler and Grinder's work (1979) demonstrates that most clinicians (and their clients) habitually encounter the world without differentiating between their sensory experience and their created abstractions about that experience. The problem is that clinicians' higher order abstractions, rather than their more immediate sensory experience, often become the primary data of therapy. Such a clinician may shut out or ignore an enormous amount of sensory based information during the course of therapy; thus, he may become disconnected from ongoing events in the social interactional field.

One might argue that the alternative is to focus on sensory based experience. Doing so would require stopping the internal dialogue of higher order abstracting, or "stopping the world," as don Juan called it. In essence, this involves pushing higher order abstractions out of consciousness to permit a more direct encounter with sensory based experience. A flower, for example, would not be experienced as the category, "flower," but as a sensory array of color, shape, and smell.

However, descriptions of sensory based experience are always connected to some sort of internalized symbolic system — such as the language one uses — that prescribes certain ways of "encountering the world" through one's senses. The fact that abstractions are mixed with sensory experience suggests that there is really no such thing as "pure sensory experience" or "raw data." Bateson (1979a) further suggests that a "necessary first postulate for any understanding of the natural world" is to realize that organisms can have no direct experience of their subjects of inquiry (p. 191). What one encounters, as we've attempted to demonstrate, are maps of maps.

A more encompassing view is that organisms experience a world by engaging in a dialectic between the abstract systems they create and the way their sense organs rub against a world. This dialectic, presented in Fig. 1 as a general dialectic between form and process, is a model of how mental process creates and organizes our world of experience. The zigzag ladder of sensory based description of process on one side and classification of form on the other represents a recursive, dialectical process.

Again, in this dialectical process, seeing a world partially follows from how we draw distinctions upon it. It is as if one's hand draws outlines on one's own retina. This process is recursive—what one draws, one sees and what one sees, one draws. Since form and process can swallow each other in a recursive fashion, it is always possible to generate different orders of view.

As we've discussed, the side of the ladder called "description of process" is primarily based on distinctions drawn by (or onto) our sensory apparatus. We can call distinctions from this column "sensory based description." The other side of the ladder, "classification of form" is derived more from our symbolic systems. Bateson saw this side as an analogue of what he called "tautology." Rather than use that term, I prefer to speak of *skeletons of symbolic relations* onto which descriptions may be structured. These skeletons provide a sort of connective tissue that enables us to link or relate diverse descriptions of process.

The notions of sensory based description and skeletons of symbolic relations should be seen as different ways of regarding how an observer draws distinctions. Using this distinction about how we draw distinctions enables us to conceptualize our world of experience as a recursive dialectic alternating between distinctions based on sensory based description and those derived from skeletons of symbolic relations.

We previously mentioned that sensory based descriptions are never actually distinct from some symbolic system or way of drawing distinctions. Similarly, we can now propose that skeletons of symbolic relations are really not distinct from the sensory data they organize. For instance, names of categories of action, including exploration, love, humor, therapy, and play are distinctions drawn by an observer on his observations of the so-called sensory data of simple action.

What we are dealing with in our distinction between sensory based description and skeletons of symbolic relations is the recursive operation of an observer drawing distinctions. Tracing this recursive operation of drawing distinctions, distinctions upon distinctions, and so on, enables us to uncover the way we construct and bind together an ecology of ideas—the construction and maintenance of a reality. Bateson (1979a) proposes that the patterns that bind ideas together "are as close as we can get to ultimate truth" (p. 191). The dances between form and process, skeletons of symbolic relations and sensory based description, letter and spirit, rigor and imagination represent, as Bateson (1979a) notes, "dialectical necessities of the living world" (p. 227). It is here that we encounter the aesthetics of change.

We can now see Fig. 1 as more clearly representing a hierarchy of *orders of recursion.*[16] None of these orders—action, context, and metacontext—is actually lower or higher than any of the others in a spatial sense; such distribution is an artifact.

One of the most frequently used examples of a hierarchy of levels is the biological universe, arranged in terms of cells, organs, whole individual organisms, social groups, and so forth. When we speak of a cell being a different level than a whole organ, say a liver, we do not think of a liver standing on top of a cell. Instead, we see an organ engulfing its component parts. The trick to seeing orders of recursion in systemic hierarchies is to view them as a cascade of Chinese boxes— systems within systems within systems. All these boxes can be seen as collapsed upon themselves, that is, seen as a monistic whole, or they can be stretched out so that different nodal points, levels, strata, or orders are identified. Each perspective, whole and parts, is different but complementary. Our epistemology is richer if we keep both punctuations.

We should remember that the complexity of human drama implies that any effort to study a particular slice of process, form, or order of recursion will inevitably lead to limited understanding. As one of Birdwhistell's (1970) students put it, "It's like trying to understand a drainage system from a 6-inch slice of river" (p. 270). Furthermore, we should not forget that the boundaries of any unit of observation are always drawn by an observer. Observers with their distinctions are always part of the observed. What a person does, including what he says, is therefore distinguished by an observer. The distinctions an observer draws in order to know a domain of phenomena may include the differences between behavior, context, and metacontext. But how real are these distinctions? They are as real as the "bubbles that come out of the mouths of characters in comic strips" (Bateson, 1979a, p. 132). In all cases, an observer simply draws an outline or, in recursive fashion, an outline of an outline.

The consequence of punctuations is aptly demonstrated by the

16. At this point we can also more clearly see how Bateson (1979a) used logical typing in a unique way. He explains:

> From this paradigm, it appears that the idea of "logical typing," when transplanted from the abstract realms inhabited by mathematical philosophers to the hurly-burly of organisms, takes on a very different appearance. Instead of a hierarchy of classes, we face a hierarchy of *orders of recursiveness.* (p. 201)

polar bear who was "framed." Bandler and Grinder (1979, p. 192) tell a story about the Denver Zoo's acquisition of a polar bear. The zoo built a temporary cage for the bear until its "naturalistic environment" could be constructed. The cage was just large enough that the bear could walk several steps in one direction, whirl around, and take several steps in the opposite direction, back and forth. When the bear's environment was finally constructed and the cage removed, the bear continued to walk back and forth within the old punctuation.

This discussion of epistemology provides a foundation for specifying the meaning of cybernetic epistemology. It should be remembered again that we are, at best, in a state of epistemological transition — that few, if any, individuals are habitually experiencing their world through cybernetic epistemology. This means that we are so accustomed to noncybernetic ways of knowing that we may distort whatever glimpse of cybernetics might fall our way. Like the bear within his imaginary frame, we may forget that our creative imagination is free to draw other distinctions. Cybernetic epistemology provides a way of discovering and constructing alternative patterns in the ecology of our experience.

DISCUSSION

THERAPIST: Please summarize what you mean by "fundamentals of epistemology."

EPISTEMOLOGIST: In the most basic sense, "fundamentals of epistemology" are a way of specifying how we help construct our world of experience. Drawing a distinction, indicating a punctuation, marking orders of recursion, and using double description can therefore be seen as epistemological tools of construction.

THERAPIST: But aren't they also descriptive tools?

EPISTEMOLOGIST: You are correct. More accurately, these tools are both descriptive and prescriptive. Their recursive connection is what this book is about.

THERAPIST: Which leads us to cybernetics?

EPISTEMOLOGIST: Indeed. Cybernetics is the world of recursive process. It provides a way of seeing these organizational patterns.

THERAPIST: I would like to have a bit of clarification regarding the difference between drawing a distinction and marking a punctuation. It seems to me that they are essentially the same.

EPISTEMOLOGIST: People often draw distinctions in order to make a punctuation. We may draw the distinction between a therapist and an epistemologist, for example. Given this difference we may then *indicate* that the epistemologist is teaching the therapist something about his craft or vice versa. The use of this distinction to make an indication of teacher and student is punctuation. So, in a way, a punctuation is a distinction that operates on itself — a second order recursion of a primitive distinction. The answer to your question is that punctuation is the same as drawing a distinction, but involves a higher order of recursion.

THERAPIST: Let me see if I have this right. If I draw a line between an epistemologist and therapist, we can speak of that difference as a primitive distinction. If I then distinguish the epistemologist as learning something from the therapist or vice versa, I am indicating a higher order difference. I'm still pointing to the same primitive distinction, but at a different order of recursion. Stated differently, the distinction between you and me enables us to indicate an infinitude of other orders of difference between us.

EPISTEMOLOGIST: I think we're speaking the same language. Incidentally, we have already been talking cybernetics. Although the author suggested that this chapter was a prelude for cybernetics, he took us right into the heart of cybernetic epistemology from the very beginning.

THERAPIST: You mean all of those references to the recursive connection of description and prescription, as well as the discussion of orders of recursion and double description were actually cybernetics?

EPISTEMOLOGIST: In part, yes. The next step is to learn some vocabulary that will enable us to more accurately articulate these patterns of recursion.

THERAPIST: Before proceeding, I would like to reexamine some of the epistemological tools already presented. Let us begin with drawing distinctions. Is the main point of G. Spencer-Brown's work the proposal that all experiential universes are invented, constructed, made up?

EPISTEMOLOGIST: It is not quite that simple. Remember that description and prescription are recursively connected. This immediately means that there are two incomplete ways of viewing an experiential universe. It is only partially true that there exists a "real" physical world outside of our skins that we are capable of perceiving. The notion that an external world lineally acts upon our sensorium in order to shape the descriptions of representations is incomplete. Similarly, it is a partial view to see the entire world as made up by our prescriptions for construction. Such a belief, called "solipsism," is a reverse punctuation of the previous lineal view. It is therefore as lineal and incomplete as the traditional perspective of an objective universe. Only the arrow of direction changes. What cybernetics pushes us toward is a way of joining both of these views. It is the recursive connection of description and prescription, as well as representation and construction, that we are after.

THERAPIST: The cybernetician is therefore trying to achieve a double view of description and prescription. The trick, I guess, is to hold each of these views together to get a higher order perspective. But what do we see when we fuse these descriptions together?

EPISTEMOLOGIST: The higher order view is cybernetics. The pattern that connects description and prescription is a pattern of recursion. Perhaps it would be useful for you to consider cybernetics, double description, and recursive process as synonyms.

THERAPIST: But you still say, time and time again, that an observer draws distinctions that construct and maintain a world of experience. As you argue, an observer chooses to construct a view of naive realism or a view that negates, or partially negates, naive realism. How do you distinguish your position from solipsism, the view that the world is only in one's imagination?

EPISTEMOLOGIST: What we have said may indeed be solipsism when we talk only about a single observer. But look what happens when we have two observers or an observer observing himself. If an observer proposes that everything appears in his imagination, he may discover that his imaginary world includes imaginary observers who also believe that they are in the midst of imaginary observers. The question then arises of which apparition is the center of the world, or stated differently, which apparition is the one creating all the others?

THERAPIST: Following Heinz von Foerster (1973b, p. 45), an Earthling and a Martian may be allowed solipsism when they are alone, but their claims fail when they get together.

EPISTEMOLOGIST: Don't forget that the very criterion you use to reject solipsism is itself a way you have chosen to punctuate the situation. The basic point is that each observer must choose whether he will view himself as the center of a solipsistic world or as part of an ecology of other autonomous observers.

THERAPIST: But is it still an observer or group of observers who create the world we know?

EPISTEMOLOGIST: Yes. We literally create the world we distinguish by distinguishing it. If a distinction is not drawn, then that which it would have specified does not exist in our phenomenal domain.

THERAPIST: Let's translate this to the world of therapy. I think you are saying that clients and therapists are members of a participatory universe in which each contributes to the construction and maintenance of a therapeutic reality.

EPISTEMOLOGIST: We must also remember that clients and therapists do not make up their reality in a lineal, solipsistic fashion. There is a larger pattern of recursion. Distinctions are drawn upon therapists and clients by each other and by the ecological system of which they are a part at the same time that each of them draws distinctions. The moiré pattern resulting from the combination of these epistemological etchings is what we can call a therapeutic reality.

THERAPIST: When a client draws a distinction, perhaps by pointing out what is troubling him, the distinction can be seen as drawn on the therapist. The therapist in turn draws a distinction, perhaps by pointing out what could be helpful. This distinction can be seen as drawn on the client. And, of course, there are distinctions being drawn on both client and therapist by the larger social system, and they, as a whole social organism, are jointly drawing distinctions. Are you saying that the interplay of all these patterns is a definition of their reality?

EPISTEMOLOGIST: That is one way of drawing it.

THERAPIST: Name another way.

EPISTEMOLOGIST: As an exercise in anthropology we could chop therapy into bits of simple action. Perhaps we would examine a videotape of a session and derive a detailed list of all discernable behavior. We might note that the therapist leans over in his chair, raises an eyebrow, folds his arms, or a client yawns, clears his throat, and peers out the window. A focus on simple bits of action would give us a long list of these types of description. If we arrange these simple actions in the order in which they occurred during therapy, we could begin looking for sequences of behavior. Have you ever been presented with what at first looked like a random list of numbers but with more examination revealed a pattern?

THERAPIST: Oh, yes. In fact I remember a simple one. Take the following series of integers: 10, 12, 15, 30, 32, 35, 70, 72, 75. With some contemplation it is apparent that this series involves a repetitive pattern. If we line it up this way, it is easy to see:

$$(10, \quad 12, \quad 15)$$
$$(30, \quad 32, \quad 35)$$
$$(70, \quad 72, \quad 75)$$

EPISTEMOLOGIST: Let's return to the list of simple actions that is a record of the behavioral flow of a therapy session. If you encounter that list like you did with your series of numbers, you may also be able to discern a repetitive pattern.

THERAPIST: I have a case in mind. Let me give you a partial list:

1. Father complains of being bored with life.
2. Adolescent daughter stays out too late.
3. Mother scolds daughter and the two have a fight.
4. Father becomes involved and effectively disciplines daughter.
5. Daughter exhibits "model behavior"; for example, one day she fixes dinner for her parents and cleans the house.
6. Mother assigns tasks to family members.
7. Father gets upset about his work.
8. Daughter skips classes at school and gets in trouble.
9. Mother gets depressed about daughter and remains in bed.
10. Father scolds daughter and takes over house chores.
11. Daughter talks about becoming a doctor.
12. Mother plans a trip to the movies for the whole family.

EPISTEMOLOGIST: And what pattern can you pull out of that list?

THERAPIST: What we have is a recurring sequence similar to one Jay Haley (1976b) often talks about:

1. Father — Incompetent
2. Child — Misbehaving
3. Mother — Incompetent
4. Father — Competent
5. Child — Behaving
6. Mother — Competent

7. Father — Incompetent
8. Child — Misbehaving
9. Mother — Incompetent

10. Father — Competent
11. Child — Behaving
12. Mother — Competent

Although the particular behaviors are different in each sequence, the same pattern of organization remains.

EPISTEMOLOGIST: Let's consider what you have done. In both the numerical and behavioral lists you have assumed that there was some underlying pattern that organized the series. You then stared at your list until a pattern could be detected.

THERAPIST: Did I invent the pattern of organization or is it really there?

EPISTEMOLOGIST: Perhaps both. Remember that prescription and description are recursively connected.

THERAPIST: Is there always a pattern underlying a sequence of events? If so, then does this imply that there is no such thing as a random event?

EPISTEMOLOGIST: G. Spencer-Brown (1957) in a tiny book entitled *Probability and Scientific Inference*, said the following:

> The essense of randomness has been taken to be absence of pattern. But what has not hitherto been faced is that the absence of one pattern logically demands the presence of another. It is a mathematical contradiction to say that a series has no pattern; the most we can say is that it has no pattern that anyone is likely to look for. The concept of randomness bears meaning only in relation to the observer; if two observers habitually look for different kinds of pattern they are bound to disagree upon the series which they call random. (p. 105)

THERAPIST: Practically speaking, it makes sense for me to approach any sequence of action and believe that there is an underlying pattern of organization.

EPISTEMOLOGIST: If you do so, you probably will be able to discern a higher order of process called interaction.

THERAPIST: When I see an interactional pattern, I assume that I am examining a higher order of recursion than simple bits of action. Looking at my list of numbers, for instance, I can detect a series of repetitive sequences. In other words (10, 12, 15), (30, 32, 35) refer to the same pattern. The particular numbers change from sequence to sequence, but the underlying pattern $(a, a + 2, a + 5)$ remains the same.

EPISTEMOLOGIST: Looking at a family, we see the same occurrence. Their particular behaviors may change, while the underlying organizational pattern remains the same.

THERAPIST: I assume that if we were to list the whole series of these sequences, we also might be able to see a larger pattern which connects each sequence. Take these sequences of numbers: (10, 12, 15), (30, 32, 35), (70, 72, 75). The pattern that sequences these sequences involves multiplying the third integer of each set by a factor of two. We move from 15 to 30, 35 to 70, and so forth, by following that rule. In this way we start a different sequence.

EPISTEMOLOGIST: Similarly, in a family the various sequences are themselves sequenced by larger patterns of organization. In human experience, patterns of interaction must change, or else we face what Bateson called "schismogenesis." If a couple continually recycles complementary relations, they will probably die of boredom. If they escalate in a symmetrical fashion, they might have a violent fight.

THERAPIST: But if they fought and someone got hurt, the relationship would shift to complementarity.

EPISTEMOLOGIST: Yes. In general, it is impossible to sustain a complementary or symmetrical relationship. Patterns of interaction must change for the participants of a relationship to survive.

THERAPIST: With this line of thinking, if we were to expand our numerical series of sequences, it might have to look something like this: (10, 12, 15), (30, 32, 35), (70, 72, 75), (75, 72, 70), (35, 32, 30) . . .

EPISTEMOLOGIST: We could hypothesize an imaginary case in which a numerical series hits a sort of threshold or upper limit when it reaches the number 75.

THERAPIST: Which, in this case, leads to the sequence reversing its direction. This is what seems to happen with social interaction. Whether the context is play, humor, fighting, or therapy, interactional sequences that escalate will eventually reach some upper (or lower) limit which reverses, alters, or changes the relationship pattern.

EPISTEMOLOGIST: Again, we are speaking of recursive process — the stuff of cybernetics.

THERAPIST: If we're always dealing with recursive process in human interaction, then we must somehow see any list, whether of simple action or patterns of action, as infolding upon itself.

EPISTEMOLOGIST: But, of course, we never get back to the "real" beginning in the sense that your list of numbers would eventually recycle to the sequence (10, 12, 15).

THERAPIST: What, then, is circular?

EPISTEMOLOGIST: The replaying of the same pattern of organization. In our list of numbers, the pattern (a, a + 2, a + 5) gets played over and over, round and round. It's like having the same music although the lyrics change.

THERAPIST: We are thus recycling the same pattern, but with different members or events. This is why it is wiser to speak of recursion rather than circularity. The pattern appears to remain the same, while the particulars appear to change.

EPISTEMOLOGIST: But at another order of process, these patterns may themselves change.

THERAPIST: Higher order recursion?

EPISTEMOLOGIST: Indeed.

THERAPIST: If I were to fully understand the epistemological tools discussed, what difference would that make in how I perform therapy?

EPISTEMOLOGIST: I don't really know.

THERAPIST: Make a guess.

EPISTEMOLOGIST: If you fully believed these ideas, then several consequences are likely. First of all, you would realize that what you see in therapy is always connected to what you do. If you become frustrated or bored or even frightened with a client, you would realize that it is necessary to vary *your* behavior.

THERAPIST: Are you implying that the therapist is solely responsible for the outcome of therapy?

EPISTEMOLOGIST: That's only one half of the relationship. Right?

THERAPIST: Double description suggests that outcomes in therapy depend upon the relation between therapist and client. Please go on.

EPISTEMOLOGIST: Another implication these tools have for therapy is that you would never settle for one view of any situation. If a wife complained of her husband's anxiety attacks, you would ask someone else, perhaps another family member or therapist, to present an alternative description of the situation. You would then try to avoid the trap of trying to find out which description is "true" or "more correct." Instead, you would attempt to fuse these descriptions into a higher order view. Some therapists, such as Selvini-Palazzoli and her Milan colleagues, go on to present a message to the family that attempts to package these double views.

THERAPIST: Please continue with how these ideas may be useful to me.

EPISTEMOLOGIST: We should not forget that all these tools are in one sense made up. They are constructions of one's imagination. We construct the idea that the world is constructed.

THERAPIST: But isn't that another example of the tools you speak of? How can we escape the recursiveness of such thinking?

EPISTEMOLOGIST: We could build a world of ideas where such self-referential paradoxes are banned and then forget that we built it. The original use of the Theory of Types, as you may recall, was to do that. On the other hand, there is a view of the world that rests entirely on paradox. The news that epistemologists like Bateson, Maturana, Varela, and von Foerster bring us is that all living and mental process involves recursion, self-reference, and paradox. This perspective is the world of cybernetics and cybernetics of cybernetics.

THERAPIST: You've not explained that latter term, but I assume that cybernetics of cybernetics is a higher order of recursion than simple cybernetics.

EPISTEMOLOGIST: Indeed. Now, to return to how this may be useful to you. If you fully accept the premise of recursion as a way of seeing events in therapy, then you will have to accept some interesting paradoxes. Most importantly, you will realize that there is no such thing as a circular or recursive epistemology that bans so-called lineal thinking.

THERAPIST: Stop! You confuse me. I thought this entire book was about giving up a lineal epistemology and moving toward a circular, recursive, or cybernetic view. What are you now talking about?

EPISTEMOLOGIST: Let us look at an example from our history books. Do you remember reading about a time when people believed that the world was a flat plane? A ship that went out too far on the ocean was believed to drop off the planet. Of course when these ships later returned, people began assuming that the world is spherical rather than flat. Photographs of the earth taken from a satellite in outer space now confirm the spherical earth hypothesis. Anyone belonging to the Flat Earth Society is seen as a bit weird.

THERAPIST: That's a nice metaphor for family therapy. Most therapists today claim to subscribe to a "circular epistemology" and castigate "lineal thinkers." A quick way to draw an indication of right and wrong in the field is to invoke the difference between circular and lineal. I cannot imagine anyone claiming to be lineal any more than I could be serious about someone claiming that the world is flat.

EPISTEMOLOGIST: G. Spencer-Brown reminds us, however, that the flat earth hypothesis is quite sensible at times. For example, if we wish to build a tennis court, draw a blueprint for a house, or navigate across the English Channel, we must use the premise that the earth is flat. I dare you to landscape a soccer field with a spherical earth hypothesis. On the other hand, if we wish to sail around the world we need to switch to a spherical hypothesis.

THERAPIST: So, in essence, we still believe that the earth is flat.

EPISTEMOLOGIST: Only when it is convenient and appropriate. And, I must add, we can believe that the earth is flat without denying its circularity and sphericality.

THERAPIST: Does your illustration extend to family therapy?

EPISTEMOLOGIST: It already has. Lyman Wynne (1982) recently wrote a paper for a book honoring the founder of structural family therapy, Salvador Minuchin. In it he praises Minuchin for being a superb "lineal" therapist. He acknowledges that this will probably be seen as a startling proposition, but argues that most effective interventions, by definition, are "lineal."

THERAPIST: Are you saying that some interventions, as well as our ways of thinking about them, should be taken as lineal?

EPISTEMOLOGIST: In the same way that you consider a flat earth hypothesis for building a tennis court. I remind you, however, that if you were to build a series of tennis courts adjacent to each other clear around the world, you would end up constructing a circle. Although each particular tennis court could be punctuated as "linear," the pattern that connects all tennis courts would clearly be "circular."

THERAPIST: Similarly, would each particular therapeutic intervention Wynne calls "lineal" be part of a more encompassing circular pattern?

EPISTEMOLOGIST: The broader patterns of organization are indeed recursive. All lineal acts and notions are actually "partial arcs," to borrow an early phrase of Bateson's, of more encompassing patterns of circularity.

THERAPIST: So what does all this suggest for the clinical world?

EPISTEMOLOGIST: It means that you do not have to throw away lineal interventions and lineal thinking, as long as you see them as approximations of more encompassing recursive patterns. Furthermore, you will not be a very effective therapist without a repertoire of lineal strategy. Who could build a tennis court without a flat earth hypothesis? There is no reason to throw away plane geometry.

THERAPIST: But you said that I must not forget that these "partial arcs" are always approximations of the more encompassing circles that incorporate them. Why?

EPISTEMOLOGIST: If you throw a ball straight up in the air, it may fall on your head. All action, when seen from the broader patterns of recursion, is recycled. If you know this, then you can shape your lineal, purposeful action to be in tune with the more encompassing patterns of ecology that connect all living process. Forgetting about these broader patterns is what gets us into trouble. Other chapters of this book have more to say about these connections. What you should remember, for now, is that it is important to hold on to both lineal and recursive punctuations.

THERAPIST: Similarly, we can hold on to logical typing as long as we remember that it is an approximation or partial arc of recursive process.

EPISTEMOLOGIST: Occasionally it is useful to unwind a recursive process and pin it on a structure of logical types. Such a method is like paper chromatography, where we get a linear record of a chemical process. This linear perspective provides a difference that enables us to discern previously inaccessible patterns. We can work with logical typing in a similar fashion as long as we think of it as a tool for marking orders of recursion. Logical typing, like the flat earth hypothesis, is sometimes a useful approximation or model.

THERAPIST: With these various double views, it is possible to proceed to the world of cybernetic epistemology?

EPISTEMOLOGIST: Again, I remind you that you have already arrived. As I previously promised, there are some interesting paradoxes in cybernetics. Perhaps I should now tell you that from this perspective there is nothing but paradox in living and mental process. Do not believe anyone who tells you that there are no paradoxes in therapy. There is nothing but self-reference, recursion, and paradox.

THERAPIST: Would you define recursion once again?

EPISTEMOLOGIST: Cybernetics, circularity, repetition, recurrence, redundancy, pattern—all refer to recursion. These terms suggest that ideas, experience, and social events do more than stretch out in lineal time. When a process infolds upon itself, we speak of recursion. The image of a circle is probably not the best way to think of recursion since we are not really referring to a return to an original beginning point in time. Each recursive loop does imply a different beginning, although in terms of the pattern of organization, it is simply recycled.

THERAPIST: That statement makes no sense to me. How can it imply both a different beginning and the same beginning? Is there a double description lurking behind this?

EPISTEMOLOGIST: What we need is a way of speaking of the simultaneity of this sameness and differentness, a double description as you suggested. Cybernetics, as the next chapter will demonstrate, is one way of articulating such a complementary relation. Stability and change, as cybernetics puts it, represent two different faces of the same systemic coin.

THERAPIST: I still want to get some more understanding of recursion. Can you give me an example of a recursive process that returns to its starting place, but marks a different order of recursion?

EPISTEMOLOGIST: Following Varela (1976b, 1979), here are some paraphrases of various recursive processes:

Mythology: Female gives birth to male who fertilizes female.

Cognition: Intuitive understanding gives a ground for logical thinking which leads to intuitive understanding.

Systems: A whole is unraveled into its parts which generate processes integrating the whole.

Therapy: A therapist treats a client who directs the therapist how to treat him.

Punctuation: A distinction is drawn that distinguishes the distinction that drew it.

Double description: A description of process is categorized by a description of form which leads to a description of process.

Drawing of a distinction: An observer draws a distinction which enables distinctions to be drawn.

Recursion: A process returns to a beginning in order to mark a difference which enables the process to return to a beginning.

THERAPIST: Is this discussion, as well as the book, filled with patterns of recursion?

EPISTEMOLOGIST: It is impossible to avoid recursion or, in the broader sense, cybernetic epistemology.

THERAPIST: The trick is to re-cognize these patterns.

EPISTEMOLOGIST: Recall the play *Le Bourgeois Gentilhomme* by Molière, where a man, nouveau riche, finds himself in a new social context. While going from one conversation to another, he discovers that he is speaking prose. He exclaims, "I am speaking prose. I have always spoken prose. Now I speak prose and I know it!" We are basically in the same situation. All living and mental process is recursive or cybernetic. We simply have to acknowledge that we always have been cybernetic epistemologists. The trick is to be a cybernetic epistemologist and know it.

3

CYBERNETIC EPISTEMOLOGY

> Don't bite my finger, look where I am pointing.
> — *Warren S. McCulloch*

Cybernetics belongs to the science of pattern and organization which is distinct from any search for material, things, force, and energy. In cybernetics, anything, or rather any idea, is "real." As Lewis Carroll said, "In my *thought,* one thing is as good as another in this world, and the shoe of a horse will do." Anyone who has made the paradigmatic leap from material to pattern will not need to read any further. What follows is an attempt to describe the difference between these two worlds of description.

A whole host of terms has been used to distinguish between descriptions of material and those of pattern. A beginning list of these metaphors can be drawn as follows:

Metaphors of Pattern	*Metaphors of Material*
Cybernetics	Physics
Mind	Body
Form	Matter
Communication	Energy
Biological world[1]	Physical world
Organization of whole	Ingredients of whole
Qualitative analysis	Quantitative analysis
Mechanistic explanation[2]	Vitalistic explanation

1. Bateson used the term "biology" in an idiosyncratic way to signify the study of "mental process," whether it be immanent in seashores, forests, computer systems, or human beings.

2. Mechanistic explanation, most simply defined, focuses on explanations of pattern and structure (see Varela & Maturana, 1973). This has been grossly misunderstood in the human sciences, where mechanistic explanation is often castigated for reducing complex living process to vulgar machine analogies. Bertalanffy (1967)

Descriptions belonging to the left column are those of pattern and cannot be depicted with metaphors derived from a material world which carries assumptions about substance, energy, and quantification. As Bateson (1974) points out, "All metaphors derived from a physical world of impacts, forces, energy, etc., are unacceptable in explanations of events and processes in the biological world of information, purpose, context, organization and meaning" (p. 26). It is not surprising that Ashby (1956) describes cybernetics as follows:

> Cybernetics started by being closely associated in many ways with physics, but it depends in no essential way on the laws of physics or on the properties of matter. Cybernetics deals with all forms of behavior. . . . The materiality is irrelevant, and so is the holding or not of the ordinary laws of physics. *The truths of cybernetics are not conditional on their being derived from some other branch of science.* Cybernetics has its own foundations. (p. 1; emphasis in original)

The difference between cybernetics and physics, pattern and material, or mind and body should not be taken as an either/or duality. In the world of cybernetics we may think of two classes of events where pattern is manifest — those involving material and those which are said to be nonmaterial. We are thus able to distinguish between the embodiment of pattern by material and the appearance of pattern in nonmaterial or imaginary worlds.

Cyberneticians remind us that physics is actually a subdiscipline of cybernetics involving the study of patterns embodied by material. From this perspective, physics and cybernetics do not represent opposite poles; instead physics is seen as a part of cybernetics. Similarly, our list of pattern and material metaphors should be seen as related, in that pattern can be embodied by various forms of material.

To clarify this idea, we can consider what is involved in the full definition of a machine. A machine is obviously more than a list of its parts or a statement about the substances that comprise it. In addition, "machine" is a term referring to a particular *organization* of

---

criticized cybernetics for its mechanistic approach and argued for a "general system theory" which is "nonmechanistic in the sense that regulative behavior is not determined by structural or 'machine' conditions but by the interplay of forces" (p. 67). He gives away his epistemology by choosing to use metaphors of force rather than pattern. Such vitalistic description, when applied to the complexities of living and mental process, actually represents the vulgar, rather than aesthetic, view.

components. Strictly speaking, the machine's pattern of organization does not require any reference to the nature of the component materials.[3] Thus, a machine is a particular case in cybernetics where a pattern just happens to be embodied by some hardware.

To know that cybernetics and physics, mind and body, form and substance, yin and yang are not two (not a symmetrical duality) requires first drawing a distinction. Such a necessity arises from a basic epistemological understanding: A world of distinctions is distinct from a world within which nothing can be distinguished. Jung (1916/1961) referred to these worlds as "creatura" and "pleroma," respectively. In an odd little paper entitled "Septem Sermones ad Mortuos," he wrote:

> Harken: I begin with nothingness. Nothingness is the same as fullness. In infinity full is no better than empty. Nothingness is both empty and full. . . A thing that is infinite and eternal hath no qualities, since it hath all qualities. This nothingness or fullness we name the PLEROMA. . . In the pleroma there is nothing and everything. It is quite fruitless to think about the pleroma, for this would mean self-dissolution. CREATURA is not in the pleroma, but in itself. . . . Distinctiveness is creatura. It is distinct. Distinctiveness is its essence, and therefore it distinguisheth. (pp. 379-380)

Epistemology emerges from creatura: Even to know that there is a world of no distinctions requires that we draw a distinction. From the perspective of pleroma, all the distinctions we create are illusion or maya, the incomplete side of a more encompassing view in which there are no distinctions. As natural epistemologists, our dilemma is having to draw distinctions in order to know a world, while knowing that these constructions are illusory. As Bateson (1975) remarked, "The mystic may laugh at us but still the task of the anthropologist is to explore the world of illusion, perhaps with the eyes and ears of the mystic" (p. 149).

Thus, to recognize that apparent dualities are not two requires first drawing a distinction. We could not realize the whole gestalt

---

3. Varela and Maturana (1973) make this same point:

We are thus saying that what is definitory of a machine structure are relations and, hence, that the structure of a machine has no connection with materiality, that is, with the properties of the components that define them as physical entities. (p. 378) without having first noted that it subsumes different parts. On the other hand, parts cannot be distinguished without having assumed a whole from which they are abstracted. In essence, we are left with the realization that the differences we draw are neither one, nor two. The world we know is not illusion, not real.

Cybernetics may be a strange world for the occidental therapist to encounter. Sometimes it is interpreted as pointing to an "invisible" world since there is nothing to count or measure, and questions regarding what is real are often irrelevant. "Seeing" a cybernetic world does require changing our habit of viewing material exclusively. At the same time, it means avoiding any lineal dichotomies between material and pattern or mind and body. An encounter with cybernetics is somewhat analogous to a Japanese landscape, where pattern, rather than objects, is primary. The objects fade into the background while pattern is brought into focus.

Our goal is to develop a double view of pattern and material, mind and body. Cybernetics enables us to encounter mind in therapy while not forgetting the bodies that embody it. Achieving such a double view requires learning to re-cognize mind. Bateson (Bateson & Rieber, 1980) put it this way:

> I believe it is much healthier on the whole to believe that the physical universe is an illusion and that the mind is real, than to believe that the mind is an illusion and the physical universe is real. But of course, on the whole neither is correct. But believing that the mind is real is one step better than believing that the physical universe is real. (pp. 250–251)

SIMPLE CYBERNETICS

That pattern organizes physical and mental process is the primordial idea that gave birth to cybernetics. Although this notion had been incubating in the history of ideas for a long period of time and was implied in the writings of the Gnostics, Samuel Butler, Lewis Carroll, and particularly William Blake, it wasn't until the middle part of this century that it hatched as a formal science. In 1943, two papers from the United States appeared that Papert (1965) describes as so clearly introducing "the new frame of thought that their publication could well be taken as the birth of explicit cybernetics" (p. xv). One of these,

by Arturo Rosenblueth, Norbert Wiener, and Julian Bigelow, set out
to identify the general principles for mechanisms that could embody
the concept of "purpose." The other paper, by Warren McCulloch
and Walter Pitts, entitled "A Logical Calculus of the Ideas Immanent
in Nervous Activity," demonstrated "the class of functions any brain
must compute in order to perceive and describe what is perceivable
and describable" (von Foerster, 1970, p. 116). These papers attempted to discern the patterns of organization that underlie purposeful behavior and perception, respectively.

At the same time, Gregory Bateson had been developing a view
of interactional process in his anthropological investigations, and
Jean Piaget had sought to identify mechanisms of knowledge by
studying their development in young children. What all these studies
shared was the "recognition that the laws governing the embodiment
of mind should be sought among the laws governing information
rather than energy or matter" (Papert, 1965, p. xvi). Papert discusses
this notion further:

> The principal conceptual step was the recognition that a host of phys-
> ically different situations involving the teleonomic regulation of be-
> havior in mechanical, electrical, biological and even social systems
> should be understood as manifestations of one basic phenomenon: *the
> return of information to form a closed control loop*. (p. xvi; emphasis
> added)

The "return of information to form a closed control loop" was
"feedback," and the Rosenblueth, Wiener, and Bigelow (1943/1968)
paper argued that "all purposeful behavior may be considered to require feedback" (p. 222). Weiner (1954/1975) records that the ideas
of their paper "were disseminated by Rosenblueth at a meeting held
in New York City in 1942, under the auspices of the Josiah Macy
Foundation, and devoted to problems of central inhibition in the nervous system" (p. 12). This meeting brought together a group of scientists who had expressed an interest in "self-regulating mechanisms"
including John von Neumann, Walter Pitts, Warren S. McCulloch,
Gregory Bateson, and Margaret Mead.[4] The participants left that

4. Bateson and Mead (1976), however, recall that the focus of the meeting was
hypnosis. The ideas from the Rosenblueth, Wiener, and Bigelow paper, entitled "Behavior, Purpose and Teleology," were actually exchanged in casual conversation and
during lunch.

2-day meeting with a sense of something paradigmatically new. Heims (1977) suggests:

> Rosenblueth, Wiener and Bigelow had, in effect, announced a new paradigm in science, according to which one seeks an overarching theory to include machines and organisms; the theory would clearly involve the ideas of information, control and feedback. (p. 143)

Following a second meeting in 1944, Warren McCulloch arranged still another conference in 1946 which involved a wider diversity of participants, including Lawrence Kubie, Heinrich Klüver, Erik Erikson, Kurt Lewin, Alex Bavelas, F. S. C. Northrop, and Heinz von Foerster. This group met biannually for several years, and most of the meetings were entitled "Feedback Mechanisms and Circular Causal Systems in Biological and Social Systems."[5]

Weiner coined the term "cybernetics" to name the new kind of thinking they had come up with. In the first edition of his book *Cybernetics: Or the Control and Communication in the Animal and Machine* (1948), he noted that "the term 'Cybernetics' does not date further back than the summer of 1947" (cited in Mihram, Mihram, & Nowakowska, 1977, p. 418). However, in 1954, in the second edition of *The Human Use of Human Beings,* he acknowledged (with no bibliographical references) the use of the term cybernetics in 14th-century French and Polish works.[6] Wiener traced its etymological origin to the Greek word meaning "steersman." In *The Republic,* Plato used the word to signify both the art of steering *and* of command. Thus, the word's original reference to both nautical and social control suggests that cybernetics is concerned with people as well as their engineering devices.

Feedback

The basic idea of cybernetics is that of "feedback," which Wiener (1954/1967) defines as follows:

> Feedback is a method of controlling a system by reinserting into it the results of its past performance. If these results are merely used as nu-

---

5. A transcript of these meetings was published by the Josiah Macy, Jr., Foundation and edited by von Foerster. A summary of the meetings can be found in Lipset (1980) and Heims (1975, 1977).

6. In an essay entitled "The Modern Origins of the Term 'Cybernetics,' " Mihram, Mihram, and Nowakowska (1977) argue that "Ampère, not Wiener, deserves

merical data for the criticism of the system and its regulation, we have the simple feedback of the control engineers. If, however, the information which proceeds backward from the performance is able to change the general method and pattern of performance, we have a process which may be called learning. (p. 84)

Stated differently, all simple and complex regulation as well as learning involve feedback. Contexts of learning and change are therefore principally concerned with altering or establishing feedback. Successful therapy requires the creation of alternative forms of feedback which will provide an avenue for appropriate change.

The classic example of feedback is the thermostatically controlled heating system. When fluctuating temperature exceeds the boundaries of a calibrated thermostat, the furnace will be triggered to turn on or off, bringing the temperature back within the desired range. The system therefore monitors its own performance and is self-corrective. This maintenance of a range of fluctuation represents a process where "feedback opposes the direction of the initial change that produced the feedback" (Parsegian, 1973, p. 67). This process, called "negative feedback," is simply "a circular chain of causal events, with somewhere a link in the chain such that the more of something, the less of the next thing in the circuit" (Bateson, 1972, p. 429). For example, the more one's traveling speed in an automobile exceeds the speed limit, particularly in the presence of a patrolman, the less likely it is that one's foot will press against the gas pedal.

In a family, an argument between two members may escalate, like the temperature of a house, until an unbearable threshold is reached. That threshold is sometimes regulated or defined, like a thermostat, by another member presenting behavior that stops the argument. For instance, a brother and sister may quarrel until the family dog begins growling. The dog's behavior diverts the siblings to approach the dog and begin playing.

Sometimes feedback works to correct deviation in the other direction. A husband and wife may be "getting along" harmoniously until a call from their grown daughter provokes them into quarelling about some relatively ridiculous issue. In this case, the escalating

---

the title of 'The Modern Founder of Cybernetics' " (p. 411). They demonstrate that Ampère had defined cybernetics as "the very art of governing and of choosing in every case what can be and what must be done."

complementarity of the couple may have reached a threshold that triggered their reaction to their daughter's call which "rescued" them from getting "too stuck together."

All families embody feedback processes that provide stability for the whole family organization. By controlling escalating bits of behavior, interactional themes, and complex patterns of choreography, the family is able to stay together. An enduring family system is said to be "self-corrective."

Rosenblueth, Wiener, and Bigelow originally suggested, however, that feedback control may lead to clumsy behavior if the feedback is inadequately structured. For example, when an individual with ataxia is offered a cigarette he will swing his hand past it in an effort to pick it up. He will then swing past it again and again until his motion becomes a violent oscillation. Similarly, a poorly designed thermostat system may send the temperature of a house into wild oscillations. In the case of an automobile's steering system, too much "lag" or slowness of response will result in the car weaving in and out of the lane. Since it takes too long for the wheels to move when the driver turns the steering wheel, he responds by turning it even more. By the time the effects of his steering change the direction of the car, he will have steered it too far in one direction. This will consequently result in a similar sequence of oversteering in the other direction. In this feedback loop, the corrective behaviors of the system appear to overshoot and result in escalating oscillations.

When a social system is caught in a feedback loop in which the corrective behaviors overshoot, its action will also appear to wildly oscillate. A classic paper by Fry (1962), entitled "The Marital Context of an Anxiety Syndrome," demonstrates that clinical anxiety sometimes oscillates between both spouses. For example, a wife may experience an anxiety attack in response to an invitation to a social party. Although the husband responds by complaining that he isn't able to see their friends because of her "condition," one implication is that her symptom serves to protect him from being "too social," something he is secretly (or unconsciously) nervous about. When his nervousness (or anxiety) about being with others calms down, his wife may begin to approach social events. This then results in the husband having an anxiety episode and the entire dramatic enactment becomes reversed. The husband now "protects" his wife, who is possibly fearful of her husband establishing outside relationships. Each spouse provides overcorrective behavior, which leaves them experiencing oscillating anxiety.

Connections of Change and Stability

It is important to realize that cybernetic process never elects a static, steady state. As Bateson (1972) notes, "Corrective action is brought about by *difference*" (p. 381). The system is technically "error activated" in that "the difference between some present state and some 'preferred' state activates the corrective response" (p. 381). Cybernetics therefore suggests that "all change can be understood as the effort to maintain some constancy and all constancy as maintained through change" (G. Bateson, cited in M. Bateson, 1972, p. 17).

For example, the term "homeostasis" is used in discussing how processes of change lead to stability. Unfortunately, the term may be a misnomer in that it is often taken to indicate some sort of "steady state." Perhaps, as Brand (1976) has suggested, it should be renamed "homeodynamics" (p. 53). "Homeo" and "dynamics," when considered together, provide a double description of the cybernetic connection of stability and change.[7]

These ideas concerning cybernetic process presuppose that all variables in a system rarely, if ever at all, can be held to an exact value. No behavior, interaction, or system of choreography is ever consistently the same. Families, for example, are perpetual climates of change — each individual varies his behavior in a whirlwind of interactional permutations.

Technically speaking, a variable will "hunt," or vary, around a "control" value. A variable in a feedback circuit will either vary within a controlled range or the range of deviation itself will be amplified. Someone may, week after week, smoke 8-10 cigarettes a day, maintaining a controlled range. Another smoker, however, may escalate the range of cigarettes smoked from 8-10 per day for one week to 20-30 per day in later weeks. In this case, the range of deviation has amplified its upper and lower limits in the same direction. Such an increase indicates a runaway in one direction.

On the other hand, the smoker could have gradually changed from 8-10 cigarettes per day to 2-30 cigarettes a day. In this case, the range of deviation has amplified its limits in opposite directions. This increase suggests an escalating oscillation of the range of deviation.

Thus, we see that there are different patterns of amplified devia-

7. The problem with "dynamics," however, is that it is too often regarded as pertaining to physical forces or energy. Perhaps we should restrict ourselves to the term "negative feedback" when indicating the cybernetic relation of change and stability.

tion. A cybernetic system may be amplifying deviation in one direction or amplifying deviation in an ever-widening range of oscillations. Runaways in one direction, such as the escalating wealth of an oil baron, are usually triggered by efforts to maximize or minimize one variable. Wild range oscillations, such as the behavior of the patient with ataxia, are usually the result of uncoordinated feedback.

The difference between seeing a range of deviation as controlled or amplified is sometimes discussed in terms of two different kinds of feedback or cybernetic systems. Maruyama (1968), for example, suggests that there are deviation-counteracting and deviation-amplifying systems that incorporate so-called "negative" and "positive" feedback, respectively.

The potential problem with this view is that it too easily depicts change and stability as a dualism of polar opposites. Families are described as either change-oriented, homeostatic, or a balanced combination of these distinct processes. This division is simply not a cybernetic view. One cannot, in cybernetics, separate stability from change — both are complementary sides of a systemic coin. Cybernetics proposes that change cannot be found without a roof of stability over its head. Similarly, stability will always be rooted to underlying processes of change. This relationship will become more apparent as we continue to examine the recursive nature of a system's feedback process.

Wiener originally proposed that there are different orders of feedback control accounting for stability and change. In other words, "Feedback can refer to the success or failure of a simple act or it may occur at a higher level when information of a whole policy of conduct or pattern of behavior is fed back, enabling the organism to change its strategic planning of further action" (Rosenblith, cited in Wiener, 1954/1967, p. 276). Wiener (1954/1967) acknowledged that this latter form of feedback "differs from more elementary feedbacks in what Bertrand Russell would call its 'logical type'" (p. 82). Such higher order feedback often provides a way of maintaining and changing a particular social organization.

As Haleys' (1973b) work masterfully demonstrates, an adolescent diagnosed as "psychotic" often signals that a family is having trouble in the developmental stage of weaning their child. The emergence of adolescent "psychotic" behavior that appears to escalate toward being unmanageable by the parents will eventually trigger a higher order of control. The parents may, for example, seek a therapist who institutionalizes the adolescent. By locking him up in a room the parents pay for, the family remains unaltered. In other words, feedback involving therapist and institution now helps maintain the family organization in a way that continues to block the adolescent's successful venture into the adult world. Effective therapy for such a complicated system would therefore necessitate establishing an alternative order of feedback process which would change the pattern recursively connecting family, therapist, and institution.

Feedback that is not subject to higher order control, that is, a situation lacking feedback of feedback, will inevitably lead to unchecked escalation and schismogenesis. Ultimately, uncontrolled escalation destroys a system. However, change in the direction of learning, adaptation, and evolution arises from the control of control, rather than unchecked change per se. In general, for the survival and co-evolution of any ecology of systems, feedback processes must be embodied by a recursive hierarchy of control circuits. Bateson (1979a) provides the example of a driver of an automobile:

> A driver of an automobile travels at 70 miles per hour and thereby alerts the sense organ (radar, perhaps) of a traffic policeman. The bias or threshold of the policeman dictates that he shall respond to any difference greater than 10 miles per hour above or below the speed limit.
>
> The policeman's bias was set by the local chief of police, who acted self-correctively with his eye on orders (i.e., calibration) received from the state capitol.
>
> The state capitol acted self-correctively with the legislators' eyes on their voters. The voters, in turn, set a calibration within the legislature in favor of Democratic or Republican policy. (pp. 198–199)

Cybernetics studies how processes of change determine various orders of stability or control. From this perspective a therapist must be able to distinguish not only simple feedback which maintains the client's presenting problem, but also *higher order* feedback which maintains those lower order processes. The therapist's goal is to activate the order of feedback process that will enable a disturbed ecology to correct itself.

An Appropriate Fiction for Behavioral Science

Von Neumann and Morgenstern (1944) once commented that someone needs to provide a fiction for the behavioral sciences that would work like the elegant fiction upon which physics was built — its Newtonian particle. Without an appropriate fiction or hypothesis,[8] no behavioral science could be built.

The idea of a recursive network with feedback structure provides a useful fiction for behavioral science. In their classic work, *Plans and the Structure of Behavior,* Miller, Galanter, and Pribram (1960) similarly propose that "the unit we should use as the element of behavior" is "the feedback loop itself" (p. 27).

Simple feedback should be taken as a beginning conceptual building block or hypothesis. Using this, we can construct the broader perspective of recursive orders of feedback process which enables us to characterize mental and living process. Complex systems involve a hierarchical arrangement of feedback. It is important to remember that such a hierarchy is a recursive network rather than a layered pyramid. When I speak of feedback process, I am referring to this recursive network.

Furthermore, I prefer to think in terms of hierarchically arranged (in the recursive sense) *negative* feedback. With this perspective we avoid the dualism that otherwise arises between "positive" and "negative" feedback. What sometimes appears as so-called "positive feedback," for example, the escalating buildup of armaments, is actually a part of higher order negative feedback. In the case of an armaments race, a nuclear war may be the corrective action in a negative feedback process. Mankind's present hope, however, rests upon the assumption that fear of such an order of self-correction (i.e., war) will itself lead to a recalibration of the arms race.

Thus, cybernetic explanation, as Bateson (1972) argued, is always "negative" (p. 399). What is sometimes called "positive feedback" or "amplified deviation" is therefore a partial arc or sequence of a more encompassing negative feedback process. The appearance of escalating runaways in systems is a consequence of the frame of reference an observer has punctuated. Enlarging one's frame of reference enables the "runaway" to be seen as a variation subject to higher orders of control.[9]

8. In one of his metalogues, Bateson (1972) defines "hypotheses" as made up notions that serve as "a sort of conventional agreement between scientists to stop trying to explain things at a certain point" (p. 39).

9. We can always choose to keep the term "positive feedback" to use as an approximation for higher orders of negative feedback. From this perspective, negative and positive feedback are complementary in the same way as recursive and lineal epistemologies.

CYBERNETICS OF CYBERNETICS

In the early days of cybernetics, engineers often made reference to the study of "black boxes." The cybernetic engineering of black boxes was restricted to examining the relation of what goes into a system (input) and what comes out of it (output). This relation was cybernetic when the output was seen as acting on the input so as to modify future output.

For example, a rocket guides itself toward the moon by recycling information about its present position to guide its future position. The shortcoming of this view is that it fails to place the observer or engineer into the picture. After a number of trial runs, for example, the engineer must calibrate the rocket's steering mechanism. This larger trial-and-error sequence is a higher order feedback process that includes the engineer.[10]

In a cybernetic system regulating house temperature, the inclusion of a human being is necessary when we remember that the house temperature's simple feedback is calibrated by a resident who adjusts the setting on the thermostat. As Bateson (1979a) proposes, "the bias (the calibration of the feedback) is itself governed by a feedback whose sense organ is located, not on the living room wall, but in the skin of the man" (p. 198). In general, any "black box" system, whether it be a rocket's steering mechanism or a simple heating system, is circumscribed by higher orders of feedback control.

The black box view which posits an observer outside the phenomenon observed often leads to the idea that the outsider is in a position to unilaterally manipulate or control the system he is observing. This perspective is sometimes useful when one is given the responsibility of managing a system. A therapist who is instructed by a court system to work with a chaotic, delinquent adolescent will be grateful for a black box view. Such a perspective, although incomplete at a higher order of recursive process, enables the therapist to discern patterns that maintain the problematic behavior and to orient his behavior in a strategic way.

The black box view, of course, is incomplete and only useful in certain situations requiring unilateral management or what McCul-

10. Bateson and Mead (1976) report that Wiener's concern wasn't restricted to input–output relations of black boxes, but included the events within the larger circuit, of which the observer is a part.

loch called a "command system" (cited in M. Bateson, 1972, p. 204). The therapist, at a higher order of recursion, is part of a whole system and subject to its feedback constraints. At this level, the therapist is incapable of unilateral control and can be seen as either facilitating or blocking the necessary self-correction.

Cybernetics moved beyond the limited punctuation of early black box engineering by acknowledging higher orders of cybernetic process. Pask (1969), for example, argued that the elementary idea of a system with a purpose did not always take higher orders of recursion into account. Rather than acknowledging different orders of purpose, early cyberneticians tended to speak of simple purposes that made reference to one particular identifiable goal. In criticizing this simplistic determinism, Bateson (cited in Lipset, 1980) argued:

> Our whole thinking about the nature of purpose and related ideas is culturally biased towards the identifiable purpose, and I suspect that this is very often too narrow a way of looking at what an organism does. For example, I can say that I have a socially mobile upward purpose of convincing you of the importance of my discoveries. . . . But actually, as an organism, I am here for much wider purposes including a sense of well-being. (p. 194)

In an attempt to expand the cybernetician's understanding of different orders of purpose, Pask (1969) differentiated two types or orders of goal directed systems — "taciturn systems" and "language oriented systems." He defines them thus:

> Taciturn systems are those for which the observer asserts or discovers the goal (purpose *in*), which is thereafter equated with the purpose *for* the systems in question. In contrast, language oriented systems can be asked or instructed to *adopt* goals by anyone who knows the object language and they may state and describe their own goals, using the same medium. (p. 25)

A "cruise control" for an automobile is a taciturn system. The driver prescribes maintaining a certain velocity for the vehicle and then leaves the system to itself to achieve that purpose. In contrast, a computer with a programming language is a language oriented system. These systems operate by asking, rather than being unilaterally commanded to achieve goals. A computer, for example, may talk back, saying that you failed to give it the appropriate information, or it may suggest alternative questions.

Taciturn systems allow an observer to act as though he is distinct from the system of interest. Toasters, radios, and televisions, for example, can be seen as having a particular purpose of operation. The higher order of recursion which involved a man prescribing a goal for the machine is conveniently forgotten. For the most part, we overlook any ongoing interaction between operator and machine. At this order of purpose we disregard any "circuit" that connects the man and toaster. Every once in while, however, we are reminded of their connection; particularly when the man gets an electrical shock from the device.

In language oriented systems, the observer more clearly enters the system by defining and requesting *his* purpose. This is a higher order of purpose in that the achievement of the system's goal requires that the observer do more than push a button to start a machine. Whereas we don't think of people contributing as much to toasting toast (other than pushing a lever) as the toaster does, we more readily recognize the computer operator as part of the system that computes. Once the computer is switched on, the computer operator must continually interact with it to achieve a goal. Here, the question "Can a computer think?" is approached by pointing to the mental characteristics of the man-computer circuit.[11]

The difference between taciturn and language oriented systems is one of recursive order. Rather than viewing these systems as a duality, language oriented systems can be seen to represent a higher order of recursion than taciturn systems. The latter is a complementary approximation of the former. Any punctuation of a taciturn system by an observer is therefore a shorthand indication of what, on a higher order of recursion, appears as a language oriented system.

Family therapists have historically encountered their clients as either taciturn or language oriented systems. The former stance views the client system as a black box that can be observed and operated on from an outside position. The latter brings the therapist into the system, prohibiting any disconnection of the therapist-client circuit.

---

11. Bateson (1972) suggests that "the computer is only an arc of a larger circuit which always includes man and an environment from which information is received and upon which efferent messages from the computer have effect. This total system, or ensemble, may legitimately be said to show mental characteristics" (p. 317).

The jump from black boxes to black boxes *plus* the observer, as well as from taciturn to language oriented systems, represents an evolution from primitive cybernetics to what has been called "cybernetics of cybernetics." As von Foerster (1973a) puts it, "It is at this point where we mature from cybernetics (where the observer enters the system only by stipulating its purpose) to cybernetics of cybernetics (where the observer enters the system by stipulating his own purpose)" (p. 31).

"Cybernetics of cybernetics," a phrase originally suggested by Margaret Mead (1968), is therefore a way of pointing to the observer's inclusion and participation in the system. In contrast to the simplistic black box approach where an outside observer attempts to detect the redundancies (or rules) in input–output relations, cybernetics of cybernetics jumps an order of recursion and places the observer as part of the observed system.

The use of cybernetic thinking in social science and psychotherapy has traditionally followed the black box model. Watzlawick *et al.* (1967) for example, argued the advantages of a black box approach:

> This concept, if applied to psychological and psychiatric problems, has the heuristic advantage that no ultimately unverifiable intrapsychic hypotheses need to be invoked, and that one can limit oneself to observable input–output relations, that is, to communication. Such an approach, we believe, characterizes an important recent trend in psychiatry toward viewing symptoms as one kind of input into the family system rather than as an expression of intrapsychic conflict. (p. 44)

The perspective that punctuates a family as a black box describes symptoms as well as a therapist's interventions as "inputs" to the box. Such a view has been quite useful for designing therapeutic strategy. Here therapists become analogous to control engineers and concern themselves with "adjusting," "recalibrating" or "changing the structural organization" of their treatment families through an explicit, purposeful design. Many important contributions to the pragmatics of therapy have arisen from this perspective.

However, the limitation of this pragmatic view is that the observer or therapist is overlooked as part of the system being observed and treated. In addition, those more complex orders of process, sometimes called "unconscious," may also be disregarded in the context of therapy.

The irony of a decontextualized pragmatic approach is that it not only puts the family into a black box, it also circumscribes the therapist as part of another black box. The even larger box, with its more complex interaction between these circumscribed systems, is easily ignored. Cybernetics of cybernetics attempts to move to a perspective in which the two separate boxes can be opened and seen as a whole recursive system.

As mentioned earlier, Wiener (1954/1975) was aware of different orders of feedback process. He realized that in the human sciences higher order cybernetic process necessarily includes the observer. Thus, he proposed that any community studied by an anthropologist will never "be quite the same afterward" (p. 163). More dramatically, he suggested that "an investigation of the stock market is likely to upset the stock market" (p. 164). Unfortunately, in the early days of "control cybernetics" these higher orders of process were not adequately articulated, and it became necessary for the field to rediscover its own recursive nature.

Howe and von Foerster (1974) note that "while cybernetics began by developing the epistemology for comprehending and simulating first-order regulatory processes in the animal and machine, cybernetics today provides a conceptual framework with sufficient richness to attack successfully second-order process (e.g., cognition, dialogue, socio-cultural interaction, etc.)" (p. 16). Simple cybernetics has provided us with notions like homeostasis and adaptation, while cybernetics of cybernetics, as will be discussed, includes concepts of self-reference, autonomy, and more complex units of mind.

SELF-REFERENCE

Errors of Objectivity

Since cybernetics of cybernetics, or what von Foerster calls "second-order cybernetics,"[12] places the observer in that which is observed, all description is self-referential. Whitehead and Russell's formulation,

12. Heinz von Foerster (Howe & von Foerster, 1974, p. 16) distinguishes *first-order cybernetics* ("cybernetics of observed systems") from *second-order cybernetics*

in 1901, of the Theory of Logical Types (see Chapter 2) was an attempt to avoid any contradictions and self-referential paradoxes in formal logic and mathematics. However, in 1931, Kurt Gödel formally proved that consistency and completeness in a mathematical theory is not possible. What he did, in effect, was prove that there is no way of getting rid of the self-referential paradoxical beasts which are a natural part of any formal system of thinking. Since those early papers, scholars such as Günther, Löfgren, and others have addressed self-referential conceptual systems and have successfully dealt with them. Von Foerster (1971) summarizes this history as follows:

> "Self-reference" in scientific discourse was always thought to be illegitimate, for it was generally believed that The Scientific Method rests on "objective" statements that are supposedly observer-independent, as if it were impossible to cope scientifically with self-reference, self-description and self-explanation—that is, closed logical systems that include the referee in the reference, the observer in the description and the axioms in the explanation.
>
> This belief is unfounded, as has been shown by John von Neumann, Gotthard Günther, Lars Löfgren and many others who addressed themselves to the question as to the degree of complexity a descriptive system must have in order to function like the objects described, and who answered this question successfully. (pp. 239–240)

The epistemological implication of cybernetics of cybernetics increasingly points to the position that "objectivity" is erroneous since it assumes a separation of the observer and observed. Along these lines, von Foerster (1976c) asks, "How would it be possible to make a description in the first place if the observer were not to have properties that allow him to generate such descriptions?" He concludes "that the claim for objectivity is just nonsense!" (p. 12).

Bateson (cited in Keeney, 1979b) provides an illustration of the foolishness that can arise when we forget that the observer is intertwined with the observed:

("cybernetics of observing systems"). This distinction is equivalent to simple cybernetics and cybernetics of cybernetics, respectively. It is unfortunate that Maruyama (1968) has used the terms "first-order and second-order cybernetics" to refer to the cybernetics of negative and positive feedback systems. His use of these terms to specify a duality rather than orders of recursion is not connected to the tradition of cybernetic thinking I have been discussing.

Somebody was saying to Picasso that he ought to make pictures of things the way they are—objective pictures. He mumbled he wasn't quite sure what that would be. The person who was bullying him produced a photograph of his wife from his wallet and said, "There, you see, that is a picture of how she really is." Picasso looked at it and said, "She is rather small isn't she? And flat?" (p. 20)

The absurdity of objectivity is further illustrated by von Foerster (1976d):

It is syntactically and semantically correct to say that subjective statements are made by subjects. Thus, correspondingly, we may say that objective statements are made by objects. It is only too bad that these damned things don't make any statements. (p. 16)

Unfortunately, the notion of objectivity with its accompanying disregard for self-reference often prevails in man's dealings with human systems. Most approaches to education, for example, follow premises of objectivity. Von Foerster (1972) characterizes this orientation as the "trivialization" of students. The student, in such a situation, begins as an unpredictable organism. He is then taught to give predictable "correct" answers. A perfect score on a so-called "objective test" is indicative of perfect trivialization: "The student is completely predictable and can be admitted into society" (p. 41). The alternative, von Foerster suggests, is to provide an educational system that in addition would ask "legitimate questions"—"questions to which the answers are unknown." In that context, self-referential dialogue could emerge where both teacher and student are recursively connected: The teacher is always part of what is learned and the student is always part of what is taught. Ideally, education would involve both "rote" learning and Socratic dialogue, joined in recursive fashion.

The same criticism could apply to therapy. Therapists who treat client systems as separate black boxes may "trivialize" a therapeutic context. These therapists view themselves as unilaterally "controlling" their clients and extoll the virtues of a so-called "objective" or "neutral" position.

One way a therapist may trivialize a client is by giving him "objective" diagnostic tests. This allows the therapist to treat a predictable category. By relating to a client's behavior as if it were a particular *category* of behavior, a therapist helps shape the "reality" of the presenting problem. This turns the therapeutic hour into an initiation rite and training session for how to be symptomatic in a particular way. In such a context, clients learn the skills necessary to be a successful category of symptomology.

Other therapists, working from a more social vantage point, may set up interactional episodes wherein the clients are led to alter their responses. In this approach, a family, for example, may be permitted to communicate only in a certain way through certain channels. Father may be instructed to tell mother how he "feels," rather than what he "thinks." At the same time, children may be kept from interrupting father's speech. In this social interactional scenario, the therapist is like a traffic cop, punctuating how the various sequences of behavior will unfold.

Whether disguised in psychometric or social interactional frames, these therapists act upon the same fundamental assumption that they are "in charge" of creating change, and that they must remain "outside" the system being treated. Cybernetics of cybernetics, as we will later see, more fully attends to the recursive relation between client and therapist—a perspective which avoids the premises of "objectivity."

Von Forester (1976c) argues, however, that one cannot negate objectivity in favor of "subjectivity" because "if a nonsensical proposition is negated, the result is again a nonsensical proposition" (p. 12). "Objectivity" and "subjectivity" represent a sort of complementary pair, like day and night or left and right. Thus, when the idea of "objectivity" is shown as nonsense, by implication this suggests that "subjectivity" is also nonsense.

Ethics of Observing

It is apparent that we need to look beyond the gestalt of objectivity and subjectivity. Cybernetics of cybernetics proposes that the alternative is *ethics*. From an ethical perspective we do not ask whether we are "objective" or "subjective." Instead, we recognize the necessary connection of the observer with the observed, which leads to examining *how* the observer participates in the observed.

This view follows from an understanding of the fundamentals of epistemology. In order to "know," one must first make a distinction. The act of making a distinction itself suggests a choice or preference. A therapist's view of a symptom therefore presupposes a particular preference, intent, and ethical base. This perspective suggests that any description says as much or more about the observer as it says about the subject of description. An obvious example is a critic labeling a particular film as "absurd." Such a description often reveals more about the critic than the film. Descriptions of clients who are institutionalized, have electrical voltage charged through their brains, or have drugs pumped into their veins give us information about their therapists.

The change to a participatory, ethical perspective is described by Howe and von Foerster (1975) as a "shift from causal unidirectional to mutualistic systemic thinking, from a preoccupation with the properties of the observed to the study of the properties of the observer" (pp. 1–2). They cite Kant as the initiator of this shift and argue that this paradigmatic change replaces our concern with objectivity to one of responsibility. Since we each prescribe particular ways of punctuating the world, it is important to examine the intentions that underlie our punctuative habits. In sum, the distinctions we make in order to know the human world arise from an ethical, not objective or subjective base.

The perspective of a self-referential, participatory epistemology rejects many of the assumptions underlying the traditional "scientific method." Accordingly, science must be redefined, particularly with regard to its application to social systems. Umpleby (1975) suggests that "cybernetics proposes to construct a more general epistemology of which the classical scientific method is a special case, a special case that is not applicable to social systems"[13] (p. 7). In a classic paper entitled "An Epistemology for Living Things," von Foerster (1976b) observes that although the physicists in the first part of this century revised the underlying notions that govern the natural sciences, the biologists are now revising the basic notions that govern all of science:

> The classical concept of an "ultimate science," that is an objective description of the world in which there are no subjects (a "subjectless universe"), contains contradictions.

---

13. Bateson (1972) has also argued that a basic science of social systems must follow an epistemology of pattern rather than classical physics:

> [My colleagues in the behavioral sciences] have tried to build the bridge to the wrong half of the ancient dichotomy between form and substance. The conservative laws for energy and matter concern substance rather than form. But mental process, ideas, communication, organization, differentiation, pattern, and so on, are matters of form rather than substance. (p. xxv)

> To remove these one had to account for an "observer" (that is at least for one subject): (i) Observations are not absolute but relative to an observer's point of view (i.e., his coordinate system: Einstein); (ii) Observations affect the observed so as to obliterate the observer's hope for prediction (i.e., his uncertainty is absolute: Heisenberg).
>
> After this, we are now in the possession of the truism that a description (of the universe) implies one who describes it (observes it). What we need now is the description of the "describer" or, in other words, we need a theory of the observer . . . this task falls to the biologist. (p. 1)

Cybernetics of cybernetics, which has been developed largely by biologists, provides us with a view of self-reference and an ethical consideration for how we participate in the construction and maintenance of our experiential universe. The avenue to correcting the potentially heartless and ethically bankrupt position of a strict application of simple cybernetics to human systems involves leaping to the position of self-reference and participation prescribed by cybernetics of cybernetics. At this higher order of process we find that we do not throw away the pragmatic advantages gained by a first-order view. Instead, the pragmatics of simple cybernetics are *contextualized* by a perspective that brings the therapist fully into therapy.

We are now ready to encounter the very core of cybernetics of cybernetics. As a means of approaching this territory, we will begin with a brief tour of the biological research that originally led to thinking about these higher orders of process. The reader should be forewarned that the pathway to understanding how a therapist is more fully a part of therapy is paradoxical. As we will see, a full consideration of a system's autonomy leads us to a richer understanding of the ecology of therapy.

AUTONOMY

Cyberneticians describe cybernetics of cybernetics as a way of viewing the "organizational closure" or "autonomy" of systems. This means that a system is viewed with no reference to its outside environment. The system's boundary is unbroken. In effect, this is an attempt to approach the *wholeness* of systems, which was the original goal of Bertalanffy's (1967) General System Theory. From this perspective, we speak of a "closed system, or more radically still, one which from the 'point of view' of the system itself, is entirely self-referential and has no 'outside,' Leibnizian for our day" (Maturana & Varela, 1980, p. v).

This orientation has been formally elaborated by the biologists Maturana and Varela. Their work began in response to the question "What is the organization of living process?" Stated differently, "What pattern characterizes the autonomy of living systems?" As a starting point, Maturana worked with his MIT colleagues Lettvin, McCulloch, and Pitts on the phenomenon of perception. In their historic paper "What the Frog's Eye Tells the Frog's Brain" (Lettvin, Maturana, McCulloch, & Pitts, 1959), they hypothesized that the frog has feature detectors built into its neurophysiology which selectively respond to particular events in its environment (e.g., color, shape, and movement of prey and enemy). This hypothesis followed the assumption that there is an objective reality or environment outside the animal which is modeled internally. Perception was therefore conceived as a matter of correlating outside environmental events with internal neural events.

This epistemology, however, began to falter when Maturana proposed a different research question: "What if, instead of attempting to correlate the activity in the retina with the physical stimuli external to the organism, we did otherwise, and tried to correlate the activity in the retina with the color experience of the subject?" (Maturana & Varela, 1980). This question, in effect, asked, "What is the relationship between an organism's eye and brain without reference to any outside stimuli?" Subsequent investigation led Maturana and his colleagues to conclude that perception is not determined by an outside environment, but is a product of the internal nervous system. Although external events can trigger the whole nervous system to act, the products of perception are internally generated. Maturana and Varela describe their fundamental discovery as follows:

> One had to close off the nervous system to account for its operation and . . . perception should not be viewed as a grasping of an external reality, but rather as the specification of one, because no distinction was possible between perception and hallucination in the operation of the nervous system as a closed network. (p. xv)

It should not be surprising that experimental epistemology discovered that the nervous system closes on itself. This is operationally necessary for an organism to be able to think about its thinking. What this perspective suggests is that sensory perception is not an internal patterning of external input. Instead, perception should be viewed "as a reflection of the structure of the nervous system" (Varela, 1979, p. 247). Cybernetics of cybernetics, as we've been hinting, turns our traditional epistemology inside out.

With this epistemology, Maturana's initial question about the organization of living systems could be answered. In sum, the autonomy of living systems is characterized by closed, recursive organization. Stated differently, all living process embodies cybernetic epistemology.

It is important, however, to realize that the order of cybernetic process that maintains a *whole* living organism is vastly more complex than that of the engineer's simple thermostat. Maturana and Varela invoked the term "autopoiesis" to refer to the order of process that generates and maintains the wholeness or autonomy of biological cells. Autopoiesis is defined by Andrew (1979) as "the capacity that living systems have to develop and maintain their own organization, the organization which is developed and maintained being identical with that which performs the development and maintenance" (p. 359).[14]

A system's *highest* order of recursion or feedback process defines, generates, and maintains the autonomy of a system. The range of deviation this feedback seeks to control concerns the organization of the whole system itself. If the system should move beyond the limits of its own range of organization, it would cease to be a system. Thus, autonomy refers to the maintenance of a system's wholeness. In biology, it becomes a definition of what maintains the variable called "living."

The ideas of Maturana and Varela are related to Bateson's work. All three argue that descriptions and relations of descriptions are generated by an observer's drawing of distinctions, which create an epistemological net ready to catch and identify a phenomenon. Furthermore, they point to the closed recursiveness of whole cybernetic systems. As Bateson (1972) put it, the cybernetic characteristics of a system "are

---

14. There is some disagreement over whether the term autopoiesis should be restricted to referring to chemical networks that produce topological boundaries, for example, living cells. Varela does not extend the concept to represent autonomy of nontopologically defined systems such as animal societies and family networks. I follow Varela's position that any characterization of an autonomous social system as autopoietic is an incorrect classification.

inherent or immanent in the ensemble as a *whole*" (p. 315). To break the circuit by punctuating an input and output is to break up the system. Following Varela (1976a) "Unless you confront the mutualness, the closure, of a system, you just lose the system" (p. 27). Varela (1979) notes that organizational closure, the highest order of feedback, differs from simple feedback in that "the latter requires and implies an external source of reference, which is completely absent in organizational closure" (p. 56). Organizational closure involves a network of interconnected feedback loops that is closed and has no inputs or outputs from an outside environment. Instead, it feeds upon itself like the recursive snake eating its own tail.

Although the organization of an autonomous system is closed, we can interact with its *wholeness* in a variety of ways. An observer or therapist can "interact with a system by poking at it, throwing things at it and doing things like that, in various degrees of sophistication" (Varela, 1976a, p. 28). These interactions represent perturbations of the stability of the whole system, which, in response, "will compensate or will not compensate" (Varela, 1976a, p. 28). What remains stable in this compensation is the system's wholeness: The system retains its identity as a particular autonomous organization. The system as a whole acts as a homeostat, that is, a device for holding its own organization within limits.[15]

An interesting example of a closed organization is provided by a field report from Darwin (cited in Ardrey, 1970):

> On a huge estancia he (Darwin) found a herd of cattle numbering over ten thousand. It seems to the unpracticed eye a disorganized agglomerate of beasts. But, as all herdsmen knew the throng was subdivided into groups of fifty or a hundred that stayed always in the vicinity of one another. Then one night came a terrifying series of electrical storms. The cattle panicked, milled, bolted, dispersed in the dark, panicked and dispersed again. By morning it was as if a deck of ten thousand cards had been shuffled and reshuffled the long night through. For the human herders, restoration of original arrangements was impossible. Yet within twenty-four hours not an animal had failed to find its original partners and with them to resume normal social life. (p. 67)

15. As Varela (1979) defines it, "an autopoietic machine is a homeostatic (or rather a relations-static) system that has its own organization (defining network of relations) as the fundamental invariant" (p. 13).

From the perspective of cybernetics of cybernetics, the electrical storm was not a lineal input-like intervention, but rather a perturbation of a closed organization. In this case, the organizationally closed social system compensated—it retained its autonomy.

The Family as Autonomous System

At its highest order of recursion, a family is an autonomous system. As a social organism, its highest order of feedback process serves to maintain its unity as a whole family creature. Stated recursively, a family is organized to maintain the organization that defines it as a family.

Families, as we've discussed earlier, can be described through various orders of process including particular bits of action, interactional episodes, and more complex systems of choreography. In this hierarchy of recursive process, the most advanced choreography is concerned with linking the lower orders of process so as to keep the organism an organism. This highest order of organization is the closed organization of the system. To change this pattern of organization is equivalent to destroying the system. When an organism cannot remain within the limits of living, it dies.

Although such a description of recursive orders may sometimes appear awkward, tedious, and complex, it is a formal way of approaching the organization of living process. We have actually already encountered this formal description in our dialectic between form and process in Chapter 2. Starting with bits of action and working up to various patterns of interaction and choreography, the zigzag ladder takes us to an upper limit. The highest order of form and process in a system is the whole system itself.

Again, the closed organization, autonomy, or wholeness of a system, say, a family, cannot change, or there would be no family. If a family system loses its autonomy, it would not be distinguishable as a unity. In that regard, it would cease to be a recognizable whole.

This is not to say that a family does not change. What changes is its structure or the way of maintaining its organization. Maturana and Varela (1980) propose that organization and structure are of different logical types.

> The relations that define a machine as a unity, and determine the dynamics of interactions and transformations which it may undergo as such a unity, constitute the *organization* of the machine. The actual

relations which hold among the components which integrate a con-crete machine in a given space, constitute its *structure*. (p. 77)

For example, when Selvini-Palazzoli and her Milan colleagues advise therapists to respect a family's homeostasis, they are referring to the highest order of homeostasis involving the closed *organization* of the family system (Selvini-Palazzoli, Cecchin, Prata, & Boscolo, 1978). On the other hand, when therapists say a symptom provides a service for a person and/or their family system, they are referring to a particular way in which that system is being *structurally* maintained as a whole. A goal of therapy may involve facilitating alternative structures to maintain the family organization.

The difference between structure and organization, as articulat-ed by Maturana and Varela, suggests a new way to understand the sys-tems adage, "The whole is greater than the sum of its parts."[16] More accurately, "The whole is the organizational closure of its parts" (Varela, 1976a, p. 29). Clearly, the organizational closure of a family is a way of pointing to the *whole family*.

DIALECTIC OF CALIBRATION AND FEEDBACK

It is important to again point out that cybernetics of cybernetics does not call for an abandonment of simple cybernetics. It does not urge us to throw away concepts of simple feedback. Rather, cybernetics of cy-bernetics is a higher order of recursion than simple cybernetics — its name is no accident. Cybernetics of cybernetics is about homeostasis of homeostasis, control of control, stability of stability, change of change, and feedback of feedback. It provides a way of constructing and discerning more complex cybernetic process through higher orders of recursion. As mentioned earlier, all systems and feedback loops are like Chinese boxes engulfing themselves.

The implication of this broad view has been stated by Beer (cited in Maturana & Varela, 1980):

It means that every social institution (in several of which any one indi-

---

16. Actually, the idea that the whole is more than the sum of its parts it partially nonsense. For example, $2 + 2 \neq 4$ is simply false. "Two plus two equals four" is a math-ematical tautology. As von Foerster (1963) points out, what we want to say is "a meas-ure of the sum of the parts is larger than the sum of the measure of the parts" (p. 28).

vidual is embedded at the intersect) is embedded in a larger social institution, and so on recursively — and that all of them are autopoietic. This immediately explains why the process of change at any level of recursion (from the individual to the state) is not only difficult to accomplish but actually impossible — in the full sense of the intention: "I am going completely to change myself." The reason is that the "I," that self-contained autopoietic "it," is a *component* of another autopoietic system. . . . An individual attempting to reform his own life within an autopoietic family cannot fully be his new self because the family insists that he is actually like his old self. (pp. 70-71)

The notion of infolded Chinese box-like systems means that an individual is part of numerous orders of organization. This, of course, has been a fundamental principle of family therapy.

One way of encountering the labyrinth of higher order cybernetic process involves using the zigzag dialectical ladder between form and process presented in Fig. 1 in Chapter 2. Recall that the dialectical map has a right column called "description of process." We previously discussed various orders of process in terms of simple action, interaction, and choreography. Translated to the world of cybernetics, this column becomes "description of feedback process."

The left column of the dialectical ladder in Fig. 1 is called "classification of form." Here, we noted, the observer classifies the organization of the process being observed: For example, "play" was proposed as a particular organization of behavior. Translated to the world of cybernetics, classification of form becomes "classification of calibration," a specification of the organization of feedback process. Using this version of the dialectic between form and process, we can construct and discern diverse orders of cybernetic calibration and feedback.

For example, the control of house temperature, at its simplest order of recursion, consists of a feedback process where thermostat and furnace respond to differences in temperature. This elementary cybernetic loop is organized by the particular setting of the thermostat, which is called the "calibration" of house temperature feedback. However, as we've previously discussed, calibration of that feedback is itself subject to higher order feedback involving the person who actually does the calibrating. People who live in bitterly cold climates and prefer staying indoors may very likely calibrate their thermostats differently than those who live in a dry, hot desert and enjoy outdoor sports. Thus, the climate and lifestyle the person experiences represent part of an even higher order feedback process which calibrates that person.

Like the dialectic between form and process, moving from one order of feedback process to another requires a dialectical swing through a classification of calibration. In the case of family interaction, a classic example involves a child's symptomatic behavior calibrating the intensity of the parents' interaction. An escalating argument, for instance, may reach a point where the child is activated to have an asthmatic attack. The child's behavior diverts the parental interaction and in this way calibrates the degree of escalation their arguing may reach.

This feedback, however, is also subject to recalibration by higher order feedback process. A therapist, for example, may restructure the family organization in a way that creates an alternative pathway for achieving stability of interaction. To accomplish this, a therapist can focus on getting the parents to calibrate their own symmetrical episodes that escalate toward runaway. By facilitating a context in which husband and wife become a self-correcting system, the therapist helps disrupt the previous calibration of their behavior by the child's symptomatic disturbance. The higher order feedback process in this case includes therapist, parents, and child. Thus, higher order feedback recalibrates lower order feedback process. Stated differently, the "therapist–parents–child system" alters the "parents–child system."

We can become aware of different orders of cybernetics through the dialectic between feedback and calibration. This cybernetic dialectic, schematized in Fig. 2, enables us to move from simple cybernetics to cybernetics of cybernetics. As the figure shows, moving from simple feedback to simple calibration accounts for the organization of simple cybernetic systems. As one ascends to higher orders of feedback process, simple feedback becomes open to recalibration — this is the level of cybernetics of cybernetics. The zigzag pattern reaches a limit, however, when one encounters the highest order of calibration and feedback in a system — what Varela and Maturana call autonomy. As discussed earlier, autonomy specifies the whole system itself, which by definition is organizationally closed.

A cybernetic dialectic may be applied to any system an observer (e.g., a therapist) happens to distinguish. Individuals, couples, triads, families, neighborhoods, and entire societies may each be punctuated by the observer as autonomous systems. It is also possible to see the

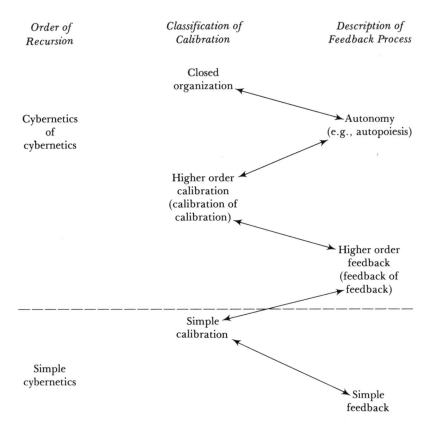

FIG. 2. DIALECTIC OF CALIBRATION AND FEEDBACK.

whole ecology of all imaginable (and unimaginable) punctuated systems as belonging to a larger autonomous system.

Mind as a Cybernetic System

One of Bateson's most important contributions has been his definition of "mind" as a cybernetic system. From this perspective, mind is an aggregate of interactive parts with feedback structure.[17] The complexity

17. Varela (1979) credits Bateson as the first to identify mind with the cybernetic system rather than what is inside the skull. Mind is therefore immanent in not only simple living systems, "but also ecological aggregates, social units of various sorts, brains, conversations, and many others, however spatially distributed or shortlived" (Varela, 1979, pp. 270–271).

of such systems ranges from simple feedback to what Bateson called an ecology of mind. Seen this way, the issue of limiting mind to within the boundaries of a skull becomes nonsense. Instead, wherever there is feedback, mental characteristics will be evident. The mind of a blind man crossing a street necessarily includes his walking cane. The cane, after all, is an active part of the feedback process that guides the man. Similarly, a musician's instrument and a carpenter's tool become parts of mental systems during the process of performance and construction. Mary Catherine Bateson (1972) proposes that the substitution of the word "mind" for the word "system" enables one to see that "mind becomes a property not just of single organisms, but of relations between them, including systems consisting of man and man, or a man and a horse, a man and a garden or a beetle and a plant" (p. 253). Such a view leads to Holt's metaphoric understanding, "The rock sculpts the sculptor, as much as the sculptor sculpts the rock" (cited in M. Bateson, 1972, p. 249). It is no surprise that the title of McCulloch's book on experimental epistemology is a pun, *Embodiments of Mind*.

The cybernetic view makes it clear that the unit of therapy is not individuals, couples, families, neighborhoods, or societies. Instead, cybernetics focuses on *mental process*. Mind in therapy may be immanent within and across a wide variety of social units including individuals, family subsystems, and whole families. The cybernetician's eye is focused on seeing these underlying patterns of feedback process.

The fullest implication of cybernetic epistemology has been summarized by Bateson (1972):

> The cybernetic epistemology which I have offered you would suggest a new approach. The individual mind is immanent but not only in the body. It is immanent also in pathways and messages outside the body; and there is a larger Mind of which the individual mind is only a subsystem. This larger Mind is comparable to God and is perhaps what some people mean by "God," but it is still immanent in the total interconnected social system and planetary ecology. (p. 461)

Cybernetics enables us to consider both the autonomy and interdependence of whole systems whether they be therapist and client or man and planet. It is ironic that a full consideration of autonomy in cybernetics leads us to a view of Mind, where all living process becomes interconnected and one. Similarly, a full consideration of the most encompassing pattern of interconnections imaginable leads us to acknowledging the autonomy of a diversity of individual systems.

These ironies, when taken as a double view, remind us of an eternal verity: In a recursive universe, the whole earth may be found in a single living cell.

CYBERNETIC COMPLEMENTARITIES

As we've noted, cybernetic epistemology proposes that we embrace both sides of any distinction that an observer draws. Throughout this book I have argued that a therapist should adopt the perspectives of both pragmatics and aesthetics, control and autonomy, simple cybernetics and cybernetics of cybernetics, and even lineal and recursive descriptions. One way of acknowledging both sides of these distinctions involves viewing them as parts of "cybernetic complementarities."

A cybernetic complementarity provides an alternative framework for examining distinctions. For the most part, people take distinctions to be representations of an either/or duality, a polarity, a clash of opposites, or an expression with a logic of negation underlying it (A/not A; right/wrong; useful/not useful; good/bad). In such a view, we speak of winning or losing in a zero-sum fashion. Varela (1976b) however, has proposed another way of looking at distinctions through the epistemological lens of cybernetics. His work is a foundation for cybernetic complementarities.

Varela begins by giving us the following basic form for viewing the sides of a distinction:

"the it"/"the process leading to it"

If you consider both sides as different, yet related, you approach a cybernetic framing of distinctions. This frame permits different sides to be seen as an "*imbrication* of levels, where one term of the pair *emerges* from the other" (Varela, 1976b, p. 64). The relationship between the sides of these distinctions is self-referential, where one side is (re)cycled out of the other. In order to generate a cybernetic complementarity, simply follow Varela's (1976b) prescription:

> To this end take any situation (domain, process, entity, notion) which is holistic (total, closed, complete, full, stable, self-contained). Put it on the left side of the /. Put on the right side of it the corresponding processes (constituents, generators, dynamics). (p. 63)

For example:

form/process
territory/map
describer/described
observer/observed
subject/object
reality/recipe
environment/system
family/individual
context/simple action
pattern of interaction/interactional process
whole/parts
circle/line
recursive/lineal
cybernetics/physics
mind/body
cybernetics of cybernetics/simple cybernetics
autonomy/control
stability/change
organization/structure
closed organization/simple feedback
aesthetic/pragmatic
art/technique
right intuitive/left logical
experiential therapy/strategic therapy
imagination/rigor
pleroma/creatura
being/becoming

It is important to note that a cybernetic complementarity involves different orders of recursion, which demonstrate how "pairs (poles, extremes, modes, sides) are *related* and yet remain distinct" (Varela, 1976b, p. 62). Cybernetic complementarities provide a way of encapsulating the recursive nature of natural epistemology.

Sometimes, however, people draw distinctions meant to indicate a pair of opposites with each side belonging to the same order of process. For example, the pair "predator/prey" is sometimes proposed as operating in terms of excluding opposites. Varela (1976b) suggests that whenever we encounter such a dualism, which he calls a "hegelian pair," we should realize that it is an incomplete sketch. What is required is to see these hegelian pairs as one side of a larger cybernetic complementarity: "For every hegelian pair of the form, A/not A, there exists a more inclusive [form], where the apparent opposites are components of the right hand side" (p. 64). In the case of the hegelian pair, "predator/prey," there is the cybernetic complementarity, "ecosystem/species interaction." If one encounters a hegelian pair where a symmetry of opposites is proposed, one can always reframe that pair as part of a more encompassing cybernetic complementarity. In the above example, the battle over food and territory between two species is only one half of the story. The larger cybernetic picture is that the battle is a means or process of generating, maintaining, and stabilizing an ecosystem.

Cybernetic complementarities, therefore, are reframings in terms of recursive process of the distinctions people draw. For example, Varela's basic form, "the it/the process leading to it," can be used to frame the pattern "stability/change." Cybernetics, as we have defined it, is, in fact, the study of this complementary relation.

The perspective of cybernetic complementarities transforms our ways of knowing toward the aesthetic vision poets have always known. Such a vision views all mental and living process as recursive and complementary. The alternative is to chop the world into innumerable dualisms that separate us from the various parts of our experience.

Regarding the distinction between aesthetics and pragmatics, a complementary view helps us avoid being split between the choice of free-associative muddle and technique untempered by wisdom. As Gregory Bateson (cited in M. Bateson, 1972) notes, "Rigor alone is paralytic death, but imagination alone is insanity" (p. 299). The aesthetic quest necessarily involves a recursive dance between rigor and imagination. We need to use our whole brain—not right, not left.

Like the early days of simple cybernetics, family therapy is engulfed in technical and control approaches to treatment. Our pragmatics need to be contextualized by more encompassing aesthetic patterns. The recursive jump from simple cybernetics to cybernetics of cybernetics provides one pathway of correction. Bateson (1972) addresses the implication of this more encompassing view:

> We social scientists would do well to hold back our eagerness to control that world which we so imperfectly understand. . . . Rather, our studies could be inspired by a more ancient, but today less honored, motive: a curiosity about the world of which we are a part. The rewards of such work are not power but beauty. (p. 269)

DISCUSSION[18]

THERAPIST: What is cybernetic epistemology?

EPISTEMOLOGIST: Cybernetic epistemology prescribes a way of discerning and knowing patterns that organize events, such as the recursive sequences of action in a family episode. This is distinct from a Newtonian epistemology concerned with knowing such matters as the nature of billiard balls and the forces that operate on them. What differentiates the work of cyberneticians is that they jump from the paradigm of things to the paradigm of pattern.

THERAPIST: Are you implying that a therapist's epistemological menu card provides a choice only between a cybernetic and Newtonian epistemology? What about all those other names I read about, such as ecosystemic, general systems, nonlineal, and circular epistemologies?

EPISTEMOLOGIST: The difference that makes the most profound epistemological difference is one of moving from descriptions of material to descriptions of pattern. Cybernetics is part of a general science that studies pattern and organization.

A "systems," "nonlineal," "ecological," or "circular" epistemology may or may not signify a cybernetic epistemology. In family therapy, for example, a "systems epistemology" is often used simply to indicate a holistic view, for example, working with families rather than individuals. Cybernetics, however, is principally concerned with changing our conceptual lens from material to pattern, rather than parts to wholes. Thus, in the world of cybernetics, both parts and wholes are examined in terms of their patterns of organization.

THERAPIST: How does this orientation connect to family therapy? Why is it important to bring cybernetic epistemology to our field?

EPISTEMOLOGIST: Cyberneticians view most of psychology and the social sciences as misguided. To put it more bluntly, they regard most of social science as insane and sometimes propose that it be buried. That, my friend, is a radical view. The social sciences' insanity has to do with their adoption of an epistemology of substance. The cyberneticians' argument is that the use of an epistemology of billard balls to approach human phenomena is an indication of madness.

---

18. Portions of this discussion appear in "What Is an Epistemology of Family Therapy?," *Family Process*, 1982, *21*, 153-168, and are reprinted by permission.

This, of course, has been suspected throughout the history of the social sciences. William James even joked that when psychology threw away mind it became mindless. More recently, humanistic psychologists under the leadership of Abraham Maslow proposed that a Newtonian physical science was an inappropriate model for psychological phenomena.

However, cyberneticians claim that these objections are often not basic enough. Remember Bateson's argument that humanistic psychologists' use of the term "third force" connected them to a vocabulary and thus an epistemology of physics. Through their choice of metaphor, their epistemology was revealed.

Bateson directed the same criticism toward family therapy, a field that also has a history of boasting about its radically different frame of reference and epistemology. He repeatedly warned family therapists that any use of physical metaphors indicates an epistemology that has nothing to do with formally knowing pattern, form, and organization of family events. The crescendo of his attack was directed at Haley, who has insistently proposed a description of family therapy in terms of the metaphor "power." Richard Rabkin (1978) identifies the Bateson-Haley disagreement as the epistemological fulcrum of family therapy. Their differing orientations signify the contrast between an epistemology of pattern and one of material.

The cybernetician's argument is that family therapy, as well as all disciplines of biology (in the comprehensive sense of that term), must embody a cybernetic epistemology if patterns that characterize living and mental process are to be encountered. Otherwise, we treat ourselves and our contexts of living as though they were heaps of bricks subject to locomotion. As the cyberneticians argue, such a position is not only "loco," but dangerous to the ecology of living process.

THERAPIST: I want to fully understand what a cybernetic epistemology of family therapy means, but I simply cannot imagine a world of human relations where "power" is not involved.

EPISTEMOLOGIST: You must realize that "seeing" power in any context follows from a way of punctuating events. If you say that a therapist and client are engaged in a "power struggle," I will say that you have punctuated the context of therapy in a way that *constructs* that view. "Power" is in the hand of the punctuator, not necessarily in the "observed." The major epistemological issues are therefore concerned with the *consequences* of particular habits of punctuation. As the ecologists have warned us, punctuating biological events in terms of physical metaphors often breeds pathology in the form of fractionation of complexity and destruction of patterns that connect. These implications of the "power" metaphor will be discussed more extensively later in the book.

THERAPIST: Let me extend your premise. If what we see is a consequence of a punctuation, then the very distinction between an epistemology of pattern and material also arises from a punctuation. Similarly, the idea of punctuating and constructing a world view is itself a particular punctuation.

EPISTEMOLOGIST: The cybernetician recognizes that one begins by drawing a distinction. For example, you may begin by indicating a distinction between yourself and the family system you treat. The cybernetician then goes on to acknowledge the domains of phenomenology that subsequently arise—the phenomenology of the punctuated system as an autonomous unit requiring no reference to outside events and the phenomenology of the interdependence of the specified system with other systems. We are therefore faced with the knots of an inseparable trio which, as Varela (1979) puts it, consists of "a system's *identity*, its performance in its *interactions* with what it is not, and how we *relate* to these two distinct domains" (p. xii–xiii).

THERAPIST: Does a cybernetic "black box" model of a family system correspond to the phenomenal domain of autonomy?

EPISTEMOLOGIST: No. This may seem a bit tricky because we tend to consider a black box something distinct from the observer. I remind you, however, that the specification of a black box is in terms of inputs from an environment that the black box transforms into outputs for the environment. Such a description refers to the interaction of the system with what is outside and is described from the perspective of the outside. The characterization of a system as a black box thus belongs to the phenomenal domain of the system's interdependence with other, outside systems.

As mentioned earlier, the contribution of Maturana and Varela to cybernetics was their description of living systems from the perspective of the whole system itself, without any reference to its environment or an outside. Let me give you an illustration of this perspective which Maturana (Maturana & Varela, 1980) often uses:

> What occurs in a living system is analogous to what occurs in an instrumental flight where the pilot does not have access to the outside world

and must function only as a controller of the values shown in his flight instruments. His task is to secure a path of variations in the readings of his instruments, either according to a prescribed plan, or to one that becomes specified by these readings. When the pilot steps out of the plane he is bewildered by the congratulations of his friends on account of the perfect flight and landing that he performed in absolute darkness. He is perplexed because to his knowledge all that he did at any moment was to maintain the readings of his instruments within certain specified limits, a task which is in no way represented by the description that his friends (observers) make of his conduct. (p. 51)

To capture a system's autonomy requires, by definition, no reference to its outside. Instead, the system must be described through reference to itself. Stated differently, the self-referentialness of a system becomes a way of pointing to the system's autonomy.

THERAPIST: When do we refer to the autonomy of a system instead of its interdependence with other systems?

EPISTEMOLOGIST: It is a matter of where you, the observer, draw the distinction. You may consider a family as organizationally closed or you may consider the pattern connecting you with them as organizationally closed. In the latter, the family and you become parts of a higher order of recursion.

THERAPIST: Does it make a difference how I draw the distinction?

EPISTEMOLOGIST: Indeed. You must recall that any act of epistemology affects how you behave as well as perceive — the two are linked as a recursive process. In therapy you may choose to behave and perceive in a way that organizes you as part of a higher order of recursion which may facilitate recalibrating parts of a family.

THERAPIST: Something is troubling me. You are speaking the language of cybernetics which includes homeostasis, feedback, learning, information, and so forth. There are some therapists who urge us to throw away those terms and begin with a new vocabulary. What do you think about such a change?

EPISTEMOLOGIST: Changing our lexicon may result in merely using new terms in the same old way. Terminology can be flexible enough to embody new ideas. In the historical context of cybernetics, the field itself evolved as a pattern of self-correction. As the field moved toward approaching higher orders of recursion, the meaning of its terms consequently evolved. The move from simple to higher order cybernetics did not entail throwing away terms like homeostasis, but enabled us to speak of higher orders of homeostasis (e.g., homeostasis of homeostasis).

THERAPIST: Is a call to throw away these terms an argument that is disconnected from the tradition of cybernetics?

EPISTEMOLOGIST: In part, yes. Our dilemma is one of choosing between the Scylla of misunderstanding and the Charybdis of talking a private language. Take the approach of Varela, for example. He is quite specific in saying that the traditional paradigm of "information" that characterizes simple cybernetics is not useful for describing the autonomy of living systems. He suggests that the jump to the order of cybernetic organization closed from an environment cannot be discussed in terms of an outside bit of information that is processed by the system and then fed back to the outside world.

Nevertheless, Varela *does not* suggest that we throw away the term "information." Instead, when looking at the autonomy of a system, he proposes that we follow its more etymological meaning as a process of "in-forming." In cybernetics of cybernetics, information becomes the in-forming of forms, or as Bateson put it, the recursive transforming of difference. When speaking of the autonomy of natural systems, information becomes constructive rather than representational or instructive. In this frame of reference, in-formation is self-referentially defined. Here, there is no outside information.

THERAPIST: What you suggest is that terms like information, homeostasis, feedback, and so on should take on different meanings in cybernetics of cybernetics.

EPISTEMOLOGIST: Yes. All descriptive language changes meaning in cybernetics of cybernetics because it is a different frame of reference. Furthermore, cybernetics of cybernetics provides us with additional terms which point to patterns we were not able to clearly discern with simple cybernetics. Autonomy, for example, is proposed as a term for the distinctive wholeness or identity of a system rather than simple cybernetic terms like homeostasis, stability, circular organization, or coherence. Autonomy more clearly specifies that we are referring to an upper limit with regard to a system's homeostasis of homeostasis, stability of stability, or coherence of coherence.

THERAPIST: Is cybernetics of cybernetics a more correct perspective for family therapy than simple cybernetics?

EPISTEMOLOGIST: That is an incorrect question. Cybernetics of cybernetics enables us to speak of the autonomy of whole systems, while simple cybernetics gives us the view of a system in the context of the inputs and outputs of various other systems. As Varela (1978) has demonstrated time and time again, each view provides a different but complementary perspective. The complete cybernetic therapist has an enriched vision that enables him to see both the autonomy and connection of diverse patterns.

THERAPIST: But when is it appropriate to use simple cybernetic description as opposed to that of cybernetics of cybernetics?

EPISTEMOLOGIST: You must never forget that the autonomy of a system is a *more encompassing* view than one that speaks of a system's inputs and outputs, simple homeostasis, simple coherence, and simple feedback. The view of cybernetics of cybernetics is one that recognizes the wholeness of a given realm of phenomena. If we wish to speak of the wholeness (i.e., autonomy) of a family, then higher order cybernetic description is appropriate. We may, however, want to view the therapist and family as distinct, but interconnected, systems: In such a case we can speak in terms of simple cybernetics. To point to the wholeness of *that* hybrid system, however, returns us again to the descriptive language of cybernetics of cybernetics.

At other times we may find it useful to dissect (i.e., punctuate) the wholeness of systems into parts and then talk about the relations among those parts. The therapist can choose to see how symptomatic behavior calibrates a particular recursive sequence of interaction. Then interventions can be discussed as if they were inputs to the family, that is, new pieces of information whose introduction to the system may provoke it to behave differently.

When whole systems, whether the family or the family-plus-therapist, are punctuated into distinguishable parts, we must remember that the parts are *approximations* of the whole system from which they were abstracted. The drawing of these partial arcs and the chopping of the world into parts provide us with various pragmatic advantages. The drawing of a difference between problem and nonproblem behavior, for example, sometimes enables a therapist to orient his behavior in a strategic fashion. The shortcoming of using the punctuation of "partial arcs" is that we may forget that they are approximations of whole patterns of cybernetic process. We set ourselves up for trouble when we forget that "interventions," "symptoms," "therapists," and "families" are approximations or metaphors for more encompassing patterns. This may lead us to see interventions and symptoms as mythical entities, seemingly real things in the fabric of nature.

This is a serious problem in the world of therapy, where punctu-ated streams of events are often reified and subjected to so-called "ob-jective" criteria. Pattern and form have no "realness," are not subject to quantification, and cannot be discussed as though they were "things" influenced by the interplay of force, power, and energy.

In sum, we are free to carve the world as we like as long as our carvings are remembered to be approximations of the more encom-passing recursive patterns from which they were demarcated. Simple cybernetics and cybernetics of cybernetics are halves of a cybernetic complementarity. The question you should have asked is "What is the appropriate use of cybernetics?" The answer to that question is that therapists should always embody an explicit sensitivity to both simple and higher order cybernetic description. Any attempt to use one per-spective without remembering the other is the error.

THERAPIST: Let me return to the drawing of a distinction. If I draw a distinction between a system and myself, I must remember sev-eral things. First of all, I must remember that I drew the frame of ref-erence. Given that frame, I can point to the phenomenal domain of the autonomous system. This requires my speaking about it without assuming that it makes any reference to an outside environment. I must speak about it as though I, the observer, did not exist to it. And finally, I can point to the phenomenal domain of the system's interde-pendence.

EPISTEMOLOGIST: You are beginning to sound like a cybernetic epistemologist. With these perspectives — a demarcation, the autono-my of a system, the system's interdependence with other outside sys-tems — one can begin thinking about a cybernetic epistemology of family therapy. Before doing so, let us focus a bit more on what these three perspectives imply.

THERAPIST: Let me guess. The drawing of a distinction or punc-tuation always means that I, the therapist, am actively participating in the construction of the reality of what happens in therapy.

EPISTEMOLOGIST: One cannot *not* draw a distinction. Any effort to not draw a distinction in itself reveals a distinction. Thus, you and your clients are always active epistemological operators.

THERAPIST: The perspective of the autonomy of a system is a bit paradoxical to me, for it seems to require that I describe a system as though I were not around to describe it.

EPISTEMOLOGIST: You are now describing your describing, which is different from pointing to the domain of phenomenology that pertains to the autonomy or closed organization of a system. In other words, your question points us toward the phenomenal domain where an observer is observing a system. This is one way of looking at how we look at systems. But with respect to the autonomy of the observed system, we can consider a phenomenal domain where it operates without reference to an outside observer. To *talk* about this phenomenal domain, however, is to reenter the domain that includes an outside observer. In sum, you are correct in assuming self-reference while being a describer or observer. This only reminds us again that you are drawing the distinctions. In general, descriptions reveal properties of the observer. What the therapist sees tells us something about his epistemology.

THERAPIST: Please explain the perspective that enables me to discuss the phenomenal domain of a system's interdependence with other systems.

EPISTEMOLOGIST: This is also a bit tricky. Let us back up again. We just implied that you cannot really describe the autonomy of a system without reference to you, the describer. Thus, what we are up against are two different ways of describing one's relation to a demarcated system. Maturana and Varela suggest that when we speak of a system's autonomy we should refer to our interactions with that system as "perturbations" rather than "inputs." This reminds us that no part of what we do to an autonomous system ever gets "inside" the system, but rather that our action interacts with the *wholeness* of the system. This is another way of saying that our interactions do not affect any one part of a system, but affect the whole organization of a system.

When we speak of the wholeness or closure of a system, we are pointing to its simultaneity of interactions. At this order of description there can be no chopping of the whole into causal loops with time delays between an input and output. Similarly, we cannot speak of the wholeness of a system in terms of hierarchy or logical typing and we cannot punctuate a beginning or end. To preserve the flavor of wholeness requires that we speak of our interactions with wholes as perturbations on a whole organization.

THERAPIST: From the perspective of a family system's autonomy, all a therapist can do is "perturb" the family and see what happens?

EPISTEMOLOGIST: This is the view that autonomy prescribes. The wholeness of a family (i.e., its closed organization) will either compensate or not compensate in response to the perturbations that act upon it. The family may compensate by altering its structure.

THERAPIST: Please give me a simple illustration.

EPISTEMOLOGIST: Let me start with a metaphoric example. Consider a balloon as an autonomous system. If you squeeze it, your action can be seen as a perturbation. You do not get inside the closed boundaries of the system, or the balloon would burst. Your perturbations on the system, if not too severe, will be compensated for by a change in the system's structure. The balloon's ability to alter its shape allows it to endure.

In the field of family therapy, Lyman Wynne (Wynne, Ryckoff, Day, & Hirsch, 1958) suggested the term "rubber fence" as a description of a form of family process. It is a mistake, Wynne argues, to think that a therapist is always "inside" a family. Sometimes the family has only altered its structure, like a rubber fence, in response to the therapist's perturbations.

THERAPIST: In sum, a family maintains itself as a viable social organism by changing its structure. Organization, however, refers to the wholeness of the family. If the organization of a family changes, the family ceases to be a family. This is again a way of speaking of the autonomy or identity of a whole system.

EPISTEMOLOGIST: Yes. I think you've got it. Let's get back to where we were. In the phenomenal domain of a system's autonomy, our interactions with a family may provoke the system to compensate by altering its structure. This order of description requires that we view whatever the autonomous system does as an effort to maintain its own organization.

In the history of family therapy, this order of process has often been called the "family's homeostasis." Unfortunately, this description is technically a category mistake. Rather than indicating simple homeostasis, what family therapists have tried to point to is the higher order, "homeostasis of homeostasis" or the autonomy of a family. Similarly, a category mistake is committed when we substitute the term "coherence" for "homeostasis" (e.g., Dell, 1982). Again, what we mean to indicate is "coherence of coherence." Any call to move us beyond homeostasis or coherence should be seen as a call to move us beyond simple cybernetics. Therefore, when therapists insist that a family's homeostasis or coherence should be respected, they are actually suggesting that we respect the family's autonomy.

THERAPIST: Okay. Now what about the other perspective we left behind? That is, what is the other phenomenal domain, which points to a system's interdepencence with other systems?

EPISTEMOLOGIST: This realm of phenomenology is concerned with those descriptions of a system which we, the observers, attribute to the system's *relationship* with other systems, sometimes including ourselves. For example, we may ascribe the characteristics of "purpose" and "causality" to a system. To say that a system has a certain purpose is to say that its relation with other systems leads to certain outcomes. When I say that the purpose of my automobile is to get me from place to place, I am actually referring to my relationship *with* the automobile. The automobile does not contain purpose. "Purpose," as Varela and Maturana argue, belongs to the phenomenal domain of a system's relationship and interdependence with other systems, not to the perspective of a system's autonomy.

This phenomenal domain of a system's ecology of relationships is expressed through what Varela calls "symbolic explanations." These explanations point to behavioral regularities of a system that are not operational for the system, but refer to observed regularities between a system and other systems or between parts of a given system. "Operational explanations," on the other hand, refer to processes of a system that make no reference to relationship with outside systems. A system's own identity-generating processes or autonomy, for example, are operational terms.

THERAPIST: When we say that a child's symptom serves to help keep his parents together, we are referring to the phenomenal domain of a child system in relation to a marital system. The purpose and function of symptoms, interventions, families, and therapists are always a symbolic description ascribed by an observer who comments on the relation between different systems.

EPISTEMOLOGIST: Correct.

THERAPIST: This clears up a controversy about the term "resistance" as it is used in therapy. Some therapists have argued that it is not a useful idea and should be abandoned. What they are actually concerned about is the term being used as if it were an operational term pointing to the phenomenal domain of the autonomous system itself. With this erroneous view, therapists may blame a client's reluctance to perform an assignment on his "resistance." Resistance, however, is actually a symbolic description pointing to the phenomenal domain of a therapist's relationship with his client. There is no need to throw away this term any more than other related terms such as "cooperation," "friendship," or "relationship." These terms are useful in orienting us to the phenomenal domain of a system's ecology of relationships.

EPISTEMOLOGIST: The trouble is seldom with the name, but with the phenomenal domain the name is assumed to be associated with. I suggest that you challenge anyone who argues for throwing away names, concepts, or ideas. The more productive approach is to discover the phenomenal domain in which the name, concept, or idea is appropriate and useful.

THERAPIST: Why is it important for family therapists to distinguish between phenomenal domains?

EPISTEMOLOGIST: This brings us back to "dormitive principles." We may, for example, see "personality characteristics" such as dependency, friendliness, or hostility as descriptions of an individual rather than descriptions pointing to the relation of that individual to another individual (e.g., the observer). A dormitive principle can now be further defined as a form of epistemological nonsense which arises when we attempt to explain a system by attributing to it descriptions that do not belong to its phenomenal domain but to its relationship with other systems.

THERAPIST: In other words, keeping tabs on these different phenomenal domains is a way of avoiding confusion and nonsense?

EPISTEMOLOGIST: Exactly. The argument of cybernetic epistemology is that the nonsense and pathology we humans generate can be traced to confoundment in these phenomenal domains. As Maturana (1980) puts it, these phenomenal domains are nonintersecting, and confusion arises from "the impossible attempt to reduce the phenomena of one of the nonintersecting domains to the phenomena of the other" (p. 46). Along these lines, Warren S. McCulloch once joked, "Psychiatry would have been a lot better off if man didn't happen to speak." Of course, the curse is also a blessing. Some of the knots we construct when we confound phenomenal domains enable us to experience patterns of art and beauty. But all that is for another discussion.

THERAPIST: Is it fair to say that all the cybernetic complementarities we have drawn, including autonomy/control, operational/symbolic explanations, cybernetics of cybernetics/simple cybernetics, whole/parts, stability/change, etc., are complementarities only in a phenomenal domain that we draw? Does this domain enable us to observe both their distinction as well as relation?

EPISTEMOLOGIST: Yes. We again return to Jung's distinction between "pleroma" and "creatura," the worlds of no distinctions and distinctions, respectively. We can only know pleroma, the whole system of no distinctions, by drawing a distinction between pleroma and creatura. This distinction, as well as the complementarity we can draw between pleroma and creatura, take place in the domain of an observer. All distinctions belong to our cognitive domain (i.e., creatura) and cannot be held as operative in pleroma.

THERAPIST: Concepts such as homeostasis, purpose, feedback, and control, which refer to relations of components of a whole system, are also specified within an observer's domain of descriptions and are not operational in the conceived autonomous system?

EPISTEMOLOGIST: Yes. We can go on to note that Varela's notion of an "operational explanation" refers to a set of terms that point to the phenomenal domain of an autonomous system. "Symbolic explanations," on the other hand, do not pertain to this phenomenal domain, but refer to the more encompassing context that links a system to other systems, or parts of a system with other parts of itself.

THERAPIST: The trouble we encounter, as we said before, arises when we mix up these two domains of description and explanation.

EPISTEMOLOGIST: Unfortunately, our culture has adopted many erroneous habits of extending symbolic descriptions into the domain of operational explanation. We therefore must back up and straighten out this muddle. As Varela (1979) puts it, "Laboring on these points and keeping good track of what terms of explanation belong to which domain is not at all a futile exercise in logic and epistemology, but a very definite need if we are to recover the usefulness of concepts such as purpose and information for natural systems" (pp. 68–69).

THERAPIST: The trouble usually begins when we forget the role of the observer. If we keep track of the distinctions we draw and the accompanying phenomenal domains they indicate, it is less likely that we will get lost in a labyrinth of confusion.

EPISTEMOLOGIST: Let us assume that we were to straighten out the terms we already have which refer to living and cognitive processes. What we would find would be an overabundance of symbolic descriptions, but a shortage of operational terms. The challenge for a science of pattern and organization is to develop an operational, or as Varela and Maturana often propose, a structural point of view. This shift is now beginning in biology with the pioneering work of Bateson, Maturana, and Varela pointing the way.

THERAPIST: In this quest for operational descriptions, such as "autonomy" and "closed organization," we should never forget the other phenomenal domain which discerns the interdependent relations between different whole systems as well as the parts of those systems.

EPISTEMOLOGIST: Indeed, for if we forget the view of interdependence of systems, we may fall into the trap of ascribing "ontological reality" to our punctuations of autonomous systems. "What is is and what ain't ain't" is only a description proposed by an observer. Varela argues that we can avoid the trap of confusing a description with "ontological reality" *only* if we remember to keep the more encompassing view of relationship.

THERAPIST: Again, both sides of a distinction we happen to draw may be seen as conceptually *connate* — the yin and yang of a cybernetic complementarity. "There is nothing mysterious about what the observer does," Varela (1979, p. 273) states. "It is no more and no less than establishing relations between parts of his own experience."

EPISTEMOLOGIST: Problems arise when a hypothesis successfully works (i.e., it is empirically, logically, or pragmatically confirmed) and is then held to be a piece of solid, ontological reality. As cybernetic epistemologists remind us, we should be very careful when we ask ontological questions such as "What is the structure of the real world?" Cybernetic epistemology directs us more toward the cognitive question "What is the structure of our experiential world?"

THERAPIST: It therefore may be misleading for therapists to talk in terms of ontology. Asking what is really real is often irrelevant. The world of therapy is one of epistemology wherein we encounter diverse patterns and structures.

EPISTEMOLOGIST: Family therapists are epistemologists in the sense that they embody patterns of knowing and constructing a therapeutic reality. As we have said before, to become aware of how one knows and constructs an experiential reality entails knowing about one's knowing. This necessarily requires that we see ourselves constructing and construct ourselves as seeing. When we jump to this order of recursion, we see that epistemology is always a self-referential, recursive process which infolds upon itself. In other words, epistemology is itself a cybernetic process. In this regard, epistemology and cybernetic epistemology become one and the same.

THERAPIST: Cybernetic epistemology is therefore neither a map, description, theory, model, paradigm nor paradigm of paradigms. It is a process of knowing, constructing, and maintaining a world of experience.

EPISTEMOLOGIST: Let me add a few pieces. If you fully consider the connection between knowing *and* constructing a world, you will realize that what we have encountered is the organization of living process. Perception and behavior are recursively linked, as the cyberneticians remind us. Remember that Maturana and Varela discovered that the nervous system is recursively organized. In the world of social organisms, experimental epistemologists such as Bateson have discovered the recursive organization of interaction. Throughout diverse orders of living process, recursive organization appears.

THERAPIST: Are you suggesting that the processes of cybernetic epistemology are the same as the processes of living?

EPISTEMOLOGIST: The identity of living process with mental process is perhaps the most profound insight of our time. Mind and nature become an inseparable unity. This is the position of Bateson, McCulloch, Maturana, Varela, von Foerster, and all cybernetic epistemologists who have fully encountered the ideas we've been discussing.

THERAPIST: A cybernetic epistemology of family therapy is therefore an epistemology of life?

EPISTEMOLOGIST: Yes. When what you do is seen as mental or living process, your action is revealed as part of a more encompassing ecological dance. Family therapy then becomes a crucible for the drama of life and mind.

THERAPIST: If I were to fully understand the insights of cybernetic epistemology, what difference would it make in the way I live my life inside and outside of my clinical practice?

EPISTEMOLOGIST: When you understand that you are a cybernetic epistemologist, you realize that you are always participating in the construction of a world of experience, including therapeutic realities. The view of a participatory universe again suggests that ethics, rather than objectivity, underlies family therapy. There is no such thing as an observer-free description of a situation which can be objectively assessed and evaluated. Instead, what one knows leads to a construction and what one constructs leads to knowing. One's knowing is recycled in the constant (re)construction of a world. As Wittgenstein asserts, ethics and aesthetics belong to the same domain. This should be clear to us now, for what we perceive is drawn by how we behave, and how we behave follows the constraints of what we perceive. The observer is in the observed, the therapist is in the clinical problem, the knower is in what is known.

THERAPIST: Where do family therapists go from here?

EPISTEMOLOGIST: As family therapists, there are several jumps that can be made. First of all, a therapist can jump from the paradigm of substance to that of pattern. This places him in the context of cybernetic epistemology. Once there, the family therapist can embody the complementary gestalt of simple cybernetics and cybernetics of cybernetics. He will then be able to jump back and forth between these orders of recursion. With this full view, a family therapist can approach the complexity and elegance of autonomous and interconnected patterns of life.

THERAPIST: Is it really necessary to fully understand cybernetics in order to be a good family therapist?

EPISTEMOLOGIST: Of course not. Cybernetics is only a raft which can carry us across the river. Other vessels are also accessible, particularly the offerings of poets. As Bateson reminded us, William Blake packaged all of these ideas in another form of symbolic system.

THERAPIST: There is a lot of work to do.

EPISTEMOLOGIST: Many of us do not yet know that how we know is inseparable from how we behave. Fewer know that cybernetic epistemology in its fullest sense is life itself. The biology of cognition, as Maturana and Varela put it, is the organization of life.

THERAPIST: A full realization of the connection between mental and living process would naturally lead one to see that mind can never be limited to what goes on within the boundaries of a skull. Mind becomes immanent in the organization of diverse patterns in our biosphere.

EPISTEMOLOGIST: We should never forget the mental system that connects diverse parts of a therapist's experience to those of a family or client system as well as to you and me as we now communicate and to all the various patterns of our biosphere.

THERAPIST: Are you suggesting that therapists, families, ecologists, cities, seashores, and forests are indistinguishable in cybernetic epistemology?

EPISTEMOLOGIST: Their distinction and connection draw a cybernetic epistemology of life and mind . . .

THERAPIST: And a cybernetic epistemology of family therapy.

4

A CYBERNETIC DESCRIPTION
OF FAMILY THERAPY

Even if the world does go round, that's no reason for
being seasick. — *Svevo*

PATTERNS OF DISTINCTION

Language is an epistemological knife. It slices the world into bits and
pieces, provides names, names of names, and names of names of
names. The first step toward generating a cybernetic description of
family therapy involves examining some of the basic distinctions our
language provides for us, such as therapist and client, pathology and
health, system and ecology. This chapter will demonstrate how these
distinctions can be used to construct a cybernetic description of family
therapy.

Self/Other

We will begin by examining how our culture distinguishes the relation
between man and environment. The idea that a human being is
separate from his environment is an epistemological distinction that
underlies most of our thinking about human interaction. This particular
indication takes many forms, including observer and observed,
therapist and client, individual and family, theorist and practitioner,
rebel and country, man and nature.

Each of these distinctions presupposes that a delimited "self" is
separate from an environmental backdrop, which is what is left over
when the "self" is abstracted out. This leads to seeing the environment
as the "other"—a separate entity with which the self interacts. Typi-

cally, the relationship is then depicted as an exchange of unilineal actions—man acts on the environment, the environment acts on man.

Such a scenario offers two basic ways of viewing man's relationship to the "other." The first is the "boxing model," where two agents symmetrically fight for victory. In other words, there is an effort to maximize or minimize some variable. Man's exploitation of earth's natural resources exemplifies this model. The other perspective is the "colleagual model" where man and environment are seen as complementary. In this case, man attempts to work with the earth instead of against it.

Both views arise from an original epistemological act that separates man from environment. In family therapy the distinction between therapist and client (or identified patient, or "customer"[1]) implies the same form of demarcation. Therapist and client are seen as distinct entities engaging in either a "boxing" or "colleagual" type relationship, or perhaps an alternation of the two. The boxing model is exemplified by theories of therapy that describe the therapist–client relationship in terms of strategies of one-upmanship, power tactics, manipulation, and control. The colleagual model tends to describe therapist and client as engaging in a mutual growth trip, co-evolutionary pilgrimage, or cooperative exploration. Again, each perspective arises from the initial distinction of separating therapist from client.

Cybernetic epistemology, however, begins by drawing a pattern of recursion through both sides of these distinctions. Rather than identifying therapist and client as separate agents who act upon each other, cybernetics looks for patterns that connect both components through a feedback structure. Looking at another example, a cybernetician does not see a separate agent turning on a furnace, but sees a pattern of feedback connecting agent and furnace. The embodiment of feedback by physical components, such as a human sensor, thermostat, and furnace is incidental.

By chopping such a recursive system into separate components, an observer breaks the pattern and obscures the view of cybernetic process. Unfortunately, most of our inherited vocabulary has been used to indicate isolated parts rather than recursive process. In family

1. Haley (1980) has introduced the term "customer" to refer to those who purchase what he has to sell.

therapy, basic terms like "system," "symptom," "identified patient," "therapist," "intervention," and so on, tend to distinguish particular pieces, entities, agents, or things of the general context called "therapy."

It is probably difficult to imagine looking at therapy without seeing a therapist and client as separate agents. Cybernetics, however, requires that we undo traditional ways of knowing and reconstruct the world in an alternative fashion by identifying patterns that recursively connect therapist and client, symptom and cure, and diagnosis and intervention. To this end, we simply must see beyond the epistemology implied by the use of nouns in describing family therapy. Since it is very unlikely that anyone is not using nouns to describe therapy (e.g., "therapist" and "client"), we should orient ourselves to use nouns in an alternative way. We have the choice of reframing nouns to signify approximations, shorthand terms, signs, or codifications of more complete patterns of cybernetic process. For example, in cybernetics, the term "observer" becomes a shorthand reference for what is more accurately an "observer–observed" relationship. Thus, symptoms, identified patients, families, therapists, and interventions are indicators of more encompassing cybernetic process. In sum, it is not necessary to throw away traditional terms in order to describe therapy. Rather, we need to reframe these terms as references to pattern and not things.

This book therefore avoids framing any either/or distinctions, including those between conscious and unconscious, individual and family, identified patient and therapist, symptom and context, behavior and interactional sequence, lineal and recursive description, and pragmatic and aesthetic orientations. These distinctions should be seen as cybernetic complementarities. The dismemberment of a cybernetic complementarity sometimes occurs, however, when family therapists and researchers dissect the natural history of family process into discrete parts, components, functions, and mechanisms. The consequence of these separations is that one may lose sight of the recursive connection of the whole family.

For example, scholars have distinguished parts of family process which are called communication, conflict, problem-solving, perception, homeostasis, and so on. If we draw rigid boundaries to indicate these distinctions, we too easily forget that they are basically shorthand indications of more encompassing cybernetic processes. To say that "homeostasis" causes a symptom to be maintained is to draw a boundary between a mechanism called homeostasis and the symptomatic behavior it is supposed to maintain. This way of thinking leads a clinician to believe that the beast "homeostasis" needs to be addressed in order to alter the symptom. At this point, not only has the therapist dissected the symptom from the thing or function called homeostasis, but has separated himself from that which he attempts to treat.

Similarly, the vocabulary that discriminates fear, rage, love, and hate too often implies that they operate separately, as isolated experiences, rather than belonging to a more encompassing ecology, that is, a recursive system of feelings. Love is a companion to hate, and careful observation shows that love and hate, among other emotions, take turns expressing themselves on the larger stage of recursive process.

Problems arise when we forget that nouns are code terms for relationship and recursive process. Part of the blame can be placed on our biological limitations. Watts (1961) explains:

> The sensation of stuff arises only when we are confronted with patterns so confused or so closely knit that we cannot make them out. To the naked eye a distant galaxy looks like a distant star and a piece of steel like a continuous and impenetrable mass of matter. But when we change the level of magnification, the galaxy assumes the clear structure of a spiral nebula and the piece of steel turns out to be a system of electrical impulses whirling in relatively vast spaces. The idea of stuff expresses no more than the experience of coming to a limit at which our senses or our instruments are not fine enough to make out the pattern. (p. 177)

Hence, when we encounter sufficient complexity, such as the recursive organization of human interaction, our inability to discern higher orders of patterns leads us to committing what Whitehead called the "fallacy of misplaced concreteness." We then "abstract from relationship and from the experiences of interaction to create 'objects' and to endow them with 'characteristics'" (Bateson, 1976a, pp. xv–xvi). Cybernetic epistemology calls for undoing these materialistic abstractions and constructing distinctions that indicate patterns of relationship and recursive process.

Dialectic in Cybernetic Description

In general, to keep sight of recursive process we must carefully construct our observations and descriptions, avoiding rigid demarcations of parts or mechanisms. To the cybernetician, any examination of the behavior or function of component parts isolated from the cybernetic processes to which they belong is nonsense. This is colorfully illustrated by McCulloch (cited in M. Bateson, 1972): "If you ask me concerning a particular cell what its function is, you've asked a question like what is the function of the second letter of every word in the English language" (pp. 65–66).

"Cybernetic description" involves preserving (and provoking) an awareness of recursively organized systems. Yet how can one use occidental language, which so often suggests either/or dualisms, to depict whole patterns of recursion? One way is to engage in a dialectic in which dismembered sides of dualisms can be reconnected.

This approach acknowledges the catch that any statement one proposes is necessarily one side of a more encompassing distinction. To get unstuck from one side of a dualistic frame is to inevitably get stuck in the other side. The process of a dialectic encourages one to continuously keep getting unstuck — from the sides of a particular distinction as well as from the whole distinction itself.

It is obvious that we cannot and should not stop drawing distinctions. We can, however, use a dialectic which continuously exposes both sides of our distinctions. Since cybernetic epistemology is itself cast in the frame of a distinction, a dialectic also must be utilized to prevent it from falling into an either/or dualism. In this sense cybernetic epistemology must continuously unravel and challenge its own propositions.[2]

An imaginary dialogue may help illuminate this process:

READER: If I understand you correctly, then all that you've said (as well as what you are going to say) about cybernetics, epistemology, and family therapy, among other topics, is not a final statement. Your ideas, in other words, are also deficient and subject to being challenged?

2. This again emphasizes that cybernetic epistemology does not merely suggest transposing one set of terms for another (e.g., family for individual, evolutionary for homeostatic, recursive for lineal, aesthetic for pragmatic), but is primarily concerned with the *context* within which distinctions are cast.

AUTHOR: I cannot say anything that cannot (or should not) be challenged, reframed, or refuted. This, of course, includes the statements I am now making.

READER: But isn't that a paradox?

AUTHOR: I cannot avoid paradox. All that I say is paradoxical in the sense that all statements uttered involve self-reference. Similarly, you cannot avoid paradox.

READER: But, following your suggestion, I might argue that paradox is a faulty idea. Perhaps I could convince you that the word "paradox" is used as if it referred to a "thing" or that things appear "paradoxical" due to a particular form of symbolic structure in the mind of the perceiver. If you reframe your way of seeing the world, paradox might disappear.

AUTHOR: I can still say that parts of your argument are paradoxical. For example, when you describe the world as separate from the one who views, punctuates, frames, or describes it, you are speaking dualistically. In this dualism you may forget that your encounter of the world is also an encounter of parts of your self (or analogues of parts of yourself). Your world will always be a house of mirrors or, as cyberneticians suggest, it will rest upon a foundation of self-referential paradox.

READER: Is what you write, then, always a self-portrait or even an autobiography?

AUTHOR: For me, possibly. What you read is your own portrait. Another view suggests that my effort to sketch some ideas for you is actually a sort of interactive product between us, as cast from my side. In other words, my best prediction of what you will be thinking helps guide what I now say. Similarly, what you get from reading my assortment of phrases is your version of the interactive dance. Your best guess of what I was thinking helps guide what you now read.

READER: Are you trying to slip in the point that the very nature of understanding our relationship — the one between author and reader — is a way to approach cybernetic epistemology?

AUTHOR: Only if we are led to seeing the broader view, which evaporates our separateness and connects us as parts of a recursive dance.

READER: Although we may dance, it still seems useful to distinguish between the two of us. Otherwise, I might argue for a share of the book's royalties.

AUTHOR: If you agree to remember that we participate in constructing the distinction between you and me and that other distinctions are also possible, I will be intellectually comfortable in hearing you speak of our "difference(s)."

READER: But aren't you really asking me to agree with your distinction about distinctions? Couldn't I begin with an alternative frame of reference and choose to not see a constructive view of the world? Suppose I deliberately start with a conventional, lineal, non-cybernetic view and decide to live comfortably within that world.

AUTHOR: If you know that you're making the choice, then you presuppose an alternative view. As long as we can acknowledge that difference, it is possible for us to become interactive parts of a larger gestalt.

Besides, if you did not choose a lineal view, someone else would have to. Or, speaking from the other direction, if you propose a recursive, cybernetic view someone else will take it as an invitation to sketch its complement.

READER: Are you saying that lineal and cybernetic views feed on one another, such that we cannot hear of one perspective without hearing of the other? Is there a cybernetic complementarity under all of this?

AUTHOR: Could I state my reply in a way that could not be regarded by some to be "lineal" and by others as "recursive"? Or could some of the *interpretations* of my proposals be seen by me as lineal and others as recursive? And could not other critics subject all of our conversation to the same differentiation?

READER: Do my questions give my epistemology away?

AUTHOR: To whom?

CYBERNETIC SYSTEMS

Definition

The previous discussion reminds us that all terms are framed by an observer's system of description. We now need to examine how basic terms in family therapy can be given a cybernetic form of description. As a starting point, a problem that has arisen within family therapy is the struggle to understand what is meant by the term "system." Most definitions have failed to identify cybernetic patterns of recursion. Too often "system" is used only to designate the *size* of the unit of observation. This noncybernetic punctuation is implied when a social organization such as a family unit is described as a system, while an individual is not.

From the perspective of cybernetic epistemology, size of social unit does not necessarily have anything to do with defining a cybernetic system. Seeing and treating couples, families, neighborhoods, or entire cultures, in itself, does not distinguish a cybernetically oriented therapist. Cybernetics simply prescribes seeing events as organized by recursive feedback process. For example, symptomatic behavior may be seen as part of a recursive sequence of an individual's behavior and experience. Using this line of description, an agoraphobic could be depicted as an individual caught in a vicious recursive sequence that includes his own problem-solving behavior. In such a case, each effort to avoid open spaces perpetuates further withdrawal from an open space. Attempts to overcome the problem help define and maintain it. Changing such a pattern may require encouraging the agoraphobic in the opposite direction (see Watzlawick *et al.*, 1974). Alternatively, symptomatic behavior expressed by an agoraphobic is sometimes part of a family's recursive pattern of interaction. In this case, the agoraphobic may be encouraged by other family members to exercise "willpower" over the condition and be instructed to follow common sense problem-solving approaches. When the family's behavior helps maintain a problematic context, subsequent intervention will require contending with their patterns of social interaction.

There are two basic rules for discerning a cybernetic system. First, recursive organization must be perceived. Thus, bits of symptomatic behavior are seen as embedded in a recursive sequence of behavior. A therapist may discover, for example, that a husband's anxiety episode is preceded by his wife's failure to prepare dinner and is followed by their son getting into trouble at school. Such a sequence, involving three people, may point to a recursive pattern that organizes the husband's anxiety.

The second and more important criterion of a cybernetic system is that it must have feedback structure, that is, the recursive process must involve self-correction.[3] A serial listing of events that occur before and after a symptomatic occurrence may not identify a cyber-

3. The order of recursion that is self-corrective is not always apparent. Recall that simple orders of recursion which appear, in isolation, to runaway or wildly oscillate, are subject to higher orders of recursive control.

netic system. If these events are recursively structured in feedback fashion, however, a cybernetic system has been detected.

In family therapy, most cybernetic systems have been identified as "homeostatic cycles." Hoffman's (1976) paper "Breaking the Homeostatic Cycle" discusses how symptomatic behavior is organized by social sequences of recursive feedback. She provides a simple example of a "homeostatic cycle" in family process which involves the triadic relationship of father, mother, and son:

> The triangle consists of an ineffectively domineering father, a mildly rebellious son and a mother, who sides with son. Father keeps getting into an argument with son over smoking, which both mother and father say they disapprove of. However, mother will break into these escalating arguments to agree with son, after which father will back down. Eventually father does not even wait for her to come in; he backs down anyway. (pp. 503–504)

The task of a family therapist, Hoffman argues, is to identify problematic recursive cycles and direct interventions at them. Hoffman summarizes several ways in which therapists demarcate these cycles: A therapist may work with a family's recursive cycle within the therapy room, or the focus may include cycles embracing larger systems outside the family (e.g., hospitals and schools). The literature of interactional and strategic therapy is particularly full of descriptions of recursive cycles of behavior and therapeutic techniques designed to interrupt them. This perspective of the recursive organization of events is clearly one of the major insights of family therapy.

Nevertheless, upon occasion, the use of cybernetic terms such as "homeostasis" or "self-correction" are criticized in family therapy. The alternative, these critics suggest, is to view living systems in terms of change and evolution[4] rather than stability and control. As we have previously demonstrated, such a perspective represents a misunderstanding of the recursive and complementary nature of cybernetics. Several decades ago, Cadwallader (1959) found a similar misunderstanding of cybernetics among sociologists:

---

4. A shift to an "evolutionary" perspective of family therapy may only lead to alternative forms of confusion and muddle. Recall William James's (cited in Perry, 1935) parody of its definition: "Evolution is a change from a no-howish untalkaboutable all-alikeness to a some-howish and in general talkaboutable not-all-alikeness by continuous stick togetherations and something elseifications" (p. 482).

Many of the sociologists who are interested in the subject of social change object to the use of all concepts of equilibrium, homeostasis or stability, arguing that to include such ideas as a central part of social theory is to preclude the possibility of dealing with change. They seem to believe that stability and change are not only contradictory ideas but that the processes themselves are totally incompatible . . . . What has been overlooked is that at least one category of stability depends upon and is the consequence of change. Just this kind of stability is of prime interest to cybernetics. (pp. 154–155)

In the case of a heating system, change within the system leads to stability of the whole system. When the system is self-corrective, fluctuations of temperature and the bending arm of a thermostat lead to constancy in the relations among components. In a family, fluctuations or differences in behavior may lead to stability of the interactional processes organizing those behaviors. In this sense, what Hoffman has called a "homeostatic cycle" is a cycle that maintains constancy of relations among interactants through the fluctuations of their behavior. "The more things change, the more they stay the same" refers to both sides of a cybernetic complementarity. Fluctuations, changes, and differences of events among component parts, maintain the sameness or stability of their recursive organization.

There are innumerable ways of drawing cybernetic systems in family therapy. For example, an "individual" may be seen as an autonomous system or as a composite system comprised of diverse forms of simple cybernetic process. In addition, parts of an individual may be recursively linked to parts outside the boundaries of his skin, for example, a blind man and his walking cane. Cybernetic epistemology suggests that there are as many forms of cybernetic systems as there are ways of drawing distinctions.

Evaluation

But does it make a difference how one draws a cybernetic system? In the context of therapy, we can identify two frames of reference that enable a therapist to evaluate a drawn system. The facilitation of symptom alleviation by the drawing of a cybernetic system is one way of determining an adequate punctuation. In the case of interactional and strategic therapies, this is typically the only criterion. Cybernetic systems are drawn as an aid in designing therapeutic strategy; if the intervention doesn't work, another system may be drawn.

For example, an interactional therapist may observe that a client who fears speaking in public habitually engages in a series of problem-solving behaviors. He may try vocal relaxation techniques, meditation, or tranquilizers prior to giving a speech. Typically, he finds that all efforts to relax result in his becoming even more nervous. As Watzlawick *et al.* (1974) suggest, successful therapy requires stopping the *class* of these purposeful solutions. The client may be instructed to begin his speeches with an announcement to the audience about his anxiety. Such a procedure alters the vicious recursive pattern organizing his behavior and may result in the disappearance of his problem and problem-solving behavior. The cybernetic system evaluated in this case is limited to the pattern recursively connecting problem and problem-solving behavior.

The other frame of reference for evaluating a drawn system involves examining the higher order effects of interventions. This entails asking whether the altered system itself introduces a higher order problem. In the previous example, we would consider whether the therapist's participation in helping solve the client's fear of public speaking generated another order of problem. Perhaps this individual will develop a habit of seeing his therapist whenever he perceives a personal difficulty. If this becomes problematic, the therapist must then treat the way he treats his client.

Alcoholic intoxication provides another example. Drinking often leads to temporary relief from a problem an individual has in sobriety. A person who does not feel part of a social group when sober may drink to have an experience of social connection. However, this temporary solution may generate and maintain a drinking problem. The drinker is then caught in a dilemma where although his drinking is an immediate cure for the problem it intends to solve, it creates and maintains another order of pathology (i.e., alcoholism) as time progresses. As the first example illustrates, therapists' interventions may be comparable in effect.

A full consideration of higher orders of cybernetic process suggests that it is possible for institutions of therapy to help maintain a population of clients. Berry (1977) even warns that wherever there is a point of ecological disconnection, whether it involves husband and wife, family and neighborhood, or politician and watershed, "the collaboration of corporation, government and expert sets up a profit-making enterprise that results in the further dismemberment and impoverishment of the Creation" (p. 137). Therapists, therefore, need to ask whether the therapeutic social systems that dispense solutions and cures perpetuate problems.

Therapists are usually not accustomed to thinking beyond immediate pragmatic outcomes. Likewise, researchers typically focus on whether the presenting problem was solved or, at best, what the success of the solution was. The latter consideration may be stated in terms of the degree of improvement or relapse or evaluated by whether other problems have arisen in the client's social context. All of these inquiries examine the effects of the therapist's intervention within simple cybernetic process. The effects within higher orders of cybernetic process are usually not approached.

It is no trivial matter to ignore higher order cybernetics. As Bateson (1972) notes, the history of DDT illustrates how little we know about higher order effects. Although DDT was discovered in 1939, it wasn't until 1950 that scientists found it to be a deadly poison to many animals. By that time he adds, industry had become committed to its production, insects were becoming immune, animals that ate the insects it was designed to destroy were also being poisoned, and the population of the world had increased. It wasn't until 1970 that we began to "control" DDT. Unfortunately, as Bateson proposes, "We still do not know whether the human species on its present diet can surely survive the DDT which is already circulating in the world and will be there for the next twenty years even if its use is immediately and totally discontinued" (p. 489).

The idea that cybernetic systems are recursively connected as parts of a whole ecology is further demonstrated in an account by Charles Elton (cited in Hardin, 1978):

> Some keen gardener, intent upon making Hawaii even more beautiful than before, introduced a plant called *Lantana camara,* which in its native home of Mexico causes no trouble to anybody. Meanwhile, someone else had also improved the amenities of the place by introducing turtle-doves from China, which, unlike any of the native birds, fed eagerly upon the berries of *Lantana.* The combined effects of the vegetative powers of the plant and the spreading of seeds by the turtle-doves were to make the *Lantana* multiply exceedingly and become a serious pest on the grazing country. Indian mynah birds were also introduced, and they too fed upon *Lantana* berries. After a few years the birds of both species had increased enormously in numbers. But there is another side to the story. Formerly the grasslands and young sugar-cane plantations had been ravaged by vast numbers of army-worm

caterpillars, but the mynahs also fed upon these caterpillars and succeeded to a large extent in keeping them in check, so that the outbreaks became less severe. About this time certain insects were introduced in order to try and check the spread of *Lantana* and several of them (in particular a species of Agromyzid fly) did actually destroy so much seed that the *Lantana* began to decrease. As a result of this, the mynahs also began to decrease in numbers to such an extent that there began to occur again severe outbreaks of army-worm caterpillars. It was then found that when the *Lantana* had been removed in many places, other introduced shrubs came in, some of which are even more difficult to eradicate than the original *Lantana*. (p. 169)

Such examples reveal both the necessity for and difficulty of attending to higher order effects of change. Although outcome studies are useful in evaluating the simple effects of therapeutic cures, the time periods involved in higher order systemic change make it difficult to assess whole ecologies. Like studying the effects of a foreign agent on a biological ecosystem, by the time we realize the higher order effects of the techniques of therapy, it may be too late to alter our action. Therapists who seriously face this dilemma will strive toward careful planning of their interventions, always with an eye toward higher order effects.

In sum, we are discussing two orders of pragmatics in which to evaluate contexts of therapy. The first is a more immediate time frame — the effects of intervention on symptomatic occurence. The latter involves a broader temporal frame — the effects of altered simple cybernetic systems on the more encompassing ecology of which they are a part.

In family therapy, Bateson has consistently called for attention to this higher order of pragmatics. He has suggested that therapists examine their interventions as thoroughly as ecologists study coal mining, petroleum engineering, insect control, and so forth. This call for an ecological view arises from a cybernetic perspective in which the recursive effects of effects are formally recognized.

PATHOLOGY AND HEALTH

Symptoms

As we've noted, cybernetics proposes that we always view symptoms within the context of recursive feedback. To fully understand this view requires that we remember that all systems, whether individuals or families, achieve stability through processes of change. There are several ways in which an individual's behavior and emotions can be seen to change. For example, a wife may alter her feelings about her husband, shifting between love, hate, frustration, excitement, and so on. If the systemic organization of her feelings is self-corrective, she will be described as having a "balanced" or "stabilized" emotional life. Another pattern of organization involves the escalation of a particular emotion or behavior. For example, an initial discouragement may escalate into metadiscouragement, or what is called "clinical depression." Or there may be an oscillation between escalated emotions, for example, manic–depressive episodes.

These patterns of organization begin to suggest how pathology or symptomology contribute to the achievement of stability through change. Namely, symptoms are a sort of "escalating sameness." What changes is the intensity of a particular emotion or the extremeness of a behavior. Symptomatic behavior is analogous to being in quicksand, where struggling in the same place results in escalating sameness.

Stated differently, symptoms indicate a system's effort to maximize or minimize a particular behavior or experience. This process results in what at first appears to be an escalating runaway. Any individual perceived as the "site" of a runaway behavior becomes socially labeled as bad, mad, or sick. The runaway behavior, however, is eventually curbed by higher order feedback processes such as encountering a therapist or policeman with their respective calibrating acts of institutionalization or sedation. It is important to realize that the social system surrounding symptomatic behavior typically calibrates its escalation.

This view of symptomology suggests that any pattern of behavior that can be characterized as an effort toward maximizing or minimizing a variable is pathological. Keith (1980), for example, has noted in the case of clinical depression that other family members who are not depressed may also be defined as pathological. Following Whitaker, he suggests that there are pathologies of "always smiling," "always being rational," and "always exhibiting 'good' behavior." Whitaker (see Neill & Kniskern, 1982) calls this category of psychopathology, "the white knight" (p. 335). Thus, a "depressed" person's escalating depression may be in synch with another person's escalating "perfect behavior," "call for hope," or "rationality." In this way the ongoing relationship between these different forms of emotions and behaviors creates a whole interactive system. Encouraging a white knight to be less perfect becomes a strategy for alleviating the presenting depression.

These observations and ideas suggest that each member of a troubled family sometimes provides related forms of escalating behavior and experience. This should not be surprising since, as we earlier proposed, bits of behavior or simple action are always organized as parts of interactive process. In the case of so-called "psychopathology," it is now evident that such behavior fits into the organization of a particular interactional context. Therefore, it is likely that each family member's pattern of behavior and experience is as pathological (or normal) as that of any other family member. This view enables some therapists to regard the whole family as the client and to engage in the technique called "moving the symptom."

However, it is important to realize that the cybernetic system maintaining a symptom does not necessarily include the whole family, nor is it necessarily limited to that social group. For example, Watzlawick and Coyne (1980) have created therapeutic interventions for treating "depression" by "interdicting the self-defeating efforts of family members to be supportive and encouraging" (p. 13). Like Whitaker, they suggest that "successful therapeutic interventions often involve changing the behavior of persons other than the identified patient" (p. 13). Their view, however, is as parsimonious as possible, attempting to attend only to those individuals who are part of immediately relevant feedback.

It follows that a symptom can be defined as a particular class of cybernetic process. In other words, symptoms represent recursive feedback cycles of escalated behavior and experience that are organized in a whole interactional system. At the order of social interaction, an individual's symptomatic behavior marks a particular kind of recursive relationship with others.

Since symptomatic behavior is part of a larger interpersonal gestalt, an individual's symptom may be taken as a metaphor about his interpersonal relationships. A husband's chronic stomachaches, for instance, may actually be a metaphor about his marriage. In this case, it would be more correct to talk about "sociosomatic" rather than "psychosomatic" illness. At a higher order of recursion, the marriage may be seen as a metaphor about an entire social ecology, possibly including offspring, parents, and grandparents. The broader view suggests that symptoms are indicators for an entire ecology of relationships.

Nathan Ackerman (see Hoffman, 1981, pp. 225-228) interviewed a family where the presenting problem was serious fighting between two adolescents. In questioning the family, he discovered that the mother had a habit of belching in her husband's face, while the father reported that he had "lost his sex." The more Ackerman probed into the family, the more difficult it was to determine which member was the "symptom bearer." More accurately, it could be seen that each family member was symptomatic in a way related to other family members' symptoms. The whole group provided a sort of balancing act through each member's unique form of bizarre behavior.

By now we should recognize that it is incorrect to assume psychiatry has "named" all symptomology. Rather, when "pathology" is identified in any social setting, it is likely that other connected members are sites of pathology. A wife diagnosed as "depressive" often signifies to the therapist a husband who is excessively enthusiastic, rational, hopeful, or well-behaved. These complementary forms of escalating behavior suggest that other labels for the diagnostician might include "neurotic normality," "psychotic hope," and "involutional happiness."

The cybernetic view does not necessarily suggest that we shift our punctuation from a "disturbed individual" to that of a "disturbed family." Rather, it identifies particular ways in which individuals *and* families maintain an organization through recursive process. Cybernetic epistemology involves moving away from blaming identified patients or their families for their problems. It sees symptoms as metaphors for a whole ecology, leading one to a stage of awareness Bateson (1958a) depicts as "humility and loneliness." This "loneliness of liberation," as Watts (1961) calls it, arises when there is no longer any gene, chemical, individual, group, or culture to blame and be angry with.

Ecological Climax

Individuals and families may organize themselves through other processes of change which are not strictly characterized by escalating sameness. In biology, when the interactions of a large number of diverse species are held in balance, the term "ecological climax" is used. This balance of diversity in an ecosystem is a way of talking about health. The alternative to health, as we've defined it, is characterized by the maximization or minimization of any variable in an ecosystem.

A unilineal focus on part of a system will disrupt and fractionate the balanced diversity of an ecosystem. An advantage for any one component will be at the expense of other components. This is what ecologists mean when they say there is no such thing as a free lunch in an ecosystem.

A paradox in ecology is that the most flexible species are the dullest. When a flexible species is not controlled by its ecosystem, ecological climax breaks down and a system of weeds remains. Bateson (cited in Brand, 1974) connects with this discussion as follows:

> The idea of sanity or health or whatever has got to be somehow related to the whole concept of climax. The definition of pathology then is: those things which destroy climax. They destroy it to the point, where 50 species lived you can now have only five. These pathologies leave a dull world. . . . The more you make these sudden changes . . . the more you fractionate down to only accept the plants we call weeds. The same is true of human society. (p. 18)

Thus, health in human ecosystems refers to a "vital balance" of diverse forms of experience and behavior. To engage in an effort of maximization or minimization, rather than diversity, leads to the escalating sameness we have defined as pathology. Maslow's (1970) studies indicate that healthy individuals escape simplistic, dichotomous forms of description.[5] These people cannot be characterized by the maximization or minimization of any particular characteristic; instead, they embody both sides of a multitude of differences. As Maslow (1970) put it, the "age-old opposition between heart and head, reason and instinct, or cognition and conation is seen to disappear in healthy people where they become synergic rather than antagonists" (p. 179).

This formulation characterizes the healthy individual as an integrated, whole unity of diverse differences. Consequently, a "whole, healthy, integrated person" is not necessarily one who can be called "symptom free." For these people, health and pathology are sides of a cybernetic complementarity. This perspective leads us to the paradox

---

5. Maslow described healthy people as escaping the dichotomies of "kindness–ruthlessness, concreteness–abstractiveness, acceptance–rebellion, self–society, adjustment–maladjustment, detachment from others–identification with others, serious–humorous, Dionysian–Apollonian, introverted–extroverted, intense–casual, serious–frivolous, conventional–unconventional, mystic–realistic, active–passive, masculine–feminine, lust–love, and Eros–Agape" (p. 179).

that pathology is an approximation or part of a more encompassing whole, called "health." A healthy individual may therefore appear to be both symptomatic and symptom free, depending upon when (and how) an observer views him.

With regard to whole families, Whitaker (1979) has described healthy families as contexts wherein role positions constantly shift, enabling the "scapegoat" function to rotate:

> I think if the family is healthy that scapegoat-role can move around so that on one day they can razz Sonny-boy for being childish, the next day they can razz Dad for being pompous, the next day they can razz Mom for being over-anxious, and the next day they can razz Sister for playing sexy games with Daddy when she should be doing the dishes. That way the scapegoat function — the "cut-em-down-to-size" function — moves throughout the family. Nobody is stuck with the horror of carrying all of the family's anxiety all the time. (p. 112)

Whitaker's view suggests that like Maslow's healthy individuals, healthy families also escape dichotomous forms of description. A healthy family will follow a choreography of diverse interactional episodes which provide a sort of ecological climax or balance. In these families, the role of scapegoat as well as white knight will constantly shift from person to person, coalitions will fluctuate between members, individuals will experience an alternation between separateness and togetherness, fights and hugs will be given fair representation, and so on.

Ecological climax is, in essence, an aesthetic metaphor for discussing health and pathology. Families, like redwood forests, are contexts with intricately woven patterns of interconnection. A healthy forest facilitates the connection and autonomy of a diverse range of species and kinds of interaction. Similarly, healthy families facilitate both diversification and connection of their members. Like a good forest ranger, a therapist should always keep his eye on the whole ecology with its different orders of process and complexity.

In earlier chapters it was argued that we should be responsive to bits of action, interactional themes, and more complex systems of choreography. We can now view health and pathology over these various orders of process. With regard to simple action, we may see escalations of the same form of action or a wider diversity of action. Moving to the order of interactional process, escalating forms of one member's action are often in synch with those of another member.

This relationship will be symmetrical, as in an escalating marital fight, or complementary, as in an escalating exhibitor–spectator relationship. Finally, choreography of interactional themes is the order of process enabling us to more clearly distinguish health and pathology. Here we see that monotonous recycling of interactional sequences signifies pathology, whereas a self-corrective organization of diverse sequences is more characteristic of ecosystemic health.

Unfortunately, much time and money has been wasted on efforts to describe bits of action that are believed to be bad, mad, or sick. As Bateson (1976c) repeatedly argued, this focus represents only "half the ass of a relationship system." Since any bit of behavior is always part of an encompassing interactional process, a larger view is required. However, like a bit of action, a pattern of interactional process is not in itself an indication of health or pathology. Observing any particular interactional episode, such as a husband and wife fighting, will not necessarily enable an observer to make an appropriate distinction between health and pathology. These interactional episodes are themselves organized by a higher order of process which we earlier referred to as involving systems of choreography.

The perspective of choreography enables us to more clearly discriminate between systems that are healthy and those that are pathological. Redundant sequences of marital fighting, for instance, may suggest pathology. This is, of course, only a formal way of stating what we already know by common sense. That is, a marital fight is in itself not a pattern of pathology, whereas nothing but marital fighting is something else again.

Thinking in terms of choreography provides a way of understanding the changing behavior and experience of individuals as well as the interactional dances embodying them. Systems of choreography indicate how lower order patterns are connected. A dramatic example of how behavior and interaction are choreographed was captured by a student of the cultural anthropologist, Hall (1977):

> Using an abandoned car as a blind, he photographed children dancing and skipping in a school playground during their lunch hour. At first, they looked like so many kids each doing his own thing. After a while, we noticed that one little girl was moving more than the rest. Careful study revealed that she covered the entire playground. Following procedures laid down for my students, this young man viewed the film over and over at different speeds. Gradually, he perceived that

the whole group was moving in synchrony to a definite rhythm. The most active child, the one who moved the most, was the director, the orchestrator of the playground rhythm! Not only was there rhythm and a beat, but the beat seemed familiar. Seeking help from a friend deeply involved in rock music, who also viewed the film several times, we found a tune that fit the rhythm. Then the music was synchronized with the children's play, and once synchronized, remained in synch for the entire 4½ minutes of the film clip! (pp. 76–77)

From such studies, Hall (1977) concluded, "People in interactions move together in a kind of dance, but they are not aware of their synchronous movement and they do it without music or conscious orchestration." (p. 71).

In this manner, therapists can learn to discern systems of choreography that connect people's action and interaction. In general, all orders of process, as well as their organized relations, should be our focus. Like the director of a symphony, we can be responsive to the individual instruments, the various ways of relating different instruments in diverse patterns of harmony and cacophony, and the music arising from the entire ensemble.

THERAPIST

Therapists affect the systems they are treating whether they intend to or not. On the other side of the relationship, the systems treated always affect the therapist. As Bateson (cited in Lipset, 1980) put it, "When the investigator starts to probe unknown areas of the universe, the back end of the probe is always driven into his own vital parts" (p. 214).

The Heisenberg-like[6] hook between the observer and the observed demonstrates that therapists do not observe clients, they observe their relationship with clients. This idea is supported by Sullivan's (1953) notion that in diagnosing, the therapist is always a part of the field being observed. Similarly, Haley (1973a) has insisted that the "therapist include himself in the description of a family" (p. 161). All of this is old hat to the cybernetic epistemologist who knows that the

---

6. Heisenberg's well-known "Uncertainty Principle" states that the observer constantly alters what he observes by the obtrusive act of observation.

map is always in the territory, the observer in the observed, the therapist in the system being treated.

What is important to realize is that a therapist's epistemology helps determine his relationship to the system he treats. For example, a therapist's relationship to a system is sometimes described with metaphors of "power." Haley, (1976b), in particular, uses this metaphor to describe a therapist as a kind of "power broker" who controls the ways in which power is distributed and used by a family. As noted earlier, this form of description differs from the position of cybernetics, which chooses descriptions of pattern rather than material and energy.

Bateson has long considered Haley's use of the metaphor of power an epistemological error that is self-validating and potentially pathological. He more recently stated (Bateson, 1976b) "Haley slides too lightly over the real epistemological differences between himself and me. . . . I believed then—and today—that the *myth* of power always corrupts because it proposes always a false (though conventional) epistemology" (p. 106).

Haley has never adequately responded to Bateson's criticism. In a footnote concerning the development of double bind theory he briefly refers to the issue:

> The issue of power and control was always a problem within the project . . . I was trying at that time to shift observation of the individual to the observation of a system and to view a power struggle as a product of the needs of a system rather than the needs of a person. I still prefer that view. . . . (Haley, 1976a, p. 78)

At the same time, Haley agrees with Bateson that to say people "attempt control" over one another is "not a way of describing two individuals *relating*," but is "putting a 'need' into them as individuals" (Haley, 1976a, p. 78).

Haley therefore makes a category mistake when he resorts to using "needs," a description appropriate for individuals, to characterize social organization. But more importantly, Haley uses a metaphor outside of cybernetic epistemology, "power," which is appropriate only for a physical, rather than mental, description of the universe.

Bateson was not playing a game of intellectual semantics in his criticism of "power." As he (1972) stated:

> What is true is that the *idea of power* corrupts. Power corrupts most rapidly those who believe in it, and it is they who will want it most. . . .

Perhaps there is no such thing as unilateral power. After all, the man "in power" depends on receiving information just as much as he "causes" things to happen. It is not possible for Goebbels to control the public opinion of Germany because in order to do so he must have spies or legmen or public opinion polls to tell him what the Germans are thinking. He must then trim what he says to this information; and then again find out how they are responding. It is an interaction, and not a lineal situation.

But the *myth* of power is, of course, a very powerful myth and probably most people in the world more or less believe in it. It is a myth which, if everybody believes in it, becomes to that extent self-validating. But it is still epistemological lunacy and leads inevitably to various sorts of disaster. (p. 486)

Part of Bateson's criticism of "power" addresses the assumption that more power will always be more powerful. This idea in its strictest sense is not applicable to ecology. Ecological products (e.g., population, oxygen, protein, money, number of clients, workshops, and so on) are intransitive and become toxic if an optimum value is exceeded. Anyone suggesting that a therapist is solely responsible for change implies a transitive and lineal relationship. It may then be assumed that the more skilled a therapist, the more "power" the therapist has to achieve change. Such an assumption is potentially toxic and after a certain point it may lead a therapist to becoming less and less flexible, less and less creative, and less and less effective as a therapist, teacher, and student.

Ecologists suggest that our planet faces certain "points of no return" owing to social policies governed by an epistemology of "power." What ecological pathologies are being constructed by therapists who implement change through an epistemology containing metaphors of "power?" Bateson continuously issued prophetic warnings in this regard.

Belief in the myth of power is self-verifying since it is a habit of punctuation. This is demonstrated by Madanes's (1981) remarks:

It has even been suggested that power may be a myth, a dangerous metaphor to be mistrusted. Yet the influence of one nation over another or the power of the rich over the poor cannot be ignored. . . . However, power is an important factor in human relations . . . . It is difficult to imagine how the relevance of power can be denied when people lock each other up, murder each other, or devote their lives to helping one another. . . . (pp. 217–218)

The cybernetician's argument is not whether "power" exists. That question is epistemologically irrelevant because it assumes that there can be an objective proof (or disproof) of its existence. The relevant criticism is directed at the *consequences* of an epistemological habit of punctuating the world in terms of power. Bateson's work attempts to demonstrate how such a punctuation reinforces greed and corruption in all those who believe in the "reality" of "social power," whether they think they have it or not. Preventing such pathology requires avoiding the use of power metaphors to punctuate the biological world.

It may seem odd to not see power in the world of human relationship. In fact it may be almost impossible for some therapists to imagine human relations without considering power. This difficulty is perhaps the most dramatic illustration of how different the world of cybernetic epistemology is from the more conventional, Newtonian world. In cybernetics, power belongs to locomotives and nuclear generators, not to mental process.

An alternative to the metaphor of power is the ecological metaphor of "part in an ecosystem." As Bateson (1974) reminds us, a crucial individual in a system (e.g., a therapist) is always *part* of that system and "is therefore subject to all the constraints and necessities of the particular part-whole relationship in which he exists" (p. 27). This perspective describes a therapist's presence in the ecosystem he treats as "part in" or "part of" the system rather than as an outside spectator, manipulator, or power broker.

A therapist may join a family (or part of a family) and nothing may appear to change, or the therapist's interventions may coincide with events of apparent change. Although a therapist's presence in a system sometimes appears to make a difference, it is important to realize that "control" refers to the whole self-corrective system, not a unilateral influence from a therapist or any other member. However, the therapist's presence helps determine how a cybernetic system is organized. The way in which a therapist is part of feedback will lead to particular ways in which family members organize their behavior around him. Their reactions, however, lead the therapist to organizing his behavior around them, and so on, round and round.

From the perspective of cybernetics, the most a therapist can do is vary his behavior, recognize the subsequent behavior of those in the surrounding social field, and modify his reactions to their reactions. If the effects of his behavior on others are used, in turn, to change his behavior, feedback is established. The therapist is not controlling their behavior, but is recognizing the response of their behavior to his and the response of his behavior to theirs.

Even the training of an earthworm does not imply that a human teacher is unilaterally controlling a worm. What the worm does and does not do helps organize the human teacher's behavior. All systems of learning utilize recursive feedback wherein information is informed. In other words, information is created within the whole cybernetic system. This follows Pask's (1973) theory which describes the learning situation as one in which teacher and student are co-learning. In a similar vein, Bateson (1972) proposes that the cybernetic system encompassing an organism and its environment is a unit of co-evolution. Therapy is such a cybernetic system, where both therapist and client are parts of co-learning and co-evolution.

To become an effective part of this system, a therapist must be able to vary his behavior and recognize the effects of all action — his as well as the other participants'. Varying one's behavior corresponds to what is traditionally called "intervention," while recognizing the effects of these interventions may be called "diagnosis." As Haley (1971) suggests, the family therapist is "interested in diagnosing how the family responds to his therapeutic interventions" (p. 282). The double view of intervention and diagnosis recognizes that they are inseparable parts of cybernetic process.

When therapy is considered to be a cybernetic system, it is impossible to distinguish what is contributed by whom. In therapy, cybernetic systems emerge from the interweaving of two major relational fields whose nodal points are represented by an "identified patient" and "identified therapist." The term "identified therapist" reminds us that the role of therapist is as flexible and indeterminate as that of identified patient. Both are merely punctuations of a whole system.

Being part of the system one wishes to know is what Maslow (1969) describes as "becoming and *being* what is to be known" (p. 50). This is a Taoist approach which is nonpurposeful, noncontrolling, and process oriented. Bateson (1972) refers to this "sense or recognition of the fact of circularity" as "wisdom" (p. 146).

In contrast, conscious, purposeful mental process cannot by itself recognize whole patterns of cybernetic process. Bateson (1972) discusses this limitation:

The cybernetic nature of self and the world tends to be imperceptible to consciousness, insofar as the contents of the "screen" of consciousness are determined by considerations of purpose. The argument of purpose tends to take the form "D is desirable; B leads to C; C leads to D; so D can be achieved by way of B and C." But, if the total mind and the outer world do not, in general, have this lineal structure, then by forcing this structure upon them, we become blind to the cybernetic circularities of the self and the external world. Our conscious sampling of data will not disclose whole circuits but only arcs of circuits, cut off from their matrix by our selective attention. (pp. 444–445)

Therapists who are responsive only to their "screen" of consciousness will more than likely be blind to cybernetic systems. The correction of this short-sightedness requires fully addressing higher orders of cybernetic process. For now, we will explore how a consideration of ecology leads us to a more complete understanding of cybernetic systems in therapy.

ECOLOGY

By drawing distinctions in therapy, innumerable cybernetic systems can be discerned. Each identified system will consequently imply a particular part/whole complementarity. For example, before a therapist meets a family, he may presume, perhaps on the basis of what he has heard from others, that the family has a particular way of recursively organizing its interaction. This initial presupposition draws a distinction between the family's organization and that of the therapist. The therapist at this point hypothesizes the family as a separate, autonomous system.

However, once a family encounters the therapist, a new system emerges. The intertwining systems of therapist and family are like moiré patterns, where two distinct patterns interact to create an autonomous hybrid pattern. It is in this moiré-like system that a therapist cannot consider himself separate from a family.

At this time, we can note that these different punctuated systems provide an initial part/whole complementarity. The whole family system alone (i.e., before encountering a therapist) becomes part of a more encompassing family-*plus*-therapist system. Extending these punctuations, observers behind a one-way mirror could draw a distinction between the hybrid system within the therapy room and a higher order system within which the observers are active parts. When

the observers provide information to a therapist that affects his subsequent action, followed by the observers giving further information
and the occurrence of subsequent modification, higher order feedback emerges. This view proposes another part/whole complementarity, with the family-*plus*-therapist as part of the more encompassing family-*plus*-therapist-*plus*-observers system.

In an experimental project at the Marriage and Family Program
of the Menninger Foundation, an even higher order of recursion was
drawn. Here, a therapist and a family were subject to calls and conferences from a team behind a one-way mirror. At another location a
higher order observer studied the interaction between family, therapist, and supervisory team. This project illustrated that diverse orders
of cybernetic process can be implemented which construct new domains of therapeutic investigation.[7]

We've discussed several ways in which cybernetic systems can be
identified over various ranges of social process. The broadest possible
view for looking at all systems, orders of systems, and interrelations
among systems is defined as ecology. As Roszak (1977) formulates it,
ecology proposes that all things in nature are systematically interrelated. He comments that if you "extend this idea as far as it will go
you can imagine the Earth at large, including ourselves and our culture as a single, evolving system of life" (p. 30). As an alternative to
distinguishing "individuals" and "families," we could therefore
choose to focus on more holistic punctuations. American Indians for
example, propose that we see the whole earth as a single organism,
with the rivers as veins and the soil as flesh (Boyd, 1974). Similarly, the
ecologist Lovelock (1979) suggests that we adopt the term "Gaia" as a
metaphor for thinking of our planet and its interlocking systems as a
whole system.

Ecological Self-Correction

When we think in terms of ecology, we encounter the Taoist position
that organisms heal themselves if not interfered with. Since the whole
ecology is recursively structured and self-corrective, any disturbed

7. It is critical to recognize that once an agent becomes an active part of a
system, he may contribute to maintaining the problem. When this occurs, the family-
plus-therapist (or any other involved agent) becomes the identified patient. Interventions must then be aimed at the family-*plus*-therapist (and, perhaps, *plus*-super-
visor).

part will adjust if we leave it alone. For example, if you reduce one of the species in a forest by a certain percentage, ten years later it will have adjusted itself to the original level (assuming no other interventions took place). The Taoist position, which attends to the whole ecology of cybernetic process, suggests that family therapy should focus on how to let an individual, a family, or a system achieve its own adjustments.

One approach to understanding how ecosystems heal themselves is to examine traditional explanations of the reorganization of personality systems. These explanations usually begin by paradoxically proposing that a personality system must dissociate in order to achieve an integration of its whole. For example, a personality system may be dissociated in terms of unconscious and conscious mind. A dialectical process between the two sides of this distinction is then enacted which enables the personality system's dissociated parts to organize into a self-corrective, integrated whole ecosystem.

Don Juan describes this dialectic as an interplay between "nagual" and "tonal," which we can roughly translate as unconscious and conscious process, respectively. For Carlos Castaneda to encounter an alternative world of experience, he had to be tricked out of his conventional ways of ordering and punctuating the world. Don Juan did this by disrupting Castaneda's routines, confusing him and trapping him in Zen-like koans. Through these disorienting techniques, Castaneda was led to experience what sorcerers call "dreaming." As don Juan (Castaneda, 1974) explains:

> "*Dreaming* is a practical aid devised by sorcerers," he said. "They were not fools; they knew what they were doing and sought the usefulness of the *nagual* by training their *tonal* to let go for a moment, so to speak, and then grab again. This statement doesn't make sense to you. But that's what you've been doing all along: training yourself to let go without losing your marbles." (p. 245)

Don Juan's explanation of "dreaming" is somewhat analogous to the way Milton Erickson described unconscious process. When conscious mind is distracted, Erickson argued, unconscious process steps forth to provide new avenues for change or the possibility of recalibration, to put it cybernetically.

Conscious and unconscious, or tonal and nagual, can also be seen as different orders of cybernetic process which are immanent in any ecology of mind. These processes do not necessarily reside within the boundaries of a person's brain, but may be part of other orders of biological and social organization. In cybernetics, the change of conscious process by unconscious process is a metaphor for the recalibration of lower order feedback by higher order feedback process.

Don Juan suggests that we momentarily let go of the tonal in order to seek "the usefulness of the nagual" and that the next step in this sequence is for the tonal to "grab again." This zigzag movement between tonal and nagual, or conscious and unconscious process, is another way of describing our dialectic of form and process. Conscious process, tonal, or left-brain mentation are therefore ways of talking about the categorization of form. Recall that this is the side of our dialectic that formally structures phenomena, whether it be the naming of form or the calibration of feedback. On the other side of the dialectic, we have unconscious process, nagual, or right-brain mentation. Here we are referring to process—the underlying Hericlitean whirlwinds that systems of punctuation order.

In the clinical world, we can refer to the dialectic of cybernetic form and process as a recursive interaction of conscious and unconscious orders of mind. This dialectical process can construct and discern relations across different orders of cybernetic feedback and calibration. A therapist helps connect a troubled situation to a higher order of feedback process which will provide correction. This higher order feedback is a cybernetic way of discussing what Milton Erickson called "unconscious mind" and what don Juan called "nagual."

One way of viewing family therapy is to depict it as a dialectical process that integrates the dissociated parts of each individual member through the medium of a social context. We can approach this perspective by examining a gestalt technique used by Satir (see Grinder & Bandler, 1976). In this technique, a therapist begins by directing a client to choose several people from a group to represent dissociated components of the client's personality system. For example, different people may be chosen to represent the client's anger, love, disappointment, hope, learning, and so forth. Using this procedure enables a therapist to help a client coordinate the behavior of a whole group by establishing self-corrective feedback for it. Through a dialectic between the feedback processes in the group and the client's efforts to recalibrate these processes, a client metaphorically achieves a recalibration of his own personality.

This gestalt technique provides a way of viewing family therapy. The individuals can be regarded as symbolic representations of the dissociated parts of each family member. When a therapist helps a whole family operate as a more coordinated unity, he enables each individual personality system to become restructured and integrated. It must be remembered, however, that this view sees each member of the family as a client — each dissociated in a different but interrelated way. By restructuring the whole family, each member becomes restructured. More formally stated, recalibration of a whole family system necessarily results in recalibration of each individual system.

Aesthetic Understanding

It is important to emphasize that a consideration for an individual's family and social niche should always be part of any therapy. Limiting treatment to individuals *in vitro* is ecologically unwise. The idea that a therapist should focus on the development of "healthy individuals" is itself an attempt to maximize only one variable — individual health. However, after a certain limit, health becomes unhealthy to another order of process. This is exemplified by the great forests in central China that died out because each individual tree was so healthy it impinged on its neighbors.[8]

The limits of individual health are controlled by the health of individuals' immediate contexts — their families. Families, in turn, must help maintain the health of the biosociocultural contexts that embody them. And so on, recursively, until we can conceive of a healthy planet.

Ecology suggests a new form of "totemism" where the general systemic structure of the world around us is taken as "an appropriate source of metaphor to enable man to understand himself in his social organization" (Bateson, 1972, p. 484). The work of Bateson, Maturana, Varela, and other cybernetic biologists is an expression of this totemism. By examining living cells, seashores, frogs, and dolphins, we are led to further understanding of human beings and the organization of their behavior in social contexts including therapy.

8. The story of China's trees may be a metaphor for contemporary times. Von Foerster (1976a) calculates that by the year 2027 "every square foot of land [will] be occupied by a person and that everyone [will] be squeezed to death" (p. 10) given the current rate of population growth.

Cybernetics encourages us to search for patterns that connect living process. As Bateson (1979a) expressed this challenge:

> What pattern connects the crab to the lobster and the orchid to the primrose and all the four of them to me? And me to you? And all the six of us to the amoeba in one direction and to the back-ward schizophrenic in another? (p. 8)

Orienting ourselves toward seeing "patterns that connect" leads us to experiencing an *aesthetics* of our ecosystem.

A metaphor for an aesthetic understanding of ecology is provided by a story from Hua-yen Buddhism, often referred to as the "Jewel of Indra" (cited in Cook, 1977):

> Far away in the heavenly abode of the great god Indra, there is a wonderful net which has been hung by some cunning artificer in such a manner that it stretches out infinitely in all directions. In accordance with the extravagant tastes of deities, the artificer has hung a single glittering jewel in each "eye" of the net, and since the net itself is infinite in dimension, the jewels are infinite in number. There hang the jewels, glittering like stars of the first magnitude, a wonderful sight to behold. If we now arbitrarily select one of these jewels for inspection and look closely at it, we will discover that in its polished surface there are reflected *all* the other jewels in the net, infinite in number. Not only that, but each of the jewels reflected in this one jewel is also reflecting all the other jewels, so that there is an infinite reflecting process occurring. (p. 2)

An awareness of the infinitely repeated interrelationships among all members of an ecosystem enables us to more fully comprehend the more encompassing recursive patterns connecting each of us. A whole ecosystem, like the Hua-yen universe, has no hierarchy, no center, or as Cook (1977) points out, "If there is one, it is everywhere" (p. 4).

The Hua-yen perspective, as metaphorized in the "Jewel of Indra," suggests that a whole is not distinct from the parts that comprise it. A person may point to his nose and say, "This is my body." But an observer to this event may draw a distinction and respond, "It is only a part of your body." Cook (1977), in explaining the Hua-yen view, observes that "it is a part of my body, but at the same time it is my body" (p. 10). Furthermore, he adds, "to insist that it is *only* a part is to fall into a fallacious view of the whole as an independent and subsisting entity to which parts belong." In ecology, the parts and whole are a cybernetic complementarity, where "what we identify as a part is merely an abstraction from a unitary whole" (Cook, 1977, p. 10).

In ecology, parts and wholes are not one, not two. The whole of our ecology necessitates the cybernetic complementarities of its parts, life *and* death, success *and* failure, health *and* pathology. With reference to the Zen Buddhist D. T. Suzuki, Cook (1977) pushes us toward a fuller understanding of this ecological view:

> As D. T. Suzuki said in his commentary on Basho's *haiku*
>
> > Lice, fleas —
> > The horse pissing
> > Beside my pillow
>
> the real world is a world of lice as well as butterflies, horse flies as well as vintage champagne, and to the person who has truly realized this, one is as good as the other. (p. 11)

The so-called "successful" therapist or physician who sets out to completely exterminate human problems and disease will be acting out of step with ecology. Such a person would be engaged in an effort to minimize the variable "pathology" and maximize the variable "health." Unfortunately, as ecologists are quick to tell us, as soon as we eradicate one disease, another appears.[9] Again, the more encompassing view of ecology depicts health and pathology as a cybernetic complementarity.[10]

Perhaps the most difficult point for occidentals (including the author of this book) to understand is that nature goes on healing itself in spite of what we do. Slater (1974) discusses this idea:

> Humans are still embedded in their ecosystem despite their grandiose fantasies, and subject to its processes — that as our mechanical mindedness reaches the danger point, corrective processes begin to occur that alter our ways of thinking and acting. (p. 180)

The ideas in this book, as well as other ideas related to it, may, in fact, be an expression of a self-corrective change process now occurring in our culture. Our only hope is that we learn to trigger the necessary higher order feedback processes before we destroy the planet.

---

9. Illich (1976) refers to "iatrogenesis" as pathology generated by doctors and warns us that modern medicine is itself a major threat to our health.

10. Bateson (1979a) for example, argues that pathology and death are necessary to exercise an "ecosystem's capacity for self-healing" (p. 222).

Efforts to minimize or maximize parts we assume to be within ourselves will be reenacted in that which is outside ourselves. Similarly, our action on what we assume is outside ourselves will be reflected within. When we understand our world of experience through cybernetic epistemology, we find that it is an ecology of mind, and as Mary Catherine Bateson (1977) proposes, "This is perhaps a basis for a new kind of respect for the structures of the world in which we live" (p. 65).

It is not enough, however, to gain an intellectual understanding of an ecology of mind. Such understanding must be the foundation for one's habits of action. What it means to embody ecology, or "cybernetic epistemology," is provided in a story told by a Buddhist priest:

> That I have been able to establish myself as well as I have has been totally because of my teacher's guidance. It was customary for him to visit the shrines of various guardians, placed around the grounds of the temple, every day after the morning service. One morning while he was making his rounds, he discovered a single chopstick in a drain. He brought it back, called me to his room, held out the chopstick to me and asked, "What is this?" I replied, "It is a chopstick." "Yes, this is a chopstick. Is it unusable?" he asked further. "No," I said, "It is still usable." "Quite so," he said, "And yet I found it in a drain with other scraps. That is to say, you have taken the life of this chopstick. You may know the proverb, 'He who kills another digs two graves.' Since you have killed this chopstick, you will be killed by it." Spending four or five hours on this incident he told me how I should practice. At that time I was seven or eight years old. His guidance at that time really soaked in. From that time on, I became very careful and meticulous about everything. (Cook, 1977, pp. 18-19)

Cybernetic epistemology insists that we *respect* all parts of our experience, whether we punctuate them as inside or outside the boundaries of our skin. As Cook (1977) reminds us, "To throw away even a single chopstick as worthless is to set up a hierarchy of values which in the end will kill us in a way in which no bullet can" (p. 19).

Bateson (1972) claimed that "the hardest saying in the Bible is that of St. Paul, addressing the Galatians: 'God is not mocked'" (p. 504). Abusing any part of an ecosystem, whether it be a chopstick, a watershed, or therapy, will trigger the surrounding ecology to correct *your* behavior. Bateson explains:

> It is of no use to plead that a particular sin of pollution or exploitation was only a little one or that it was unintentional or that it was commit-

ted with the best intentions. Or that, "If I didn't, somebody else would have." The processes of ecology are not mocked. (p. 504)

DISCUSSION

THERAPIST: What is the most important point to remember when constructing a cybernetic description of family therapy?

EPISTEMOLOGIST: We should never forget that the cybernetic system we discern is a consequence of the distinctions we happen to draw.

THERAPIST: Several ways of drawing a system have been discussed, such as a whole family, a family-*plus*-therapist, a family-*plus*-therapist-*plus*-observers, and so on. Which of these punctuations is the most appropriate?

EPISTEMOLOGIST: Appropriate for whom and for what? Your question needs to be recycled back to you, the observer, who is constructing the drawn system.

THERAPIST: Let me try a different question. Which of those punctuations of cybernetic systems correspond to simple cybernetics and which to cybernetics of cybernetics? In other words, do some of these distinctions point to a black box system while others indicate an autonomous system?

EPISTEMOLOGIST: Any system one decides to draw can be marked as autonomous or as open to the inputs and outputs of other systems. For example, a family watched by an observer from behind a one-way mirror may be considered an autonomous system. If we observe it that way, we then view our action on the family as perturbations rather than inputs. Here, we do not follow a black box model with its punctuation of "something in/process/something out." Instead, we look at how a system alters its structure in order to maintain an invariant organization.

THERAPIST: Yes, I remember that vocabulary. What I'm really trying to ask is what does the punctuation of autonomy do for us?

EPISTEMOLOGIST: First of all, let me remind you that the perspective of autonomy is not a new idea in therapy. In fact, before anyone had heard of family therapy, the idea of autonomous individuals was at the core of our thinking about behavior.

THERAPIST: Then why is autonomy considered a new idea?

EPISTEMOLOGIST: Historically, we have limited the idea of autonomy to a description of individuals. Today we are beginning to punctuate other orders of systemic process as autonomous.

THERAPIST: Such as whole families, family-*plus*-therapist, and family-*plus*-therapist-*plus*-observers?

EPISTEMOLOGIST: Each of these demarcated cybernetic systems can be punctuated as autonomous. From this perspective, we discover that it is restrictive to view any particular system as strictly autonomous since we can also see the system as interdependent or part of another higher order system. The way in which we move from seeing whole families, family-*plus*-therapist, and so on, indicates what we could call a dialectic of autonomy and interdependence.

THERAPIST: In other words, by viewing a whole family as autonomous, we are only marking a beginning?

EPISTEMOLOGIST: Yes. When a therapist, another autonomous system, enters the stage, we can draw other phenomenal domains. The interaction between these two autonomous systems can be seen as perturbations. In this case, the two systems are, as Varela and Maturana say, "structurally coupled." We can, however, draw a higher order autonomous system which subsumes the two systems as interdependent parts.

THERAPIST: Which perspective is more correct?

EPISTEMOLOGIST: Remember that each perspective is drawn by an observer and that the difference between autonomy and interdependence can be seen as a cybernetic complementarity—not one, not two.

THERAPIST: So, in sum, we should hold on to both perspectives and jointly use them as a form of double description?

EPISTEMOLOGIST: I think so. If a therapist is hypothetically capable of chopping therapy into an infinitude of distinctions and then indicating an infinitude of these autonomy/interdependence complementarities, he will have, as the cyberneticians say, more requisite variety.

THERAPIST: Do you mean that he will be able to generate an endless number of ways of drawing cybernetic systems?

EPISTEMOLOGIST: Indeed.

THERAPIST: So what?

EPISTEMOLOGIST: If a therapist can draw a wide variety of models, then he is less likely to get stuck.

THERAPIST: If a drawn cybernetic system, or model as you say, does not lead to the desired outcome, whatever you define that to be, then another can be drawn?

EPISTEMOLOGIST: That's it.

THERAPIST: So any theorist, researcher, teacher, or practitioner who argues that any one perspective or model is more correct than others is admitting that he has chosen a certain way of being inflexible. He has, in other words, decided to punctuate his world of therapy in a limited way. His clients may then suffer if they, like the graduate student's ferrets, do not fit into his punctuated frame of action.

EPISTEMOLOGIST: Not only his clients, but his students and colleagues may suffer. At this point, I need to warn you that although we can acknowledge the usefulness of drawing a wide variety of models, it makes a hell of a difference which model you happen to use. In general, we can state that each particular situation in therapy requires a unique form of model.

THERAPIST: The trick is to know when the model you have constructed is useful and when it is not.

EPISTEMOLOGIST: If you can draw the distinction between what is useful and not useful, you will be able to know when you should change your model of a cybernetic system. Doing this when working with a client establishes feedback.

THERAPIST: Therefore, if I follow you, discerning the way a therapist constructs models of cybernetic systems and subsequently changes his models (based on his interaction with a client as prescribed by these models) is another way of seeing cybernetic process in therapy.

EPISTEMOLOGIST: Indeed. Cybernetics, or to use another metaphor, *mind* is immanent in the organization of all living process.

THERAPIST: Would you say that this book is a living creature?

EPISTEMOLOGIST: Your question reminds me of a statement Gregory Bateson once made: "My book is a living thing. Every day I water it with my tears to help it grow."

THERAPIST: Then, you, me, this book, and the experiences of therapy, among other phenomenal domains, are parts of living process. This brings us to ecology, once again.

EPISTEMOLOGIST: Yes. A full consideration of autonomy will always take us to the whole that connects each part of our experience. Considering the autonomy of an individual leads us to seeing the individual as part of an autonomous family system, which in turn can be seen as part of a more encompassing, autonomous ecology.

THERAPIST: How can family therapy be seen through the perspective of ecology?

EPISTEMOLOGIST: What do you wish to connect?

THERAPIST: There are so many views and models of family therapy, I cannot imagine seeing a pattern that connects all of them.

EPISTEMOLOGIST: Perhaps a *conscious* model of this pattern is beyond any of us.

THERAPIST: Then how can I approach the differences the field encompasses?

EPISTEMOLOGIST: Let's try an experiment, an exercise therapists sometimes refer to as a "guided fantasy." Imagine that you could arrange a major conference for all the differing schools of thought in family therapy. Perhaps you would invite Haley, Minuchin, Watzlawick, and Whitaker, among others. Now that you have all these people together in the same room, I would like for you to imagine that the conference is called to order by a Zen master, who in his earlier days was a gestalt therapist. After a few preliminary announcements, he proposes that he would like to begin by asking for a volunteer. It so happens that you end up on stage with this Zen master. He asks if you are willing to participate in a "gestalt parts party," a procedure, you may recall, that was discussed in this chapter. The Zen master explains that he has learned to use this technique in a special way which may be beneficial to therapists, rather than their clients. Can we begin?

THERAPIST: Yes, I am willing to try it out.

EPISTEMOLOGIST: The Zen master is now asking you to choose different people to represent different parts of your own understanding of family therapy. Some of these parts may represent past orientations you once followed or partially followed, but have now placed out of your immediate memory due to conversion to alternative models. Perhaps some of the teachers of these different views are in the audience, and you could ask them to come on stage and enact the parts of your ecology of perspectives.

THERAPIST: I have learned how to organize my behavior in therapy from Haley, Minuchin, and Watzlawick. Therefore, I must bring them on stage. At the same time, Bowen once reminded me that on some order of process I am a knot of recycled biography. Let's bring him up, too. In addition, when I experience Whitaker's work I cannot deny that there is something more to therapy than conceptual understanding, family reincarnation, and strategic technique. I need Whitaker on stage to acknowledge that part, whatever it is. I could go on and on.

EPISTEMOLOGIST: Let's assume that you have all the people on stage who represent the dissociated parts of your entire history of orientation to family therapy. At this point, the Zen master begins helping you coordinate these parts to work better as a whole organization. He tells you that pragmatics and aesthetics, left- and right-brain mentation, strategy and experience, do not have to be seen as either/ or dichotomies. Instead, he shows you how to see them as parts of cybernetic complementarities. Through his coaching, you are able to construct a conference where Haley and Whitaker, Watzlawick and Bowen, and others, engage in a true dialogue. This conference, as the days go by, does not become a symmetrical battle of who is right and who is wrong. Rather, it becomes a ballet of differences. You, with the help of the Zen master, orchestrate it to be so.

THERAPIST: And what does the audience see?

EPISTEMOLOGIST: The audience, at first, thinks it is seeing an unusual example of a gestalt parts party. They see a Zen master acting as though he were a therapist, working with a therapist who acts as though he were a client. By helping you, the therapist, coordinate the dissociated parts of your understanding of family therapy, an entire conference is constructed. The audience, of course, soon catches on, and begins to see that the Zen master's experiment with you was really a trick to get the leaders of different viewpoints in the field of therapy to engage in a dialogue, rather than a battle for territory. Did you, as the volunteer client, have that sense?

THERAPIST: After a while, I think I began to catch on. Through coordinating the diverse parts of myself, I did notice that I was helping the Zen master create an entire conference. It was an odd experience.

EPISTEMOLOGIST: What you did, in this fantasy, was prescribe a way of organizing what are often taken as either/or perspectives of family therapy. In cybernetic terms, by calibrating the way your group of family therapists interacted with each other, you achieved a recalibration of your own epistemology of family therapy.

THERAPIST: What did the coordination of these various parts of family therapy look like?

EPISTEMOLOGIST: The cybernetic organization of diverse parts of family therapy could only be seen by examining the whole confer-ence. Any excerpt of an exchange between, say, Haley and Whitaker, would not capture the more encompassing patterns. The pattern that connects each of them as well as their differences involved the whole conference.

THERAPIST: Why doesn't someone set up such a conference in order to recalibrate the field of family therapy? There seem to be many trivial battles and disagreements in our field which could be properly put into perspective by such a conference.

EPISTEMOLOGIST: There is no need to plan such a conference, for the conference has always been happening. In other words, the entire history of the family therapy field is the conference we've been speak-ing of. The battles, debates, and disagreements are all necessary com-ponents of this more encompassing conference.

THERAPIST: Is this conference part of its topic, as the observer is in the observed?

EPISTEMOLOGIST: Yes. We return to another cybernetic comple-mentarity.

THERAPIST: Before proceeding, I would like to address something that confuses me. I'm not quite certain what it means to view the en-tire history of family therapy, and therapy in general, as a conference or "parts party," as you put it. If we are basically concerned with co-ordinating a diversity of different parts, why is it that the field contin-ues to argue, debate and generate differences?

EPISTEMOLOGIST: The field must change in order to stabilize its organization. Cybernetics, as you recall, concerns the complementary relation of change and stability, or in the case you now present, dif-ference and harmony, or disagreement and resolution. The idea that stability, harmony, or resolution means the absence of change, differ-ence, and disagreement is absolute nonsense. The two sides of these distinctions are cybernetically related.

THERAPIST: Does this mean that I should believe all views of fam-ily therapy? Some therapists, for example, attempt to construct an "eclectic view."

EPISTEMOLOGIST: I must introduce another paradox. It is impor-tant that you decide to believe in a single perspective, at least for a while. Such a perspective may be called "structural," "strategic," "in-teractional," "experiential," or as you have suggested, "eclectic." By holding on tightly to the tenets of one perspective, you are prepared to discern and encounter a different perspective. In such an encounter, your *conversation* will become the more encompassing side of a cybernetic complementarity.

THERAPIST: Can I have the conversation with myself?

EPISTEMOLOGIST: It is possible if you can maintain the appropriate distinctions. I would think that such an attempt might, at times, be a bit crazy-making.

THERAPIST: So, in effect, you are saying that it is important to choose a partial view and hold to its premises. One's encounters with other partial views then generate the more encompassing perspective, which is not immediately accessible to either side of the dialogue.

EPISTEMOLOGIST: All therapists need this double view. On the one hand, a particular framework is held onto; on the other hand, the framework is acknowledged as incomplete and requiring the self-correction of a more encompassing dialogue with a different framework.

THERAPIST: So what position does the author of this book take?

EPISTEMOLOGIST: It is named "cybernetic epistemology."

THERAPIST: If a therapist chooses this path, who would his teachers be?

EPISTEMOLOGIST: I'm not certain how to answer that question. I could point out that everyone the therapist encounters, including his clients, is potentially a teacher. This is a way of acknowledging the higher order processes of learning that occur when dialogue is allowed to happen. Or I could respond to your question by listing some of the books about therapy that seem to exemplify the path of cybernetic epistemology.

THERAPIST: Let me guess the latter. I would say that the work of the Mental Research Institute has provided the cornerstone for the application of simple cybernetics to therapy. This work has historically included the contributions of Beavin, Fisch, Haley, Jackson, Watzlawick, and Weakland, among others.

EPISTEMOLOGIST: I cannot imagine being part of the path of cybernetic epistemology in therapy without fully acknowledging their work. It is no accident that the name of their organization points to "mind." Given their contributions, we can move on to acknowledge higher orders of cybernetics—what has been termed cybernetics of cybernetics. It is here that we understand how differing perspectives are valuable in the context of dialogue. The more encompassing patterns of cybernetic process lead us to an entire ecology of mind, where everyone, as well as every situation, is seen as a valuable teacher.

THERAPIST: As this chapter argued, even the old chopstick which was thrown away is valuable.

EPISTEMOLOGIST: As well as the act of having thrown it away.

5

CYBERNETICS OF
THERAPEUTIC CHANGE

> DIOGENES: Everything always changes: We are never the same.
> ALEXANDER: *(Slaps him in the face.)*
> DIOGENES: Why do you slap me?
> ALEXANDER: I didn't slap *you*; if I understood correctly, I must have slapped somebody else.

Change and stability represent a complementary gestalt in cybernetics. Thus the French proverb "The more things change, the more they remain the same" can be stood on its head: "The more things remain the same, the more they are changing." The tightrope walker must continuously sway in order to remain in balance. Similarly, the way to remain balanced while standing in a canoe is to make it rock. Applying this perspective to social systems, Bateson (cited in Bateson & Brown, 1975) proposes, "You can't have a marriage and not quarrel with your wife" (p. 47).

Whether it be the acrobatics of tightrope walking or marriage, what remains "stable" or "balanced" is a self-correcting cybernetic system. What changes are behaviors within a cybernetic system — the interlinked parts change to keep the whole a whole. However, a whole system itself is part of a higher order cybernetic system, and so on, ad infinitum. To account for the stability of higher order systems, we must point to higher orders of change.

In the context of therapy, questions of change become problematic whenever we attempt to specify what should change — the "it" to be changed. Should an individual's character change, a marital relationship, a family structure, or neighborhood ecologies? Cybernetic epistemology reframes our orientation by proposing that questions of change are always about cybernetic process.

Our goal in this chapter is to develop a cybernetic understanding of therapeutic change. Although we will be using the specific term "change," we should never forget that it is one half of a more encompassing cybernetic complementarity, "stability/change." The reader should therefore view any reference to change as a shorthand indication of this particular complementarity.[1]

MODELING PATTERN

In the early days of the double bind project, even before "double bind" had been proposed, Bateson and his colleagues were having some problems understanding the nature of schizophrenia. Norbert Wiener provided some advice to Bateson, in the form of a request: "I am an engineer and you, my customer, must specify to me what characteristics you will require in a machine to say that that machine is schizophrenic" (Bateson, 1979b). This proposal encouraged them to construct a formal model. They subsequently came up with the following description: "A telephone exchange could be called 'schizophrenic' in a formal sense if it mistook numbers mentioned in the conversation between subscribers for those numbers which are the names of subscribers" (Heims, 1977, p. 151). For example, if I were talking to you over the phone and happened to mention that I live at 1497 Main Street, the telephone exchange, at that point, would dial the number 1497. Like a schizophrenic who makes a category mistake, the telephone exchange would confuse a numerical description of my address with a request for dialing another person.

Wiener's advice to the Bateson project provides direction for a therapist: Whenever a problem or symptom is encountered, a therapist can respond by constructing or identifying a model of the presenting problem. It is important to realize that this refers to a mechanistic model — only pattern and relationship are of interest, not the particular materiality embodying it.

1. Accordingly, the title of this book should be reread as *Aesthetics of Stability/Change*.

A therapist who follows cybernetics will always begin by constructing models that embody the relations of the problem at hand. These models may be drawn from a client's own life or from more diverse topical domains. The formal relations of a couple's sexual difficulties may be modeled in their dining habits.[2] Or a therapist may find a related pattern in a myth connected to the couple's own natural history. Therapists who explore past events in order to construct a family myth for battling its present dilemma demonstrate this latter approach. For example, those who follow the early Milan team style of family therapy will dig up "data" about a family's past events in order to construct a story or "hypothesis" about why the family is currently stricken with trouble and pain. Implicit in their work is the idea that if the story is in some way a model, isomorph, or caricature of the family's present way of organizing itself, then presenting the model in a modified way to the family will be useful. Milton Erickson was one of the most creative innovators of therapeutic models. He had the ability to model a client's problematic context using an incredible range of explanations, stories, and prescriptions.

Although there is more to successful therapeutic intervention than creating models, we should recognize that the starting point for a cybernetic understanding of therapeutic change is to learn to identify form and pattern in therapy.

As we will demonstrate, discerning pattern requires working backwards. The pattern one wishes to know arises from the comparison of different models of the observed situation. This operation is illustrated by the optical trick invented by Sir Charles Wheatstone, a discovery described by Land (1977):

> In 1838, Sir Charles Wheatstone held a cubic block in front of him and made two drawings, one of the appearance of the cube from the position of his right eye and a second of the appearance of the cube from the position of his left eye. He arranged a set of mirrors so that he could look back at the drawings, seeing simultaneously with his right eye only the drawing made from the right eye point of perspective and with the left eye only the other. There came into existence for him a real three-dimensional cubic block. (p. 2)

---

2. See Haley (1973b, pp. 27–28) for an illustration of how Milton Erickson used such a strategy.

In other words, by modeling the perspective of each eye and then looking at them simultaneously through an apparatus called a stereo-scope, he could encounter the higher order pattern called "depth per-ception."

This brings us back to the notion of "double description" set forth in the discussion of fundamentals of epistemology. It was sug-gested that a description of social interaction could be derived by con-sidering the views of each interactant simultaneously. In this way, a higher order pattern was constructed.

The Perception of Difference

Binocular vision, double description, and the creation of moiré pat-terns provide evidence for a basic discovery by Weber and Fechner that what we always perceive is "difference." The idea that differences are the "food for perception" is implicit in cybernetic epistemology and was seized upon by Bateson (1979a) as a fundamental that "every schoolboy should know." In the world of pattern, events are primarily triggered by difference rather than force and energy. The invitation you didn't receive in relation to the invitations your friends received (as well as to the invitation you thought you would receive) is a differ-ence that can trigger your interaction with a party's host. Bateson re-alized the function of difference when he considered what gets from a territory to a map. What crosses this border is "news of difference" — a difference that makes a difference. Differences immanent in the material world, such as the boundaries between sea and shore, are what get on to geophysical maps. Not *things* but *difference* always gets from a territory to a map.

The notion that mental process works in terms of difference is supported by neurophysiological and perceptual research. A com-mon experience is our awareness of the absence of noise when an air conditioner shuts off. What we attend to is the difference between the air conditioner's noise and absence of noise; what remains the same disappears from our awareness. For example, research shows that if you achieve an unchanging retinal image, or what is technically called a "stabilized retinal image," the object you are looking at becomes in-visible to you. Furthermore, if you continue to focus on that object while it is invisible to you, it will again appear, but only to eventually disappear again. What is concealed will be revealed, but what is revealed will again be concealed.[3]

To keep the perceptual world from flipping between visibility and invisibility, our eyes constantly change their position. Thus, we create a cybernetic system wherein different images are created in order to perceive a stable world. In general, every perception we are aware of is constructed from multiple views of the world. In order to see any pattern, different models of the pattern must be drawn.

Like an eyeball which must constantly move in order to create different images, a therapist must use his epistemological knife to carve different models of the therapeutic situation or he will become stuck in the same dilemma as a retina that encounters a stabilized image. Such a therapist will be disoriented and unable to see what is going on from moment to moment, session to session. Therapy to this therapist will be a world of oscillation, like the shifting visibility and invisibility of stablized retinal images.

Family therapy has a built-in advantage of providing a clinician with multiple views from a diverse population of lenses: Each family member presents his own perception to the therapist. To get a glimpse of the whole ecology, the therapist must be able to construct patterns connecting these diverse views. He can achieve this higher order view through an epistemology in which bits of simple action and interaction are connected to more encompassing patterns. The use of double description is one way a therapist can discern higher order patterns of social choreography.

Changing Patterns

Before proceeding, we should remind ourselves that the particular patterns we perceive are always a consequence of our learned habits of punctuation. This is dramatically demonstrated by experiments involving what are called "displaced images." The American psychologist G. M. Stratton invented special eyeglasses which used mirror sys-

3. Some researchers (see Pritchard, 1972) have covered subjects' eyes with contact lenses upon which a small projector is mounted. The contact lenses, which move with the eyeball's saccadic jerks, are coupled with the image projector tube so that stabilized retinal images are achieved. After a certain period of time, a subject viewing a stabilized image will report that image to fade and disappear. After another period of time, the image will reappear, and on and on.

tems and telescopes to alter retinal images. These bizarre eyeglasses restructured the world by inverting it both vertically and horizontally. After continuously wearing these lenses for several days, Stratton was amazed to discover that everything he observed became "normal." He could even walk with ease and enjoy seeing the natural world. After living for a while in this altered visual world, Stratton decided to remove the spectacles. At that moment he found that "the reversal of everything from the order to which I had grown accustomed during the last week, gave the scene a surprising bewildering air which lasted for several hours" (cited in Gregory, 1971, p. 205). He then had to relearn how to see what to others was an "undistorted world," which now appeared to him as "distorted."

A lens, or frame of reference, determines the pattern we see, whether it is up or down, distorted or not. A change of lens always invokes a period of initial confusion or transition. If an observer can endure the crisis of transition, a new frame will result in an alternative order. The task of epistemological change, although dramatically more difficult, is comparable. Through the lens of cybernetic epistemology, an alternative world will eventually emerge. In Castaneda's (1974) terms, with "unbending intent" one can "stop the world" and "see."

Artists have always known this. In addressing a complaint that his portrait of Gertrude Stein did not look like her, Picasso replied, "Never mind, it will." Similarly, constructing and perceiving higher order patterns of cybernetic organization requires patience, practice, and unbending intent.

ORDERS OF LEARNING

When constructing models that embody the formal relations of a particular situation, it may be necessary to acknowledge the order of learning the situation requires. It is therefore vital that we understand more precisely what is meant by "orders of learning." To accomplish this, we need to turn to one of Bateson's most important papers, entitled "The Logical Categories of Learning and Communication" (Bateson, 1972).

As a starting point, he describes "zero learning," where the "causal links between 'stimulus' and 'response' are, as engineers say, 'soldered in'" (Bateson, 1972, p. 284). This refers to those responses that are solely determined by genetics or are so automatic that no correction appears possible. All other orders of learning involve "trial and error"; thus, an organism's behavior is potentially subject to correction, so that when a behavior is marked as wrong, the organism can try another behavior until it gets it right.

"Learning I" refers to a situation where the perceived choices are within a particular set of behavioral alternatives. This order of learning is usually the focus of experimental psychology with its classical, instrumental, and rote learning models. Note that all stochastic learning — learning involving "trial and error" — can be discussed in terms of feedback process. An organism's behavior is recursively linked to another system's behavior such that the effect of a behavior modifies subsequent behavior. The specification of how these corrections are made is determined by the particular context of learning.

Whereas Learning I deals with "change in the specificity of response" or the learning of a particular simple action within a given context, Learning II refers to learning *about* a particular context of learning. This essentially involves learning how to identify and organize one's action as part of a specific context. For example, each time a trainer teaches a dog a new trick (Learning I), he goes through the same instrumental procedure. After a series of these learning episodes the dog learns that these different scenarios signify the same form of organization — that is, the dog learns that he is engaged in an instrumental relationship with the trainer. The dog can then be described as having learned to identify and organize his behavior as part of a particular context.

In Learning II, learning does not arise from comparing different behaviors, but from comparisons across various learning opportunities. Thus, after repeated experience in an instrumental type of learning context a dog will "learn to learn." He then habitually punctuates future encounters with the trainer as "instrumental learning."

As Bateson (1972) proposes, "*What* is learned in Learning II is a way of *punctuating events*" (p. 300) rather than a specific behavioral response. He goes on to suggest that any particular way of punctuating events is adaptive only up to a certain point. A habit of punctuation leads to difficulties when the set of alternatives it specifies does not provide an appropriate solution. Consider the example, in Chapter 2, of the dog in Pavlov's experiment who learned to punctuate the laboratory as a context requiring that he discriminate between an ellipse and a circle. When an experimenter made it impossible for the dog to make that particular discrimination, the dog was put into a different learning context. The new context was one in which the dog was punished for being right: In essence, he was doing the right thing, but in the wrong or inappropriate context.

For the dog to do the right thing in the new context, he would have to recognize the context as being different. If he actually discerned the new context he would probably choose to take a nap or bark at the experimenter rather than fool with the ellipse and circle. On the other hand, organizing his behavior in a way appropriate for the context of ellipse–circle discrimination leads to a "Pavlovian neurosis" or a "Batesonian psychosis." Any effort to discriminate between the two geometrical shapes results in an inappropriate order of change, or what Watzlawick *et al.* (1974) term "first-order change."

If the punctuated context, rather than the specific response, is the primary source of error, then a different contextual punctuation must be learned. This change indicates a "revision of the *set* from which the choice is made" (Bateson, 1972, p. 287) or what Watzlawick *et al.* (1974) call a "second-order change." In the case of Pavlov's dog, the set of alternatives prescribed by the original context of discrimination involved all behavior that might indicate a difference between a circle and an ellipse. All changes of behavior that represent attempts to make that indication signify first-order change. For the dog, second-order change would involve moving to a different set of alternatives: The dog might take a nap, bark, or even urinate on the experimenter.

The feedback process for initiating second-order learning and change necessarily involves the comparison of different contexts, frames, or punctuations. This may be done by putting the animal in the wrong, as Pavlov did, but with a difference — the experimenter, trainer, or therapist must occasionally throw in a random reward. Bateson illustrates this higher order learning in the training of dolphins at the Ocean Science Theatre in Sea Life Park, Hawaii. Here the trainers carefully reward their dolphin with a fish whenever the dolphin's behavior approximates the trick being taught. Bateson noted that after the creatures have acquired several tricks they, like other animals, learn to learn other tricks: That is, it becomes easier for the trainer to teach them new tricks. However, Bateson observed that if an experimenter held back from rewarding a dolphin who had already learned several tricks, the dolphin would try various sorts of behavior, as if it were trying to discover which particular action of its behavioral repertoire the trainer wanted. If none of its behaviors were systematically reinforced, an incredible event would occur: The dolphin would suddenly begin exhibiting behavior never seen before in dolphins. In other words, the dolphin became what might be called "creative." The dolphin jumped an order in learning by changing from a habitual set of behaviors to an entirely new set of behaviors which had not been seen before.

Karen Pryor (1975), one of the dolphin trainers, reports what happened when this knowledge was subsequently used to train a dolphin to be "creative":

> And when she finally caught on to what was happening, when she began to understand that what she had to do to get us to blow the whistle was to do something *new,* she really went wild. . . . She had been in the habit of offering two or three types of responses per session. Now in one session she offered us eight types of responses, four of which were completely new, and two of which, the flip and spin, were elaborate and perfectly performed from the beginning. She gave 192 responses in that session, nearly nine per minute, compared to a previous rate of three or four per minute, and instead of slowing down, at the end of the session she went faster and faster, until she was in such a wild flurry of swipes, leaps, splashes, tail slaps, and careening around that she was outstripping our ability to describe what was going on, even with three of us talking at once. (pp. 241-242)

It is important to note that these dolphins were in a "metacontext" somewhat different from that of Pavlov's dogs. In the dolphin pool, human trainers nurtured affective relationships with their creatures and could not bear to see them suffer. Thus, they would every once in a while throw in a fish at random in order to preserve their relationship with the dolphin. Pavlov's dogs, subject to the cruelty of experimental control, did not fare as well and consequently went mad.

Nevertheless, the pattern of organization that constrained Pavlov's dogs was *generally* similar to that of Pryor's dolphins. In both cases the creatures were part of a genus of metacontextual pattern called "double bind." The difference between the pattern which shaped psychosis and that which shaped creativity was the random fish. In the latter case, this reinforcement helped preserve the integrity of the relationship between man and creature.

Clinicians are sometimes faced with a similar situation in therapy. The trick is to put a client in the wrong, but at the same time to occasionally throw in a random reward to preserve the therapist–client relationship. Similarly, a Zen master must put his student in an impossible situation, such as having him meditate on a koan. At the same time he must occasionally demonstrate that he cares, perhaps by whacking the napping student with a stick.

Bateson (1972) proposes that there is also "Learning III" which represents "a corrective change in the *system* of sets of alternatives from which choice is made" (p. 293). Here change does not refer to change of a specific response (Learning I) or contextual punctuation (Learning II), but refers to change of the premises underlying an entire system of punctuation habits. This order of learning is very difficult and rare, Bateson notes, although it sometimes occurs in "psychotherapy, religious conversion, and in other sequences in which there is profound reorganization of character" (p. 301).

The problem with aspiring to Learning III is that we tend to overlook that most of our punctuations arise from the same premises for punctuating. Comparing different punctuations that arise from the same premise merely generates Learning II — we become more skilled at inventing new punctuations within the same system. For example, in occidental culture most of us work from the same basic premises involving distinctions between the observer and observed. A change in these epistemological premises, however, results in the creation of an alternative system of punctuations. Such a conversion represents Learning III and embodies the transition sometimes called change of epistemology.

In sum, different orders of learning and change indicate that people or systems of people may be classified as being caught in a frame, a set of frames, or a system of sets of frames. The order of being stuck determines the required order of solution.

Therapists who continually see the world in one way are stuck in the self-verification of a particular habit of punctuation. These therapists seem to encounter clients with complementary punctuation habits. Therapists who think in terms of hierarchical social control, for instance, will probably end up treating a large number of troublesome adolescents who require effective parental discipline.

Learning an alternative way of punctuating constitutes a second-order change (Learning II). Therapists who engage in such learning, however, may shift from one theoretical punctuation to another and find themselves wondering what to do with a variety of views. Some may simply continue to move from one case of myopia to another. Others, believing that no single theory can corner truth, may attempt to hold on to a diversity of views.

One way of incorporating a diversity of views is to become an eclectic. For instance, a therapist may use "gestalt work" at one time and "strategic family therapy" at another. This therapist's theories and techniques are like an eclectic concert program — different music is played at different times.

Another approach to incorporating diverse perspectives involves combination. Here the clinician takes bits and pieces from various approaches and "integrates" them into his own unified model. It is an illusion to view this as an eclectic approach. More accurately, any combination of views is itself a new theory. Combining Beethoven and Bach gives you neither, but something else. An "integrated theory" simply becomes another theory which an eclectic may add to his files.

All of these efforts to avoid an addiction to any one punctuation habit involve Learning II. At this order of change, a clinician can only continue learning to learn variant punctuations. However, as we mentioned, another jump in learning is possible. Third-order change, or Learning III, emerges when different epistemologies are discerned. Entering the labyrinth of epistemological comparison means going beyond theory and becoming aware of a difference that may make the most profound difference in one's orientation to clinical understanding and action.

UNCONSCIOUS PROCESS

Higher orders of learning and change can be described in terms of unconscious mental process. To orient ourselves to this perspective, we need to begin by acknowledging that the more "fundamental" a premise, the less accessible it will be to consciousness. As Samuel Butler proposed, the more one "knows" something the less aware one becomes of that knowledge. In addition, it is economical that premises controlling vital habits of action such as breathing and perceptual process are wired in at more inaccessible orders of mental process.

Bateson often cited the experiments of Adalbert Ames as illustrations of our unconscious premises regarding perception. One of these is the Ames Room Illusion which demonstrates that perception of an object's size becomes distorted in a nonrectangular room that is assumed by an observer to be rectangular. In this illusion, an observer peers through a hole into a nonrectangular room where two people are standing in different corners. One corner is much farther away from the observer than the other. Since the room is *assumed* to be rectangular due to unconscious premises organizing perception, the people in the room appear as a midget and giant, although they are actually equal in height.

What is intriguing about this illusion is that even if an observer is shown how it is set up and told how it works, he will continue to distort the visual field. Conscious understanding of the Ames Room Illusion does nothing to alter one's unconscious premises for organizing perception. It is also interesting to note that people from cultures accustomed to living in round-shaped houses often do not experience the illusion. Those people carry around different epistemological premises for "seeing rooms."

Premises which are deeply habitual and consciously inaccessible specify unconscious orders of mind. The major characteristic of unconscious orders of mind is that they embody *premises of relationship* which can never specify any particular side of a distinction, tense (time), or negative. In other words, unconscious mental process can never literally communicate "it," "did," "will do" or "never." Unconscious process cannot directly specify the "it" that must change. It cannot explicitly indicate that a past action, interaction, or system of choreography needs to be changed, nor can it propose that it could change. And finally, unconscious process cannot directly or explicitly say "no." Unconscious process communicates, as we will later see, in an indirect fashion.

The Structure of Calibration

Since premises of unconscious mind are concerned only with relationship, they embody the more encompassing patterns of cybernetic epistemology. The distortion of these whole patterns of recursion and relationship by conscious orders of mind is potentially pathological. For example, the whole recursive organization of man-and-environment may become broken into either/or dualisms of man versus environment. Correcting such a distortion requires reconnecting it to the more encompassing unconscious premises of whole relationship.

This idea has been implicitly understood by therapists such as

Milton Erickson who describe unconscious mind as a healing agent. Because it is recursively organized, unconscious process is a self-correcting system. When therapists and clients abandon their conscious, purposeful strategies of action and attend to the "doing of nondoing" or the wu-wei of the Taoist, they attend to unconscious orders of mind. Jung (1939) advised, "Wait for what the unconscious has to say about the situation" (pp. 31–32). A fundamental premise of ecology which seems beyond the understanding of a great portion of occidental culture is that an ecosystem will heal itself if left alone. An ecosystem is self-corrective because, as we've noted, it embodies a recursive organization of feedback processes. Letting an ecology heal itself does not mean being lazy or unresponsive. Rather, the doing of nondoing is a call for a higher order of action. Therapy thus becomes a context wherein a system finds its own adjustments.

One way a system begins to adjust itself is by generating symptomatic behavior. Such behavior is comparable to an "itch," "beacon of light," or "bugle call" in that it attracts the attention of quite a few people. Family, friends, neighbors, and therapists, for example, may attempt to be "helpful." Their attempts will organize the problem either as part of a process of self-correction or runaway and oscillation.

The latter consequence is dramatically exemplified by an alcoholic who swings back and forth between sobriety and drunkenness. With each full swing, the problem intensifies and if unchecked the extent of drunkenness will eventually be fatal. Embedded within this oscillatory pattern are runaway sequences of behavior. Each drinking binge is itself a runaway phenomenon where one drink always proposes another drink. This escalating pattern is eventually calibrated by higher order feedback. For example, the alcoholic may eventually pass out or will not be given another drink. Calibration helps lead the victim back to sobriety. The process underlying sobriety, however, may also be depicted as an escalating runaway. This runaway pattern, which often includes the "helping behavior" of others, is eventually calibrated when the temptation to take a drink becomes too overwhelming, thus initiating another runaway drinking bout.

Each episode of drinking and sobriety is itself organized within a larger oscillatory pattern which swings between episodes of sobriety and drunkenness. The range of this oscillation will also increase (i.e., runaway) until it, too, is checked by higher orders of feedback process. The cybernetic organization of such an ecosystem may therefore include escalating patterns of drinking and sobriety, as well as escalation of the intensity of these escalations.

We can generally propose that any cybernetic system entering therapy has been problematic in the sense that it has wildly oscillated or has gone into runaway. The challenge for a therapist is to join that system in a way that will promote appropriate self-correction. Unfortunately, family therapists have often referred to negative feedback (or self-correction) as a way families maintain symptomatic behavior, while positive feedback is regarded as the process of therapeutic change. The more encompassing perspective is that symptomatic behavior is always subject to some form of higher order control.[4] The avenue to therapeutic change is initiating an alternative form of higher order self-corrective feedback. This alternative self-corrective change attempts to generate a more adaptive way of maintaining the whole organization of a system.

It is important to note that the cybernetic system that emerges when a therapist joins a family will also be self-corrective, oscillating or going toward runaway. There is simply no way a therapist can avoid being part of a cybernetic system recursively connecting his behavior with that of other members of the treatment ecology. The goal of therapy, then, is to activate this cybernetic system to provide an alternative higher order feedback correction of the lower order process involving symptomatic escalation.

Patterns That Connect and Correct

Bateson's (1971) analysis of alcoholism provides a cybernetic way of thinking about how people aid in either maintaining or correcting problematic behavior. His theory claims that what is fundamentally wrong with an alcoholic is a dissociated epistemological premise, usually some variation of self versus environment or body versus mind. (These disconnections refer to what was earlier called distortions of unconscious premises of relationship by conscious orders of mind.) Bateson depicts an alcoholic as engaged in a battle arising from a false separation between mind and body, which is sometimes expressed as

4. Recall the argument in Chapter 3 that any punctuation of positive feedback or runaway can be seen as part of more encompassing negative feedback processes.

"My 'will' can resist my body's 'hunger' to drink." "Will" represents a part of conscious *mind* that attempts to control the *body's* "hunger" for alcohol. In this contextual structure body and mind do not represent a cybernetic system with corrective feedback, but a symmetrical battle.

For an alcoholic, the battle is first expressed as "I can control my drinking." The symmetrical relation between mind and body helps construct another erroneous epistemological premise called "self-control," the idea that one part of a system can have unilateral control over other parts. Although an alcoholic's challenge of self-control provides the motivation to attain sobriety, achievement of sobriety destroys the very challenge that generated his sobriety. In other words, the more he tries to stay sober, the more likely he is to get drunk, and vice versa.

When psychotherapeutic, family, and social network interventions reassure and console an alcoholic with an emphasis on "You'll do better next time," the premise of self-control, with its underlying disconnection of self and body, is reinforced. What the alcoholic hears is "You'll conquer your hunger for booze next time." This helps trigger the vicious oscillatory pattern again. Unfortunately, with each oscillation between sobriety and drunkenness, the intensity steps up. Attempts to control drinking then change to trying to stay sober, and finally, trying to stay alive.

Other forms of symptomatic behavior also involve this type of escalating process. In general, the more a client tries to control his symptom, the more the erroneous epistemological premise of "will" versus "symptom" is reinforced. The client will subsequently be caught in an escalating runaway until a "bottom," or threshold, is hit. The intensity of an "anxiety episode," for example, builds as the victim attempts to stop it. The battle against panic causes it to escalate until the patient gives up and declares a kind of helplessness, at which time the anxiety may be relieved.

Another function of symptoms in a self-correcting system is to provide communication to the social context surrounding them. Watzlawick *et al.* (1967), for example, propose that a symptom is a way of communicating "It is not I who does not (or does) want to do this, it is something outside my control, e.g., my nerves, my illness, my anxiety, my bad eyes, alcohol, my upbringing, the Communists, or my wife" (p. 80). Epistemologically, part of the message of a symptom is quite accurate—it is a message that "self-control" is an illusion and that one is always part of a more encompassing self-corrective system. Seen in this light, symptoms represent communication regarding higher order cybernetic process.

Along these lines, Bateson (1972) sees the alcoholic's battle to prove control, sobriety, or survival as a "determined effort to test 'self-control'" with the "unstated purpose of proving that 'self-control' is ineffectual and absurd" (p. 327). In general, we can view symptomatic behavior as striving toward higher orders of self-correction. Symptomatic behavior starts this process by attempting to negate the distorted premises organizing a problematic sequence of experience and interaction. In this way, an ecosystem can begin healing itself. Therapeutic change is only possible when an ecosystem becomes appropriately responsive to symptomatic behavior: It is not enough for a symptom to be spoken, it must be heard by the entire system.

Unconscious process can never literally say, "Something is wrong" or "Change the frame, premise, or punctuation." At unconscious orders of mind, negation is communicated by acting out the proposition to be negated. For an alcoholic, "hitting bottom" represents a behavioral reductio ad absurdum of the premise of self-control. Moments of "hitting bottom" typically occur when a person realizes that he doesn't have control over a situation. The experience is a "panic of discovering it (the system . . .) is bigger than he is" (Bateson, 1972, p. 330). Through an experience of hitting bottom, a symptom leads its victim to self-correction, epistemologically speaking, in that the dissociated dualism between self and symptom is reconnected.[5]

Unfortunately, at the moment of correction (or immediately thereafter) an individual's social context often tends to reinforce the old mind–body dualism by suggesting that he try again. Even if a patient continues to recover, relapses may occur if he is congratulated for "his improvement," "willpower," or "self-discipline." In this manner, dismembered epistemological premises may be reinforced, helping to maintain the problematic context.

Therefore, successful intervention must block these reinforcements and allow a system to heal itself. One responsibility of a thera-

5. More precisely, a symptom leads to a "correction" of the dismembered epistemological premise by reconnecting mind and body as a complementary rather than symmetrical relationship.

pist is therefore to encourage clients to avoid doing battle with their symptoms. This does not mean that a therapist should be unresponsive to a client's dilemma, if that were even possible. On the contrary, a therapist must help structure a context of learning where both therapist and client can sucessfully respond to the self-corrective communication of symptomatic behavior.

The success of therapeutic maneuvers that encourage symptomatic behavior have long been known in family therapy and hypnotism. These so-called "paradoxical interventions"[6] are explained by Watzlawick *et al.* (1967) as follows:

> If someone is asked to engage in a specific type of behavior which is seen as spontaneous, then he cannot be spontaneous anymore, because the demand makes spontaneity impossible. By the same token, if a therapist instructs a patient to perform his symptom, he is demanding spontaneous behavior and by this paradoxical injunction imposes on his patient a behavioral change. (p. 237)

This explanation can be further elaborated by noting that the message of prescribing a symptom is actually congruent with the messsage a symptom proposes. That is, the premise of self-control is negated. By being instructed to spontaneously generate a symptom, a patient finds that self-control is not possible. One cannot purposefully "will" a symptom to occur any more than "will" it away. By experiencing this demonstration, a system can learn that efforts of self-control with regard to symptomatic behavior are absurd.

Whitaker's "psychotherapy of the absurd" has also recognized the relation between prescribing a symptom and "reducing to absurdity the escalating process of the family struggle" (Whitaker, 1975, p. 11). He describes this reductio ad absurdum in the following metaphoric language (Whitaker, 1975):

---

6. Whether a therapist is justified in calling an intervention "paradoxical" depends in part on which particular species of paradox is involved. Self-referential paradoxes, for example, are part and parcel of *all* human interaction. Naming a "paradoxical intervention" requires specifying whether one is referring to the phenomenal domain of an observer's description, the relation of therapist and client, the effect of an intervention on a client or therapist, and so on. For example, is there paradox in the logical structure of one's description or in the structure of a social interaction? Stated differently, is there paradox in the map or the territory? Can one recognize paradox in the latter without recognizing it in the former? Or vice versa? Is that paradoxical? To whom? Etc.

It's as though an individual patient comes with a leaning tower of Pisa and the therapist, instead of trying to straighten the tower, builds it higher and higher and higher until, when it falls, the entire building falls rather than just the construct that the therapist has helped with. (p. 12)

A family therapist (de Shazer, 1980) once developed a reputation for treating clergymen who claimed to have "lost God." Such a clergyman, after failing to resolve his problem through self-effort and numerous encounters with other therapists, would come to this therapist's office and relate a sad story of how "God had left his life." Being a clergyman, this was not a very useful frame within which to practice his livelihood. The therapist prescribed that the clergyman take an architectural tour of all the churches in the town where he lived. If he was not successful in "locating God" in his own town, he was to plan trips to other towns in order to explore other churches.

The bewildered clergyman would then be dismissed to immediately begin his "search for God." In the process of going from church to church the client would eventually encounter a wall of absurdity, a sort of hitting bottom. In that moment, the dismembered epistemological premise separating "man from God," or in more general terms, "self from others," would evaporate in the experience of a reductio ad absurdum. Consequently, the client could no longer take his "problem" seriously.

Perhaps the greatest master of staging a reductio ad absurdum was Milton H. Erickson. A therapist following his orientation might instruct a "bed wetter" to purposefully urinate in bed for six nights *prior* to going to sleep, only allowing the seventh night for a rest. Or a therapist might recommend to a psychotic who carries around a wooden cross that he construct another cross. Erickson's own view was that he "accepted" whatever a client brought to him as an indication of what to do. Haley (1973b) reports Erickson's explanation as follows:

> The analogy Erickson uses is that of a person who wants to change the course of a river. If he opposes the river by trying to block it, the river will merely go over and around him. But if he *accepts* the force of the river and diverts it in a new direction, the force of the river will cut a new channel. (p. 24)

Symptoms therefore provide a road map for a therapist and signal where therapy should begin. In sum, symptomatic behavior enables a cybernetic system to communicate that a particular epistemological premise is distorted, erroneous, or ineffective. Correction, arising from unconscious process, takes form through an enactment of a reductio ad absurdum. This enactment provides a platform for changing the distorted epistemological premise.

SOCIOFEEDBACK

The goals of therapy are twofold: (1) enabling a symptomatic enactment to unfold and thereby produce a reductio ad absurdum, and (2) helping a system evolve toward an alternative structure for maintaining its organization. In terms of cybernetics, the first goal involves establishing appropriate self-corrective feedback. This occurs when symptomatic behavior can be expressed in a way that allows an individual, couple, or family to encounter the absurdity of the premises underlying their behavior, interaction, or choreography. The second goal of change concerns the alternative structures a system will generate following correction of its erroneous premises. We will soon see that the new patterns and structures a system evolves are usually a surprise to both therapist and client.

As we've suggested, any therapist who blocks a symptomatic enactment will probably reinforce an erroneous epistemological premise and risk escalating a system to a higher order of pathology. Cybernetics prescribes that techniques of therapy must allow symptomatic behavior to create a dramatic scenario for the problematic system; by cooperating with symptomatic communication, clients may go through the ritual of reductio ad absurdum. These "cooperative"[7] therapeutic techniques may include prescribing the symptom, positively connoting the symptom, and deliberately escalating the absurdity of the symptom.

By facilitating a reductio ad absurdum, a family therapist becomes the director of a play: a symptom generates the script while a family becomes the cast. Like a director, the therapist can only set the stage and help facilitate the unfolding scenario. Similarly, Watts (1961) has summarized the "teacher of liberation" as one who struc-

7. Steve de Shazer (1982) has proposed that family therapy should be couched in terms of family–therapist *cooperation* rather than resistance, power, or control. This helps remind a therapist that he is always part of a more encompassing system.

tures a situation where the false premises of a "student" are amplified to demonstrate their absurdity:

The "guru" or teacher of liberation must therefore use all his skill to persuade the student to act upon his own delusions, for the latter will always resist any undermining of the props of his security. He teaches, not by explanation, but by pointing out new ways of acting upon the student's false assumptions until the student convinces himself that they are false. (p. 68)

The therapist, too, must carefully promote the unfolding of symptomatic behavior to create a theatre of the absurd.

A therapist's participation in therapy thereby helps create *sociofeedback:* That is, the hybrid system merging family and therapist is analogous to a social form of biofeedback. In biofeedback, a person learns to bring about a particular physiological change, such as voluntarily producing an "alpha wave" of bioelectrical activity. To do so requires that the individual's brain be coupled to a machine capable of feeding back to that person the results of his cortical behavior. A therapist and family, at a higher order of process, represent a similar form of cybernetic system. When a family therapist "recognizes" a family's relevant activity he can signal that back to them. Following this metaphor, the therapist must lock in on symptomatic communication and mirror or feed it back to the family. In this way, the family encounters its own "absurdity."

A therapist must therefore be able to create "transforms" of a system's symptomatic communication. We discussed earlier that a therapist perceives pattern in therapy by constructing different models. The creation of a transform involves the same process.

The use of the term "model" indicates how a therapist comes to know the system he treats. The term "transform" refers more to how a therapist shapes his response to that system. In other words, models and transforms are complementary sides of the systemic pattern involving description and prescription, respectively. Seen this way, sociofeedback in therapy again suggests that diagnosis (knowing) is inseparable from intervention (action).

The process of creating transforms is demonstrated when a therapist extends the propositions of his clients. If a wife complains that she can't tolerate her husband, a therapist, following Whitaker (1975), can create a transform of this communication by commenting, "Why haven't you divorced him?" or "Why don't you have an affair?" or

"Why don't you have him eliminated?" When the client claims that such a statement is ridiculous, nonsensical, or absurd, the therapist can insist that he is being "therapeutically logical," "professional," "trying to help," and so on. By following this process a reductio ad absurdum is created within the therapeutic system. By fully encountering this absurdity, an erroneous premise can be negated and corrected. Consequently, a family may then generate an alternative structure for maintaining its organization.

Like all processes of stochastic learning and evolution, alternative structures are partially drawn from the so-called random. The leap toward a structural change necessarily requires that there be something "new" from which to create an alternative structure. As Bateson (1979a) states, "Ross Ashby long ago pointed out that no system (neither computer nor organism) can produce anything *new* unless the system contains some source of the random" (p. 174).

Therefore, a necessary ingredient of effective sociofeedback in therapy involves the introduction of random "noise." Some noise, of course, is introduced by any effort to create a transform of symptomatic behavior. The process of therapeutic change, however, usually requires a bit more precision. The cybernetic system of therapy must therefore provide sufficient noise from which an alternative structure can be constructed.

The task of introducing noise in therapy can be likened to that of presenting a "Rorschach" to the client. Not just any Rorschach will do; the client must assume that there is meaning or order in it. His search for meaning will then generate new structure and pattern. A part of therapy must always be presenting meaningful Rorschachs which clients (and sometimes, therapists) believe to contain "answers" and "solutions." These Rorschachs may be constructed from family history, cultural myth, psychobabble, religious metaphor, stories about other clients (fictional or not), and so forth. The explanations clients propose or request usually provide a clue for what form of Rorschach will be useful. A student of Eastern thought might be given a reading from the *I Ching*, whereas a deacon of a Baptist church may require some obscure Biblical reference. A client who happens to be a family therapist, however, may have to be given a theoretical mythology, such as Bowenese, Whitakerese, or Weaklandese.

Thus, a cybernetic orientation to therapy centers around the construction of transforms that model symptomatic communication.

These transforms must be "packaged" to provide an adequate source of random noise as a basis for structural change. The packaging can be regarded as a Rorschach or crystal ball which helps a troubled system create a new pattern and structure. The particularities of the presenting problem, as well as the way it is presented, direct how a therapist should construct and package a transform.

The recursive cycling of transforms in sociofeedback constitutes the context of therapeutic change. When a therapist constructs a transform of symptomatic communication with a little noise sprinkled in, the client then constructs a transform of that transform. The therapist subsequently transforms it, and so on, round and round. The cybernetic system becomes a recursive flow of different transforms.

A recursive cycle occurs whenever a transform of symptomatic communication is constructed. With every recycling of interaction, a different order of recursion is generated. A therapist must be able to utilize the difference between these orders of recursion as a guide for creating his next transform. This is, of course, another way of saying that a therapist must use the effect of his intervention to shape subsequent intervention. Such a feedback process reminds us that clients help shape their therapist's interventions and that therapists help shape their client's behavior. Both are interlocked in feedback.

The Cybernetic Therapist

A therapist who attempts to avoid mistakes or errors might be disastrous to clients. The very basis for cybernetic self-correction arises from the generation of error or difference, which enables future behavior to be altered. Oscar Peterson (cited in Lyons, 1978), widely acclaimed as the jazz pianist's jazz pianist, was once asked how he feels when he hits an occasional wrong note. He responded as follows:

> My classical teacher used to tell me, "If you make a mistake, don't stop. Make it part of what you're playing as much as possible . . . ." One thing I try to convey to my students when I'm teaching is the relativity of notes. From a melodic standpoint, there are no wrong notes because every note can be related to a chord. Every note can be made part of your line depending on how fast you can integrate it into your schematic arrangement. (p. 31)

Peterson's point applies to the world of therapy. A therapist can view every action, including those called "intervention," as part of a creative unfolding. In this sense there are no mistakes per se, but only action that is connected to a structured sequence of action. This perspective suggests that looking for the "right" intervention or the "correct" behavior simply misses the larger point. The therapist should focus on discovering the broader structure that always encompasses any particular bit of behavior.

These considerations suggest that a therapist needs several basic skills: an ability to vary his behavior and an ability to discern and use the effects of that behavior to direct his subsequent behavior. These therapeutic skills correspond to the ways a therapist operates as an "effector" and "sensor." The task of creating difference concerns one's "effectors," whereas discerning difference is the job of one's "sensors." When the relationship between effector and sensor, or intervention and diagnosis, is recursively organized, we may speak of a cybernetic system.

In general, any problematic system requires three ingredients for correction. First, a sufficient range of sensors to detect difference. Second, a sufficient range of varied behavior to facilitate the creation of difference. And finally, and most importantly, the system must be able to recursively link sensors and effectors so as to provide self-correction. The therapist's task is to enter a system and participate in a way that connects their sensors and effectors as recursive parts of self-corrective feedback. This process constructs sociofeedback in therapy.

The clinical world sometimes punctuates its activity by separating the processes of clinical practice, theory, and research. For instance, specialists may be trained in these three areas and then housed in separate offices or academic departments. This separation is an appropriate metaphor for the dismemberment of effector, sensor, and their feedback relation in the process of therapy.

A cybernetic therapist is always a practitioner, theorist, and researcher. To be effective, a therapist must be able to construct models, package them as interventions, and discern what happens. Cybernetics reconnects these arbitrarily punctuated facets of therapeutic process as parts of a more encompassing process called sociofeedback.

Stewart Brand once proposed the question "What color is a chameleon on a mirror?" This riddle helps us understand sociofeedback in therapy. Cybernetically, a chameleon in the context of its mirror image demonstrates a feedback process wherein perceived changes of color in the mirror image lead to changes of color in the chameleon. If there is a significant time lag between the creature's sensor and effector, the color it perceives will be out of phase with the color it generates. This results in the creature trying to make corrective adjustments to reduce the difference. Every effort of adjustment, however, only leads to the same recursive corrective process being played over again. In such a case, the solution helps to maintain the problem.

If the color the creature perceives is in synch with the color it generates, the system will maintain a stable range of color. It is a mistake, however, to think that this chameleon and mirror are not locked in feedback. The mirror image and chameleon are constantly changing color in relation to one another. In this case, the feedback relation between these changes maintains what an observer perceives as a stable range of color values.

In sum, a chameleon sitting on a mirror cannot avoid changing its color. The relevant issue concerns what form of stability is being maintained. In the one case, color is stabilized within a range we perceive as varying around a particular color value. In the other, the range of stability may encompass the whole spectrum of the chameleon's color-generating domain. An observer not accustomed to thinking in terms of recursive process might provide a different description of the latter form of stability. For this observer, the color changes may look like an escalating runaway, stepping up from red to orange to yellow to green to blue (this is a hypothetical chameleon). With repeated observation, the individual might speculate that the color blue is a sort of threshold which triggers the process to start from the beginning again. Using the perspective of cybernetics, he would be able to see that the escalating runaway process was, all along, only part of a more encompassing self-corrective recursive system.

In therapy, the outcome of sessions can be similarly analyzed by examining the feedback between therapist and client. The mirroring operations of therapy include interpretations, dramatic announcements, ambiguous stories, free associations, rituals, and behavioral assignments. More broadly, all the therapist's responses can be seen as mirroring the problematic system. In addition, an observer could argue that all responses of a client are a mirroring of the therapeutic system. Like a chameleon on a mirror, this system will achieve some form of stability. The therapist will help initiate a different order of problem or help shift the problematic context to a different way of correcting itself which is more satisfying to both client(s) and therapist(s).

Cybernetics provokes us to consider who is the chameleon in therapy. Is the therapist an active mirror who helps trigger a troubled system's own resources to steer the course of therapy? Are symptoms a kind of appropriate "coloration" to their surrounding context? Is the client an active mirror who helps trigger a therapist to construct a useful transform? Are interventions a kind of appropriate "coloration" to their surrounding context? Is therapy, to borrow a phrase from Truman Capote, "Music for Chameleons"?

DISCUSSION

THERAPIST: How is symptomatic behavior an appropriate "coloration" to the context that surrounds it?

EPISTEMOLOGIST: Gregory Bateson (1976d) once had a schizophrenic patient who asserted, "I am an end table made of Manzanita wood." The patient was refusing food at the time and the institution wanted to force-feed him.

THERAPIST: So his metaphoric communication had to do with people treating him like a thing? Was his schizophrenic utterance an appropriate "coloration" to his institutional life? Is this what you mean?

EPISTEMOLOGIST: There is more to the story. Bateson, in fact, asked the patient the very same questions you now propose. He got nowhere, however. Thinking that his patient might respond differently if he were in a different context, Bateson strategized to get him to a restaurant in another town. What he did was arrange to take the patient on a trip to visit his parents. This enabled them, while en route, to pull over to the side of the road and eat in a restaurant—a place where food would obviously be in a different context.

When the waitress presented the menu, Bateson ordered ham and eggs. His patient subsequently said that he would like ham and eggs *and* toast. When the food arrived, Bateson ate everything but his toast. The patient, after staring at Bateson's toast, said that he would like to eat it. He then proceeded to devour all of the remaining food, including his own meal. After a second cup of coffee, he leaned back and said, "Manzanita [man's an eater]. If the circumstances were resolved, he would [wood]."

THERAPIST: So his statement was not only a metaphor about his situation, it was also a request to be in a different context. His "coloration" changed, so to speak, when he got into that restaurant.

EPISTEMOLOGIST: Don't forget the nature of his relationship with Bateson. The sequence involving the toast also provided a difference that made a difference.

THERAPIST: Would you say that the schizophrenic offered the first toast, perhaps an invitation for a friendly encounter? After all, he specified that he wanted ham and eggs *plus* toast. Bateson reciprocated by leaving his toast on his plate—shall we say, a toast of toast?

EPISTEMOLOGIST: It's interesting to note that they went on to have quite an interesting conversation after this exchange.

THERAPIST: I'm curious. Whatever happened to this schizophrenic?

EPISTEMOLOGIST: I don't know, but there is something else that might interest you. Bateson asked him what was wrong with the therapy people were giving him. He replied, "A contrivance to change the color of a man's eye to please a psychologist is too much. And you're all psychologists, though some of you turn and become medical doctors for that part of you which hurts. Never mind thinking of the man who is so sick he has to munch on his own."

Our chameleon riddle returns: An impasse may occur when there is an attempt to change the color of a man's "I" to suit a therapist.

THERAPIST: Did this schizophrenic ever attempt to explain why he went mad?

EPISTEMOLOGIST: He once stated, "Bateson, you want me to come and live in your world. I lived in it from 1920 to 1943, and I don't like it." The patient was born in 1920 and hospitalized in 1943; this utterance occurred in 1957. When Freida Fromm-Reichmann came through Palo Alto, Bateson asked her what she would have said. She replied, "Yes, I once had a patient who said something like that and I said, 'But I never promised you a rose garden.'"

THERAPIST: I would like to know what to do when I actually practice therapy. What does a cybernetic understanding of therapeutic change propose with regard to the pragmatics of carrying out an intervention?

EPISTEMOLOGIST: Remember, your behavior should always be a transform of a client's symptomatic communication.

THERAPIST: How do I know what is really his symptomatic communication?

EPISTEMOLOGIST: That is an important question. I can now tell you that we have actually been using the notion of symptomatic communication as a useful fiction. In the pragmatics of therapy, you really don't need to worry about what is symptomatic, problematic, troublesome, and so on. You simply transform whatever the client brings to you.

THERAPIST: What? I thought my job was to identify the presenting problem and then treat it. What are you talking about?

EPISTEMOLOGIST: The cybernetic orientation to therapeutic change presented here only requires that a therapist construct transforms that *model* a client's communication. If a client says he is well, then the therapist responds with a transform of that message. He could recommend, for example, that the client take a vacation to test his recovery. Of course, he should probably add that it is likely that the client's problem will return.

THERAPIST: Why do that?

EPISTEMOLOGIST: We need to remember that it is incomplete to imagine change without stability in cybernetic systems. The two come hand in hand. Therefore, when a client says "Change me," he is actually saying two things, "Change me and stabilize me." Sometimes therapists refer to this as a double message of "Change me but don't change me." The cybernetic view is to see all requests for change as requests for change *and* stability. Similarly, a request for or statement of stability also proposes change.

THERAPIST: Troubled families, of course, have their own unique ways of requesting change and stability. This cybernetic complementarity may be couched in terms of the distinction between closeness and distance, individuation and togetherness, control and spontaneity, absurdity and seriousness, chaos and order, health and pathology, recovery and relapse, and so on.

EPISTEMOLOGIST: A therapist with a cybernetic world view will know that what to others appears as an either/or issue is often an analogue or metaphor of a system's underlying complementary relation between change and stability. With this insight, a therapist can acknowledge and prescribe both sides of an issue.

An awareness of cybernetic complementarity in family process explains a number of interesting observations long known to therapists. For instance, prescribing a symptom while scheduling another session to work on the problem is a way of requesting both change and stability. On the other hand, both messages may also be proposed to a family that reports symptom disappearance — warning them of a relapse while simultaneously giving them a vacation from therapy.

THERAPIST: Does the process of creating transforms in therapy always involve constructing these double messages which address change and stability aspects of a troubled system?

EPISTEMOLOGIST: In part, yes. At this point we should recall that a cybernetic system encompasses a recursive, complementary relation between processes of change and stability. Stated more formally:

$$\text{Cybernetic System} = (\text{Stability/Change})$$

THERAPIST: Given this view, what is the goal of therapy?

EPISTEMOLOGIST: The goal of therapy is simply to alter the way a problematic system maintains its organization through processes of change. Thus, interventions attempt to facilitate a more adaptive ontogeny of the presenting system. Note that family therapists often make a category mistake when describing the development of a family system in terms of "evolution" rather than "ontogeny." As Varela (1979) states, "It is inadequate to talk about evolution in the history of change of a single unity in whatever space it may exist; unities only have ontogenies" (p. 37). The goal of therapy can be stated formally thus:

$$(\text{Stability/Change})_1 \xrightarrow{\text{Intervention}} (\text{Stability/Change})_2$$

where the cybernetic system at time_2 is more adaptive than it was at time_1.

THERAPIST: What changes in therapeutic change?

EPISTEMOLOGIST: Therapeutic change of a cybernetic system, whether the system is punctuated as an individual, couple, whole family, neighborhood, or entire society involves change of change — change of how a system's habitual process of change leads to stability.

THERAPIST: How does one create such change?

EPISTEMOLOGIST: Following Ashby, Bateson argued that adaptive change requires both a source of the random and a source of order that serves to draw distinctions upon the random. Note that this definition of order, if closely examined, prescribes a restriction regarding what is to be taken as a "source of the random." Specifically, by the random we mean some arrangement of events that can be meaningfully punctuated by a system's source of order. Such a definition suggests a complementary relation between random and order.

THERAPIST: This means that not all ways of introducing the random will be useful. A troubled social system must confront some source of the so-called random in a way that will facilitate the generation of a new pattern or structure for organizing its experience, behavior, and interaction. Such a relevant source of the random has been called a "meaningful Rorschach."

EPISTEMOLOGIST: We can now model the process of therapeutic change as follows:

$$(\text{Stability}/\text{Change}) / \text{Meaningful Rorschach}$$

This expression indicates the emergence of a cybernetic complementarity of higher logical type. If we simplify the left side of this distinction, we can see this more clearly:

$$\text{Cybernetic System}/\text{Meaningful Rorschach}$$

This complementarity, in turn, can be seen as an isomorph, transform, analogue, or model of our most elementary cybernetic complementarity:

$$(\text{Stability}/\text{Change})$$

Here, stability refers to the stabilization of a cybernetic system's wholeness or autonomy and change refers to the construction of different patterns and structures that serve to maintain the whole system.

THERAPIST: Effective therapy can therefore be described as a context that enables a cybernetic system to calibrate the way it changes in order to remain stable. This "change of change" requires that a therapist help the troubled system encounter a meaningful Rorschach.

EPISTEMOLOGIST: In an earlier chapter it was proposed that an idea central to many schools of therapy is that a client, whether an individual or whole social group, can be depicted as an ensemble of uncoordinated parts. The task of therapy, following this way of thinking, is to integrate these parts into a balanced, self-corrective, unified whole.

For the sake of parsimony, we can imagine the parts that therapy organizes as being expressed through three voices. As we've mentioned, there is a voice that requests change and a voice that requests stability. If a therapist pays too much attention to the former, an observer may say that the part requesting stability "resists" the therapist's interventions. On the other hand, too much attention given to stability may lead a client system to demand that the therapist take them more seriously. This may happen to therapists who, in their efforts to be strategic or systemic, do nothing but prescribe the symptom or positively connote it. Effective therapy requires responding to the voices of both change and stability (see Keeney, 1981).

THERAPIST: Is the third voice the random noise from which a troubled system can create, construct, or invent a new structure or pattern?

EPISTEMOLOGIST: Yes. This third voice is a meaningful Rorschach for the client. Although the client may believe that a solution is being given to him, the client actually constructs his own alternative structure out of this Rorschach.

THERAPIST: I agree that all clients complain that they want to change some aspects of their situation. At the same time, clients present a message, often covert, that they want to remain stable. Clients, of course, are not aware that they are communicating these different messages. To successfully work with both of these messages requires having the client system encounter a higher order complementarity that encompasses its voices of change and stability. This is done, as you suggest, by presenting a Rorschach to the client system, which, like a mirror, enables the client system to construct its own solution.

EPISTEMOLOGIST: It is important to remember that clients are never consciously aware of all the multiple messages they communicate. If a therapist points out to a client that he is covertly communicating something, he will more than likely respond as if someone had spoken to him in Swahili. A therapist should not simply articulate or underscore the voices of change or stability. The trick is to embrace both in a way that helps construct a higher order of complementarity. As we've proposed, one way of doing this is to package a transform that models three voices, messages, or parts: (1) a meaningful Rorschach, (2) a request to change, and (3) a request for stability. This approach can be resketched as follows:

$$\left(\frac{\text{Request for Stability}}{\text{Request for Change}} \right) \Big/ \frac{\text{Presentation of}}{\text{Meaningful Rorschach}}$$

A therapist can package these voices in dramatic announcements, behavioral assignments, stories, jokes, rituals, or interactional
episodes. Therapists who work as a team may even divide the voices
among themselves. In such a case, one therapist can propose change,
another stability, and another, perhaps through a message sent from
behind a one-way mirror, can propose a Rorschach. Whether working as a soloist or as a member of a group, therapists must orchestrate
these three voices of therapeutic change.

THERAPIST: Would you give me an example?

EPISTEMOLOGIST: Let's examine one of the most fascinating examples of how a therapist became part of sociofeedback. I'm speaking
of a case report from Milton Erickson. The following excerpts are
Erickson's own description of this case (cited in Haley, 1967, pp.
501–502):

> George had been a patient in a mental hospital for five years. His
> identity had never been established. He was simply a stranger around
> the age of 25 who had been picked up by the police for irrational be-
> havior and committed to the state mental hospital. During those five
> years he had said, "My name is George," "Good morning," and "Good
> night," but these were his only rational utterances. He uttered other-
> wise a continuous word-salad completely meaningless as far as could
> be determined. It was made up of sounds, syllables, words, and incom-
> plete phrases. For the first three years he sat on a bench at the front
> door of the ward and eagerly leaped up and poured forth his word-
> salad most urgently to everyone who entered the ward. Otherwise, he
> merely sat quietly mumbling his word-salad to himself. Innumerable
> efforts had been made by psychiatrists, psychologists, nurses, social
> service workers, other personnel and even fellow patients to secure in-
> telligible remarks from him, all in vain. George talked only one way,
> the word-salad way. After approximately three years he continued to
> greet persons who entered the ward with an outburst of meaningless
> words, but in between times he sat silently on the bench, appearing
> mildly depressed but somewhat angrily uttering a few minutes of
> word-salad when approached and questioned.
>
> The author joined the hospital staff in the sixth year of George's
> stay. The available information about his ward behavior was secured.
> It was learned also that patients or ward personnel could sit on the
> bench beside him without eliciting his word-salad so long as they did
> not speak to him. With this total of information a therapeutic plan was
> devised.

THERAPIST: Let me guess what he might do. From a cybernetic point of view, Erickson should construct a transform that models George's symptomatic behavior. From what has been said, we know that George has invented a particular language and that he greets people while sitting on his bench, as well as allowing them to sit with him. Somehow, Erickson must work with that data.

EPISTEMOLOGIST: In order to construct an adequate transform of George's behavior, Erickson needed to do some more homework. He had to learn some patterns in George's language. As he describes this next step:

> A secretary recorded in shorthand the word-salads with which he so urgently greeted those who entered the ward. These transcribed recordings were studied but no meaning could be discovered. These word-salads were carefully paraphrased, using words that were least likely to be found in George's productions and an extensive study was made of these until the author could improvise a word-salad similar in pattern to George's, but utilizing a different vocabulary.

THERAPIST: In other words, Erickson's choice of transform involved modeling patterns of George's language, but with a difference. This difference arose from using a different vocabulary. The patterns were the same, while the particulars were simply noise.

EPISTEMOLOGIST: What Erickson did was develop a way of packaging his transforms. By responding to George with an isomorphic language, he could package a wide range of transforms. The different vocabulary, as you suggest, allowed for some noise. Let's go on with the story:

> Then all entrances to the ward were made through a side door some distance down the corridor from George. The author then began the practice of sitting silently on the bench beside George daily for increasing lengths of time until the span of an hour was reached. Then at the next sitting, the author, addressing the empty air, identified himself verbally. George made no response.

THERAPIST: What can we say about this interaction, other than the fact that Erickson is modeling or providing transforms of George's silence? Or is it that George is transforming Erickson's silence?

EPISTEMOLOGIST: We have a recursive system, where both are providing transforms of each other. We could also say that Erickson has chosen to begin his relationship with George by not doing what others have previously done. He does not try to secure intelligible remarks, nor does he ask any questions. By sitting silently on the bench, he draws a distinction. In effect, he proposes that their relationship will be different. By increasing the period of time they sit in silence, another pattern is drawn. Namely, he marks that any message proposed can be escalated or amplified. Stated differently, their silence proposes stability while their escalating periods of silence propose change. Having set this context, Erickson verbally identifies himself. This signals the beginning of a different order of encounter.

> The next day the identification was addressed directly to George. He spat out an angry stretch of word-salad to which the author replied, in tones of courtesy and responsiveness, with an equal amount of his own carefully contrived word-salad. George appeared puzzled and, when the author finished, George uttered another contribution with an inquiring intonation. As if replying the author verbalized still further word-salad.
>
> After a half dozen interchanges, George lapsed into silence and the author promptly went about other matters.

THERAPIST: We can now clearly see sociofeedback in this cybernetic system. After Erickson's identification proposed a different way of encountering one another, George responded with angry word-salad. Subsequently, Erickson transformed that word-salad, followed by George's transforming, and on and on, round and round.

EPISTEMOLOGIST: Let's map a part of their sequence as follows:

1. George: Angry word-salad
2. Milton: Courteous word-salad (with different vocabulary)
3. George: Curious word-salad
4. Milton: Courteous word-salad (with different vocabulary)

Using our frame of cybernetic complementarity

(Stability/Change)/Meaningful Rorschach

we can dissect Erickson's transforms as follows: His courteous intonation indicates change, while his use of a similar *form* of word-salad indicates stability. And finally, by using a different vocabulary, George is provided with a Rorschach from which an alternative pattern can be constructed. George responds to this transform by altering his angry intonation to an inquiring intonation.

George and Milton Erickson, during this recycling of transforms, become part of a self-corrective feedback process. A context for therapeutic change is being constructed. Erickson's account continues:

> The next morning appropriate greetings were exchanged employing proper names by both. Then George launched into a long word-salad speech to which the author courteously replied in kind. There followed then brief interchanges of long and short utterances of word-salad until George fell silent and the author went to other duties.

THERAPIST: Would you say that a context for therapeutic change is still being built?

EPISTEMOLOGIST: Indeed. George and Milton Erickson are building a relationship through their recursive interaction. Their communication is connecting them as much, if not more, than any "logical" or "rational" exchange. By using the effect of each behavior to shape consequent behavior, each participant is locked in feedback. When George proposes a long word-salad speech and Erickson responds in kind, George is then put into the position of reacting to Erickson's response to his response. He simply cannot avoid a relationship with Erickson. We cannot say that Erickson is controlling George, for his communication is only a transform or mirroring of George's behavior. Similarly, it is incomplete to suggest that George controls Erickson, for he appears to mirror Erickson's behavior. Both of them transform each other's behavior. To return to Erickson's narrative:

> This continued for some time. Then George, after returning the morning greeting made meaningless utterances without pause for four hours. It taxed the author greatly to miss lunch and to make a full reply in kind. George listened attentively and made a two hour reply to which a weary two hour response was made. (George was noted to watch the clock throughout the day.)

THERAPIST: The more encompassing cybernetic system now more clearly appears to be correcting George's (and Erickson's) behavior. After all, George has now consciously coupled his behavior to the flow of clock time.

EPISTEMOLOGIST: Indeed. The subsequent event should not surprise you:

> The next morning George returned the usual greeting properly but added about two sentences of nonsense to which the author replied

with a similar length of nonsense. George replied, "Talk sense, Doctor." "Certainly, I'll be glad to. What is your last name?" "O'Donovan and it's about time somebody who knows how to talk asked. Over five years in this lousy joint" . . . (to which was added a sentence or two of word-salad). The author replied, "I'm glad to get your name, George. Five years is too long a time" . . . (and about two sentences of word-salad were added).

THERAPIST: Erickson had helped create a different context for his interaction with George, analogous to Bateson's breakfast with his schizophrenic. In this different context, they could even talk about the odd way in which they occasionally communicated.

EPISTEMOLOGIST: The different context, in George's case, was a situation where he could use both of his languages — English and schizophreneze.

THERAPIST: What accounts for this change?

EPISTEMOLOGIST: As we've learned, cybernetics defines therapeutic change in terms of sociofeedback. In sociofeedback, symptomatic behavior can unfold into a reductio ad absurdum. After hours and hours of uttering schizophreneze and having to listen to as much, we could say that George was led to encounter the absurdity of his situation. At that point, a sort of "hitting bottom," he decided he had had enough and requested that Erickson "talk sense."

THERAPIST: What happened after their first rational conversation?

EPISTEMOLOGIST: Erickson sums up the case as follows:

The rest of the account is as might be expected. A complete history sprinkled with bits of word-salad was obtained by inquiries judiciously salted with word-salad. His clinical course, never completely free of word-salad which was eventually reduced to occasional unintelligible mumbles, was excellent. Within a year he had left the hospital, was gainfully employed and at increasingly longer intervals returned to the hospital to report his continued and improving adjustment. Nevertheless, he invariably initiated his report or terminated it with a bit of word-salad, always expecting the same from the author. Yet he could, as he frequently did on these visits comment wryly, "Nothing like a little nonsense in life, is there Doctor?" to which he obviously expected and received a sensible expression of agreement to which was added a brief utterance of nonsense. After he had been out of the hospital continuously for three years of fully satisfactory adjustment, contact was lost with him except for a cheerful postcard from another city. This bore a brief but satisfactory summary of his adjustments in a distant city. It was signed properly but following his name was a jumble of syllables. There was no return address. He was ending the relationship on his terms of adequate understanding.

THERAPIST: Can we map all of Milton H. Erickson's work in terms of sociofeedback?

EPISTEMOLOGIST: Not only Erickson's, but any process of therapeutic change can be mapped in this fashion.

THERAPIST: It again seems to me that cybernetics is more than a map. It is also a prescription for a way of working. I am interested in further exploration of that territory.

EPISTEMOLOGIST: That task is for another book.

THERAPIST: Before proceeding, I need to discuss something else. Throughout this book it has been implied that pragmatic applications of cybernetics are sometimes decontextualized with respect to the aesthetic patterns of a whole ecology. Please tell me how a cybernetic understanding of therapeutic change, as discussed in this chapter, avoids being a decontextualized bag of tricks, insensitive to ecological considerations.

EPISTEMOLOGIST: If a therapist becomes a mirror, he avoids any attempt to change a patient's "I" to fit his own world view. As we've suggested, a therapist must package three basic messages to a troubled ecology — a message of change, stability, and a relevant Rorschach. The nature of these messages, however, is not solely determined by a therapist. A therapist always follows and uses what a client brings to him.

THERAPIST: If I follow you, such a therapist is not really "manipulative" or "tricky" in the bad sense of those terms. Instead, this therapist is only a mirror directing a client to direct him. We earlier put this in terms of a recursive definition of therapy: "A therapist treats a client who directs the therapist how to treat him."

EPISTEMOLOGIST: We can also see the behavior clients present as nonpurposeful and beyond their conscious control. Clients, like therapists, mirror the contextual structure embodying them. There are no power games in therapy, although therapy is sometimes punctuated and believed to be organized that way. The more aesthetic view prescribes clients and therapists as parts of more encompassing patterns of cybernetic process.

THERAPIST: Like the jeweled net of Indra, a therapist's mirror helps connect him to diverse orders of recursive process immanent in the whole ecology. A therapist with this insight might work at polishing his mirror.

EPISTEMOLOGIST: Therapeutic change always polishes one's mirror.

6

AN AESTHETIC BASE
FOR FAMILY THERAPY

I believe that action, if it be planned at all, must always be planned upon an aesthetic base. — *Gregory Bateson*

CONSCIOUS PURPOSE

Conscious purpose, with its aim of achieving specific goals, cannot take into account whole ecological contexts. Unfortunately, this limitation often leads to cybernetic disconnections: For example, a client's conscious effort to "control" symptomatic behavior helps structure a symmetrical battle between mind and body.

Throughout this book we have hinted that pathology arises from distortions of epistemology that are rooted to conscious orders of mind. These distortions are evident in how we regard conscious transforms or models of recursive process. Rather than seeing a conscious transform as an approximation of a more encompassing pattern of recursion, we may make the error of believing that the approximation is a complete isomorph of what we are dealing with.

Conscious mind, for example, may model a recursive process in terms of lineal structure. Sometimes this is useful — we may want to design a flat tennis court for our lawn. At other times, the approximation is dangerous. In these cases, our interaction with a system, based on an incomplete model of that system, threatens its organization. By constructing lineal structure we tend to choose maximization or minimization of variables in our world, leading to ecological fractionation and pathology. For example, if we perceive a shortage of fuel, we simply set out to create more coal mines and oil wells. The way in which these natural resources are part of an interlocking ecology is often ignored. Similarly, we minimize pests through insecticides in order to maximize crop yields. The recursive nature of the cybernetic system comes back to haunt us in the future when we discover poison in our own bodies.

The same argument concerning conscious purpose applies to change of individuals and social systems in therapy. We can therefore be equally critical of approaches to therapy that emphasize purpose, control, and technique. For example, there are an ever increasing number of technical approaches that attempt to "distill" Milton Erickson's artistry into packaged cookbooks on how to do therapy. Speaking of "cookbook" therapists, Bateson (cited in Keeney, 1977) proposed that "Milton worked in the weave of the total complex, whereas they come away with a trick which is separate from the total complex. This disconnected trick therefore goes counter to the whole and helps perpetuate an illusion of power" (p. 60).

Perhaps we should regard any "bag of tricks" for curing or preventing pathology as ecologically dangerous, potentially leading to higher order problems. An alternative position is to contextualize the techniques of therapy as part of a more encompassing aesthetic base. From this perspective, problems only arise when our technique is not adequately tempered by higher orders of cybernetic process. As Bateson (1972) explains:

> Mere purposive rationality unaided by such phenomena as art, religion, dream, and the like, is necessarily pathogenic and destructive of life; . . . its virulence springs specifically from the circumstance that life depends upon interlocking *circuits* of contingency, while consciousness can see only such short arcs of such circuits as human purpose may direct. (p. 146)

This view suggests that pathology may be perpetuated by therapists who work without an aesthetic orientation. A therapist who sees himself as a unilateral power broker or manipulator is dealing with partial arcs of cybernetic systems. Such a position threatens the recursively structured biological world in which we live. Only wisdom, that is, "a sense or recognition of the fact of circuitry" (Bateson, 1972, p. 146), can safely and effectively deal with ecosystems.

Bateson (1972) suggests that medical science is an example of how unaided consciousness works.

Being doctors, they had purposes: to cure this and that. Their research efforts were therefore focused (as attention focuses the consciousness) upon those short trains of causality which they could manipulate, by means of drugs or other intervention, to correct more or less specific and identifiable states or symptoms. Whenever they discovered an effective "cure" for something, research in that area ceased and attention was directed elsewhere. We can now prevent polio, but nobody knows much more about the systemic aspects of that fascinating disease. Research on it has ceased or is, at best, confined to improving the vaccines.

But a bag of tricks for curing or preventing a list of specified diseases provides no overall *wisdom*. The ecology and population dynamics of the species has been disrupted; parasites have been made immune to antibiotics; the relationship between mother and neonate has been almost destroyed; and so on. (p. 145)

Again, intervention strategies that do not fully consider the ecology of the problems they attempt to alter will help breed higher orders of pathology. We are therefore responsible for contextualizing our techniques, whether they belong to medicine, education, engineering, or psychotherapy. An aesthetic base for our interventions requires that technique be adequately coupled to higher orders of mental process, that is, unconscious orders of mind.

Throughout our discussion it has been suggested that unconscious orders of mind are connected in recursive relationship. More broadly, we have proposed that divergent disciplines of study ranging from neurophysiology to psychotherapy converge on the generalization that recursive structure organizes the biological world — whether in the domain of cellular activity, body metabolism, emotional life, or interpersonal relationship. To understand the pathologies of biology requires knowing how epistemological premises of recursive relationship, what we might call "biological eternal verities," become distorted. Distortions arise when conscious transforms of unconscious process are not subject to subsequent correction by unconscious process. This view suggests that conscious mind is not to be blamed for pathology; similarly, unconscious process is not the root of our problem. Pathology arises when conscious and unconscious orders of mind are not recursively connected as parts of self-corrective feedback.

We are free to consciously construct lineal approximations of recursive process as long as unconscious orders of mind are allowed to correct any misuse or misunderstanding of these incomplete models. Thus, consciously planned therapeutic strategy should be subject to higher order correction. In sum, an aesthetic base for therapy arises when conscious *and* unconscious orders of mind provide self-corrective feedback.

Unfortunately, knowing more about cybernetics and ecology may not help alleviate the errors of conscious purpose. What is needed is a feedback connection of conscious knowledge with higher orders of mental process. One way of achieving this connection is to develop a *respect* for ecology, as Rappaport (1974) suggests:

> It could be argued that increased knowledge of ecosystems results in decreased respect for them, and thus leads men to be guilty of, and subsequently to be punished for, what might be called ecological hubris. It is perhaps the case that knowledge will never be able to replace respect in man's dealings with ecological systems . . . . (p. 59)

This idea is further exemplified by a story about a conference organized for people who were experts on running conferences. As Bateson (1979b) reports:

> Everyone who is an expert in running conferences knows that the first half of your conference will always be wasted on nonsense — ego values, establishment of positions around the table, debating the room temperature, etc., etc. At approximately the half-way point, people realize that they are not getting anywhere and they begin to work. Now, the people at that conference of professional conference-makers knew this fact and were therefore not worried that the first half of their conference was wasted. They assumed they would later begin productive work. Unfortunately, it is a necessary condition for your later productivity that you be worried about the phase in which you're not saying anything important. At this conference, they went on talking nonsense until the very end of the conference — because it never worried them.

Conscious knowledge of the recursive nature of ecosystems does not necessarily breed wisdom. Respect for ecology, however, is a different order of knowing. Cybernetic epistemology suggests that respect for ecosystems follows naturally when a therapist views and conducts himself as part of a more encompassing mental system. Experientially, this form of respect involves an awareness that any particular feeling, perception, or idea is always a fragment of the whole system or context that embodies it.

ART AND CRAFT

A therapist can be described as either an artist or craftsman. Those who exclusively practice, teach, and evaluate particular sets of skills and techniques characterize "craftsmen" or "technicians." These therapists occasionally imply that therapy is analogous to repairing a car or broken chair, that is, therapy is a craft involving useful skills — "I will fix it."

For an artist, the skills and techniques of therapy are secondary to a more encompassing perspective. Art is concerned with the ecological implications of a course of action as it is woven into a total context. For an artist, the practice of a skill has importance in terms of the way it becomes part of a whole ecology — personality, social context, and world.

As Collingwood (1938/1975) points out, craftsmen and artists both utilize the same skills and techniques toward a particular goal, such as the construction of a building. However, to the artist there is a difference that extends beyond the conscious working-out of the means to a preconceived end. This difference concerns how the particular achievement is connected to the context of which it is a part.

Stated differently, art is concerned with the recursive relation between unconscious and conscious orders of mental process. Bateson (1972) summarizes this understanding of art:

> It is not that art is the expression of the unconscious, but rather that it is concerned with the relation *between* the levels of mental process. From a work of art it may be possible to analyze out some unconscious thoughts of the artist, but I believe that, for example, Freud's analysis of Leonardo's *Virgin on the Knees of St. Anne* precisely misses the point of the whole exercise. Artistic skill is the combining of many levels of mind — unconscious, conscious, and external — to make a statement of their combination. It is not a matter of expressing a single level. (p. 464)

Since art involves the recursive relation of diverse orders of mind, it can amend the limited view proposed by "unaided consciousness." As Bateson suggests (1972), art may have a "positive function in maintaining what I call 'wisdom,' i.e., in correcting a too purposive view of life and making the view more systemic . . . " (p. 147).

When art is seen as a bridge between parts of mind, it is clear that an artist invokes a recursive relation between so-called left- and right-brain mentation. In the case of art in Zen Buddhism, a student chooses a discipline to master, such as archery, calligraphy, or tea-serving. Learning technique proceeds through daily practice of particular skill components. Any conscious attention to the "personal growth" or "enlightenment" of the student which distracts from learning technique is summarily dismissed. While mastering technical skills the student is also given an experiential dilemma such as a koan. This "impossible riddle" helps temper any erroneous sense of pride which might arise with mastery of technique. In Western vernacular, the student's ego is kept in check. More accurately, dualisms are curbed — one does not atrribute mastery to one's self, but to a more encompassing context of which the self is part. The overall effect is that the Zen student's technique is organized as a complementary part in a broader ecosystem.

Thus, art, whether in therapy or a concert hall, requires *both* left and right brain mentation. This reminds us, first of all, that art always includes technique. One can never play music unless some form of technique has been previously assimilated. Any attempt to be in the context of art without having learned sufficient technique can only lead to free-associative muddle. In therapy, "experiential approaches" are sometimes interpreted to mean a gushing out of unconscious process. This is not art. At the same time, an emphasis on technique without regard for the more encompassing aesthetic patterns leads to a mechanical, sterile performance. Such is the case with "strategic approaches" which may ignore any aesthetic base and focus on a purposeful, chess-like punctuation of therapy gamesmanship. This is also not art. Art emerges when head and heart become parts of a cybernetic system capable of ecological self-correction.

PRACTICE

Each of us chooses or accepts the context within which our life is governed. Changing to a different context eventually leads to an alteration of our habits of action and experience. For example, a student of biology will patiently study mathematics and science until finally the bits of information begin to coalesce into meaningful patterns. Suddenly, he may awaken to discover he is becoming a biologist. Similarly, a music student will discipline himself to practice exercises that may seem trivial until the joy of being "musical" finally evolves. Commitment to the *discipline* a context prescribes is the choice that makes a difference.

Similarly, a therapist must practice and wait patiently in order to achieve an epistemological conversion. The nature of "practice" is further illuminated in Bateson's account of an interview (Bateson & Brown, 1975):

> I was interviewing a Japanese girl in the war on respect in the Japanese family. She was describing what happens when dad comes home from work. I asked my questions, and it was all beautifully detailed, all beautifully coming out. Then she said, "But in Japan we do not respect the father." "Wait a minute. What have you been telling me?" "Well, you see, we *practice* respect for the father." "Why do you do that?" "In case we need to respect somebody."
>
> Now, the joke of that is that the Japanese idea of practice is different from the Occidental idea of practice. Occidentals laugh, more or less, when they hear this. We practice in order to get a skill, which is then a tool—in which I, unchanged, now have a new tool, that's all. The Oriental view is that you practice in order to change yourself. You incorporate the discipline of practice in you, and you come out of the practice as a different sort of person. This is the whole theory of Zen practice, Zen and archery, all those things. (p. 41)

Commitment to an aesthetic base for therapy requires that we see therapy as a form of practice. Like Zen, the practice of therapy becomes a context of higher order learning for a therapist.

In his classic book *Zen in the Art of Archery* (1953/1971), Eugen Herrigel presents a personal account of the years he spent in a Zen monastery. It is a story of epistemological change and the experiences characterizing such a transition. Throughout his Zen training in archery, Herrigel clearly understood that "bow and arrow are only a pretext for something that could just as well happen without them, only the way to a goal, not the goal itself" (p. 22). Similarly, therapy can be seen as a vehicle for the therapist's epistemological change. In other words, therapy, as well as archery, is simply a context for practice.

In his 6 years of training, Herrigel encountered periods of intense confusion in trying to master the Zen approach to archery. Over and over, his Master would proclaim: "The right art is purposeless, aimless! The more obstinately you try to learn how to shoot the arrow for the sake of hitting the goal, the less you will succeed in the one and the further the other will recede" (p. 51). The context of therapy is comparable: Sometimes the more a therapist tries to affect change, the further from success he drifts. The challenge is to learn to be patient and wait properly.

This patience, or waiting properly, is metaphorically described by Herrigel's Zen Master:

> It is all so simple. You can learn from an ordinary bamboo leaf what ought to happen. It bends lower and lower under the weight of snow. Suddenly the snow slips to the ground without the leaf having stirred. Stay like that at the point of highest tension until the shot falls from you. So, indeed it is: when the tension is fulfilled, the shot *must* fall, it must fall from the archer like snow from a bamboo leaf, before he even thinks it. (p. 71)

In this interactive dance, a whole pattern of organization rather than conscious intent or purpose triggers action. Sociofeedback in therapy also demonstrates this process. Here, a whole pattern of cycled transforms triggers change, rather than the conscious purpose of an individual. Like snow falling from a bamboo leaf, a troubled system is naturally led to dropping its problematic behavior and recalibrating itself.

When a therapist is recursively connected to a troubled system through sociofeedback, the two become a self-corrective cybernetic system. The Zen archer similarly becomes one with the bow, arrow, and target. In this system, the hand on the bow is recursively related to the center of the target. When this realization is achieved in Zen, another recursive relation emerges, "where teacher and pupil are no longer two persons, but one" (Herrigel, 1953/1971, p. 91).

Herrigel (1953/1971) concludes his story with his Master's farewell:

> I must only warn you of one thing. You have become a different person in the course of these years. For this is what the art of archery means: a profound and far-reaching contest of the archer with himself. Perhaps you have hardly noticed it yet, but you will feel it very strongly when you meet with your friends and acquaintances again in your own country: things will no longer harmonize as before. You will see with other eyes and measure with other measures. It has happened to me too, and it happens to all who are touched by the spirit of this art. (p. 92)

When therapy is seen as a vehicle for epistemological change, the consequence is identical. A therapist who is part of such a learning context will eventually experience his world in a profoundly different way — he will have learned to discern and construct patterns that connect.

STORIES: THE ROYAL ROAD TO EPISTEMOLOGY

Our habitual ways of drawing distinctions sometimes distort our awareness of relationship by directing us to only one side of a distinction, a problem discussed in a previous chapter. As suggested earlier, one way of avoiding this distortion is to talk about both sides of a distinction simultaneously, that is, to invoke double description. In this way, distinctions can be used to create descriptions of pattern and relationship.

Stories provide a way of building double descriptions and enabling higher order patterns to be discerned. As Bateson (1979a) suggests, "A story is a little knot or complex of that species of connectedness which we call *relevance*" (p. 13). By transferring our stories from situation to situation, we create contexts that provide meaning and structure for what we do.

In therapy, what emerges are stories and stories about stories. Stories reveal how people punctuate their world and therefore provide a clue for discovering their epistemological premises. In general, therapy is a process of weaving stories between therapist and client systems. Attending to symptomatic communication is one way of hearing a story. In psychoanalysis, for example, "The analyst must be stretched or shrunk onto the procrustean bed of the patient's childhood stories" (Bateson, 1979a, p. 15). The therapist then builds his own story in response to the one he has been told. From a cybernetic perspective, when an exchange of stories is structured in terms of feedback, self-correction becomes possible.

The stories people live as well as their stories about those stories are all that a therapist has to work with. In this sense, therapy is a conversation, an exchange of stories. This perspective is discussed by Szasz (1978): "Seeing therapy as conversation rather than cure thus requires that we not only consider the error of classifying it as a medical intervention, but that we also look anew at the subject of rhetoric and assess its relevance to mental healing" (p. 11).

We earlier mentioned that Warren McCulloch (1967) once joked that "psychiatry would have been a lot better off if man didn't happen to speak" (p. 421). His point is that therapists always deal with "disorders of symbolic structure." From this perspective, we can easily see how Laing's (1970) book of poetry, *Knots*, is a more accurate catalogue of psychopathology than any present or future version of DSM. Laing's poetic sketches capture pattern and relationship; they are not static reifications, such as "bipolar depression" or "schizophrenia." Instead, Laing uses language to construct poetic stories that embody particular skeletons of pattern. We recognize the "knot" in the whole story, rather than in any single element.

In a paper entitled "In Praise of Muddleheaded Anecdotalism," Simon (1978) claims that scholars such as Bateson and Laing are anecdotalists. He distinguishes "anecdotalists," who communicate analogically from "orthodox empiricists," who work more digitally. Simon (1978) describes the work of anecdotalists thus:

> They "muddle" their theories with statements about the contexts and relationships among messages. In place of single referents, they present us with levels and layers of meaning. In place of "either-or" thinking, they offer us "both-and" thinking. In place of discrete categories, or even linear dimensions, they offer us hierarchical orderings. (p. 24)

Simon follows Bateson in suggesting that anecdotes provide an alternative to "dry, statistical summaries." As he notes, "If the 'melody' without is harmonious with a 'melody' within, we're likely to achieve a kind of phenomenological understanding — Verstehende" (Simon, 1978, p. 28). In stories we find a matrix for encountering these interweavings.

It should be no surprise that poets are well aware of these matters. Gary Snyder (1979), for instance, describes the poet as "myth-handler-healer":

> The poet as myth-handler-healer is also speaking as a voice for another place, the deep unconscious, and working toward integration of interior unknown realms of mind with present moment immediate self-interest consciousness. The outer world of nature and the inner world of the unconscious are brought to a single focus occasionally by the work of the dramatist-ritualist-artist-poet. That's another layer. Great tales and myths can give one tiny isolated society the breadth of mind and heart to be *not* provincial and to know itself as a piece of the cosmos. (p. 33)

Poetry, to Snyder, is "a tool, a net to trap, to clutch, and present; a sharp edge; a medicine, or the little awl that unties knots" (p. 29). This provides a tidy metaphor for therapy, where knots of mental process are embodied in the stories clients and therapists construct. Therapy, like poetry, attempts to untie these knots.

A BEGINNING

It is natural that a book like this should end with an invitation to begin. In this spirit, I would like to present such a request. The following proposal was written by Gregory Bateson for a conference he and I designed in 1979. I urge you to accept it as a formal invitation to continue considering what it means to fully encompass an aesthetic base for therapeutic change.

> Many sequences are wrong or painful, socially destructive or individually insane. These may need active intervention. But this is not our focus of attention.
>
> I hope that we may examine some of the presuppositions and habits of thought which lie behind such social and individual pathologies. And also the presuppositions of health.
>
> In our social, individual and psychiatric adaptation—in our very *ideas* of "adaptation"—there is a syndrome arising out of imperfect balance-or-harmony between quantity and pattern.
>
> William Blake tells us *"Bring out weight and measure in a year of dearth"* and hints that quantitative judgement has no useful function in a time of plenty. But we in 20th century middleclass America, living in a matrix of unheard-of plenty, use weight and measure at every turn and in every context, appropriate and inappropriate. Commercialism combines with fashionable styles in scientific method to seduce us into an orgy and/or nightmare of quantity. A bland nightmare of homogenization.
>
> I hope that we may focus not upon gloom which would be easy, but upon *understanding*. If indeed there is an over-development of quantitative perception, there must also be an under-development of perception and understanding of quality and pattern. It is to this lack that I hope we may address ourselves—positively—attempting to remedy the weakness or deficiency.
>
> A simplified parable may make the matter clearer. A square has "more" sides than a triangle and a doughnut (torus) has "more" holes than a solid. But these quantitative comparisons give no hint of the

rich *formal* insights which topological mathematics will build upon the contrasts of pattern.

As our conversation bounces off the quantitative towards pattern and quality, we shall inevitably (I hope) encounter considerations of *aesthetic*. I hope that these may become the main theme of our discussion.

Is there a world of determinism — an interlocking network of *necessary* truths — without which no pragmatic understanding of human events is complete? Does action — purposive action — become arid and pathogenic when such principles are ignored or contravened? Could we, perhaps, at a venture, begin to make a list of such truths? About rhythm? Spatial pattern? Limits of organization? Modulations of form? Of utterance? Are there *necessities* of poetry, without which prose is pathogenic?

I suggest as starting points for thinking and discussion that attention to quantity rather than pattern leads us to ignore aesthetic necessities:

> In child rearing and family.
> In architecture and diet.
> In speech and rhetoric.
> In education.
> In athletics and games.
> In politics and leadership.
> In science.
> In the applications of science.
> In medical and psychiatric practice.
> In international affairs.
> In philosophy and religion.
> Even in art — poetry.

In every one of these fields of human activity — even in crime — there are problems of pattern, about which very little formal thought has been done. The result is a splitting of discourse between the pragmatic and the aesthetic, the structural and the functional, the eternal and the secular.

An aesthetic base for family therapy requires that we have the courage to construct and encounter difference. In the context of dialogue, we find a truth of recursive connection. As Bateson (cited in Brand, 1974) reminds us, "The truth which is important is not a truth of preference, it's a truth of complexity . . . of a total eco-interactive on-going web . . . in which we dance, which is the dance of Shiva" (p. 32). The dance of Shiva includes all cybernetic complementarities —

good/evil, health/pathology, aesthetics/pragmatics, whole/part, family/individual, cybernetics of cybernetics/simple cybernetics, recursive/lineal.

The wisdom or respect for ecological diversity and complexity suggests a cybernetic meaning of love that encourages us to cut across the boundaries of individual skin and embrace more complex mental systems. Mary Catherine Bateson (1977) proposes that this "definition of *love* or of *mind* invites us to generate whole new orders of being to be valued or loved, as we perceive ourselves entering into various kinds of relationship, and thereby being changed" (p. 68). In therapy it is necessary that we bring this form of love and wisdom to the mental systems we encounter and become part of. In this way, our different journeys become a shared co-evolution.

Isak Dineson (1961) has stated with aesthetic elegance what all this discussion has attempted to point toward:

> "Madam," said the Cardinal, "you speak frivolously. Pray do not talk or think that way. Nothing sanctifies, nothing, indeed, is sanctified except by the play of the Lord, which is alone divine. You speak like a person who would pronounce half of the notes of the scale—say, *do, re* and *mi*—to be sacred, but *fa, sol, la* and *ti* to be only profane, while, Madam, no one of the notes is sacred in itself, and it is the music, which can be made out of them, which is alone divine. If your garter be sanctified by my feeble old hand, so is my hand by your fine silk garter. The lion lies in wait for the antelope at the ford, and the antelope is sanctified by the lion, as is the lion by the antelope, for the play of the Lord is divine. Not the bishop, or the knight, or the powerful castle is sacred in itself, but the game of chess is a noble game, and therein the knight is sanctified by the bishop, as the bishop by the queen. Neither would it be an advantage if the bishop were ambitious to acquire the higher virtues of the queen, or the castle, those of the bishop. So are we sanctified when the hand of the Lord moves us to where he wants us to be. Here he may be about to play a fine game with us, and in that game I shall be sanctified by you, as you by any of us." (pp. 14–15)

DISCUSSION

THERAPIST: What must I do to become an artist of therapy?

EPISTEMOLOGIST: A starting point is practice.

THERAPIST: Through practice I can polish my mirror?

EPISTEMOLOGIST: That is only a beginning. Remember that a

mirror proposes an outside which it reflects as well as someone who polishes it. You eventually must go beyond these distinctions. Shen-hsiu, the head monk under the Fifth Patriarch once said:

> Our body is the Bodhi tree,
> Our mind is a mirror bright.
> By polishing, from dust keep free
> And let no more alight.

To complete his partial glimpse, Hui-neng, the Sixth Patriarch responded:

> There is no Bodhi tree,
> Nor mirror to wipe.
> With all completely void,
> Where can dust alight?

THERAPIST: But, there is a more encompassing side to any distinction that dissolves the distinction. The cybernetic complementarity of pleroma/creatura or whole/part surrounds all our knowing.

EPISTEMOLOGIST: Drawing a distinction is like carving a notch in a boat to mark where you are in the water.

THERAPIST: So why should I draw distinctions?

EPISTEMOLOGIST: Perhaps, as a form of practice, it will help you understand how to be an artist in therapy.

THERAPIST: Will this make me an artist?

EPISTEMOLOGIST: I'm reminded of a story: One day a devoted Zen student named Baso was practicing a rather awkward posture, which made him look like a frog. A Zen master walked by and asked, "What are you doing?" "I am practicing Zen," Baso replied. "Why are you practicing?" "I want to attain enlightenment and be a Buddha," the student said.

The Zen master then picked up a tile and started to polish it. The devoted student asked the master, "What are you doing?" The Zen master responded, "I want to make this tile into a jewel." With a puzzled expression, the student asked, "How is it possible to make a tile into a jewel?" "How is it possible to become a Buddha by practicing Zen?" the master replied.

THERAPIST: How is it possible to be an artist, to be part of the Tao, to be a complementary, humble part of our ecosystem? How can I know?

EPISTEMOLOGIST: Kuan Tsu once said, "What a man desires to

know is *that* (i.e., the external world). But his means of knowing is *this* (i.e., himself). How can he know *that*? Only by perfecting *this*."

THERAPIST: I have one final question. What would an artist say to my questions? More specifically, how does an artist explain what he does?

EPISTEMOLOGIST: I'm reminded of one final story, told by Chuang-tzu (cited in Watts, 1975):

> Ch'ing, the chief carpenter, was carving wood into a stand for hanging instruments. When finished, the work appeared to those who saw it as though of supernatural execution. And the prince of Lu asked him, saying, "What mystery is there in your art?"
>
> "No mystery, Your Highness," replied Ch'ing; "and yet there is something. When I am about to make such a stand, I guard against any diminution of my vital power. I first reduce my mind to absolute quiescence. Three days in this condition, and I become oblivious of any reward to be gained. Five days, and I become oblivious of any fame to be acquired. Seven days, and I become unconscious of my four limbs and my physical frame. Then, with no thought of the Court present in my mind, my skill becomes concentrated, and all disturbing elements from without are gone. I enter some mountain forest. I search for a suitable tree. It contains the form required, which is afterwards elaborated. I see the stand in my mind's eye, and then set to work. Otherwise, there is nothing. I bring my own natural capacity into relation with that of the wood. What was suspected to be of supernatural execution in my work was solely due to this." (pp. 110-111)

REFERENCES

Andrew, A. M. Autopoiesis and self-organization. *Journal of Cybernetics*, 1979, *9*, 359–367.

Ardrey, R. *The social contract.* New York: Atheneum, 1970.

Arnold, M. Stanzas from the Grande Chartreuse. In W. E. Buckler (Ed.), *The major Victorian poets: Tennyson, Browning, Arnold.* Boston: Houghton Mifflin, 1973. (Originally published, 1855.)

Ashby, W. R. *An introduction to cybernetics.* London: Chapman & Hall, 1956.

Auerswald, E. H. Families, change and the ecological perspective. In A. Ferber, M. Mendelsohn, & A. Napier (Eds.), *The book of family therapy.* Boston: Houghton Mifflin, 1973.

Bandler, R., & Grinder, J. *Frogs into princes: Neurolinguistic programming.* Moab, Utah: Real People Press, 1979.

Bateson, G. Language and psychotherapy—Frieda Fromm-Reichmann's last project. *Psychiatry*, 1958, *21*, 96–100. (a)

Bateson, G. *Naven* (2nd ed.). Stanford: Stanford University Press, 1958. (b)

Bateson, G. Psychiatric thinking: An epistemological approach. In J. Ruesch & G. Bateson, *Communication: The social matrix of psychiatry.* New York: W. W. Norton, 1968. (Originally published, 1951.)

Bateson, G. The cybernetics of "self": A theory of alcoholism. *Psychiatry*, 1971, *34*, 1–18.

Bateson, G. *Steps to an ecology of mind.* New York: Ballantine, 1972.

Bateson, G. Draft: Scattered thoughts for a conference on "broken power." *CoEvolution Quarterly*, 1974, *4*, 26–27.

Bateson, G. Some components of socialization for trance. *Ethos*, 1975, *3*, 143–155.

Bateson, G. Foreword: A formal approach to explicit, implicit and embodied ideas and to their forms of interaction. In C. Sluzki & D. Ransom (Eds.), *Double bind: The foundation of the communicational approach to the family.* New York: Grune & Stratton, 1976. (a)

Bateson, G. Comments on Haley's history. In C. Sluzki & D. Ransom (Eds.), *Double bind: The foundation of the communicational approach to the family.* New York: Grune & Stratton, 1976. (b)

Bateson, G. Personal communication, October 28, 1976. (c)

Bateson, G. Personal communication, October 29, 1976. (d)

Bateson, G. The thing of it is. In M. Katz, W. Marsh, & G. Thompson (Eds.), *Explo-*

rations of planetary culture at the Lindisfarne conferences: Earth's answer. New York: Harper & Row, 1977.

Bateson, G. The birth of a matrix or double bind and epistemology. In M. Berger (Ed.), Beyond the double bind. New York: Brunner/Mazel, 1978.

Bateson, G. Mind and nature: A necessary unity. New York: E. P. Dutton, 1979. (a)

Bateson, G. Personal communication, September 6, 1979. (b)

Bateson, G., & Brown, J. Caring and clarity. CoEvolution Quarterly, 1975, 7, 32-47.

Bateson, G., & Mead, M. For God's sake, Margaret. CoEvolution Quarterly, 1976, 10, 32-44.

Bateson, G., & Rieber, R. Mind and body: A dialogue. In R. Rieber (Ed.), Body and mind. New York: Academic Press, 1980.

Bateson, M. Our own metaphor: A personal account of a conference on the effects of conscious purpose on human adaptation. New York: Alfred A. Knopf, 1972.

Bateson, M. Daddy, can a scientist be wise? In J. Brockman (Ed.), About Bateson. New York: E. P. Dutton, 1977.

Berry, W. The unsettling of America. New York: Avon Books, 1977.

Bertalanffy, L. Robots, men and minds. New York: George Braziller, 1967.

Birdwhistell, R. Some meta-communicational thoughts about communicational studies. In J. Akin, A. Goldberg, G. Myers, & J. Stewart (Eds.), Language behavior. The Hague: Mouton, 1970.

Bloch, D. The future of family therapy. In M. Andolfi & I. Zwerling (Eds.), Dimensions of family therapy. New York: Guilford Press, 1980.

Boyd, D. Rolling thunder. New York: Dell, 1974.

Brand, S. Two cybernetic frontiers. New York: Random House, 1974.

Brand, S. Homeostasis. In K. Wilson (Ed.), The collected works of the Biological Computer Laboratory. Peoria, Ill.: Illinois Blueprint Corporation, 1976.

Bugental, J. Challenges of humanistic psychology. New York: McGraw-Hill, 1967.

Cadwallader, M. The cybernetic analysis of change in complex social organizations. American Journal of Sociology, 1959, 65, 154-157.

Carroll, L. Alice in wonderland (D. Gray, Ed.). New York: W. W. Norton, 1971. (Originally published, 1865.)

Castaneda, C. The teachings of don Juan: A Yaqui way of knowledge. New York: Ballantine, 1968.

Castaneda, C. A separate reality: Further conversations with don Juan. New York: Pocket Books, 1971.

Castaneda, C. Journey to Ixtlan: The lessons of don Juan. New York: Simon & Schuster, 1972.

Castaneda, C. Tales of power. New York: Simon & Schuster, 1974.

Collingwood, R. G. The principles of art. London: Oxford University Press, 1975. (Originally published, 1938.)

Cook, F. H. Hua-yen buddhism. University Park, Pa.: Pennsylvania State University Press, 1977.

de Mille, R. Castaneda's journey: The power and the allegory. Santa Barbara, Calif.: Capra Press, 1976.

de Mille, R. The don Juan papers: Further Castaneda controversies. Santa Barbara, Calif.: Ross-Erikson, 1980.

de Shazer, S. Personal communication, November 8, 1980.

de Shazer, S. *Patterns of brief family therapy: An ecosystemic approach*. New York: Guilford Press, 1982.

Dell, P. Beyond homeostasis: Toward a concept of coherence. *Family Process*, 1982, *21*, 21–41.

Dinesen, I. *Seven gothic tales*. New York: Vintage Books, 1961.

Eliot, T. S. *Four quartets*. New York: Harcourt, Brace & World, 1973. (Originally published, 1943.)

Evans, R. I. *R. D. Laing: The man and his ideas*. New York: E. P. Dutton, 1976.

Fry, W. The marital context of an anxiety syndrome. *Family Process*, 1962, *1*, 245–252.

Fry, W. *Sweet madness: A study of humor*. Palo Alto, Calif.: Pacific Books, 1963.

Goguen, J., & Varela, F. Systems and distinctions: Duality and complementarity. *International Journal of General Systems*, 1979, *5*, 31–43.

Gregory, R. *Eye and brain*. New York: McGraw-Hill, 1971.

Grinder, J., & Bandler, R. *The structure of magic* (Vol. 2). Palo Alto, Calif.: Science & Behavior Books, 1976.

Haley, J. (Ed.). *Advanced techniques of hypnosis and therapy: Selected papers of Milton H. Erickson, M.D.* New York: Grune & Stratton, 1967.

Haley, J. Family therapy: A radical change. In J. Haley (Ed.), *Changing families*. New York: Grune & Stratton, 1971.

Haley, J. Beginning and experienced family therapists. In A. Ferber, M. Mendelsohn, & A. Napier (Eds.), *The book of family therapy*. Boston: Houghton Mifflin, 1973. (a)

Haley, J. *Uncommon therapy*. New York: W. W. Norton, 1973. (b)

Haley, J. Development of a theory: A historical review of a research project. In C. Sluzki & D. Ransom (Eds.), *Double bind: The foundation of the communicational approach to the family*. New York: Grune & Stratton, 1976. (a)

Haley, J. *Problem-solving therapy*. San Francisco: Jossey-Bass, 1976. (b)

Haley, J. How to be a marriage therapist without knowing practically anything. *Journal of Marital and Family Therapy*, 1980, *6*, 385–391.

Hall, E. *Beyond culture*. New York: Anchor, 1977.

Hardin, G. *Stalking the wild taboo* (2nd ed.). Los Altos, Calif.: William Kaufmann, 1978.

Heims, S. Encounter of behavioral sciences with new machine–organism analogies in the 1940's. *Journal of the History of the Behavioral Sciences*, 1975, *11*, 368–373.

Heims, S. Gregory Bateson and the mathematicians: From interdisciplinary interaction to societal functions. *Journal of the History of the Behavioral Sciences*, 1977, *13*, 141–159.

Herrigel, E. *Zen in the art of archery*. New York: Vintage Books, 1971. (Originally published, 1953.)

Hoffman, L. Breaking the homeostatic cycle. In P. Guerin (Ed.), *Family therapy: Theory and practice*. New York: Gardner Press, 1976.

Hoffman, L. *Foundations of family therapy*. New York: Basic Books, 1981.

Howe, R., & von Foerster, H. Cybernetics at Illinois. *Forum*, 1974, *6*, 15–17.

Howe, R., & von Foerster, H. Introductory comments to Francisco Varela's calculus for self-reference. *International Journal of General Systems*, 1975, *2*, 1–3.

Illich, I. *Medical nemesis.* New York: Pantheon, 1976.

Jung, C. *The integration of personality.* New York: Rinehart, 1939.

Jung, C. *Memories, dreams, reflections* (A. Jaffé, Ed.). New York: Vintage Books, 1961. (*Septem sermones ad Mortuos* originally published, 1916.)

Keeney, B. *On paradigmatic change: Conversations with Gregory Bateson.* Unpublished manuscript, 1977.

Keeney, B. P. Ecosystemic epistemology: An alternative paradigm for diagnosis. *Family Process,* 1979, *18,* 117-129. (a)

Keeney, B. P. Glimpses of Gregory Bateson. *Pilgrimage: The Journal of Existential Psychology,* 1979, *7,* 17-44. (b)

Keeney, B. P. Pragmatics of family therapy. *Journal of Strategic and Systemic Therapies,* 1981, *1,* 44-53.

Keeney, B. P. What is an epistemology of family therapy? *Family Process,* 1982, *21,* 153-168.

Keith, D. V. Family therapy and lithium deficiency. *Journal of Marital and Family Therapy,* 1980, *6,* 49-53.

Keys, J. *Only two can play this game.* New York: Julian Press, 1972.

Konorski, T. The role of the central factors in differentiation. In R. Gerard & J. Duyff (Eds.), *Information processing in the nervous system.* Amsterdam: Excerpta Medica Foundation, 1962.

Korzybski, A. *Science and sanity* (4th ed.). Clinton, Mass.: Colonial Press, 1973.

Laing, R. D. *Knots.* New York: Vintage Books, 1970.

Land, E. *Process as reality.* Paper presented as Phi Beta Kappa Oration, Harvard University, June 14, 1977.

Lettvin, J. Y., Maturana, H., McCulloch, W., & Pitts, W. What the frog's eye tells the frog's brain. *Proceedings of the IRE,* 1959, *47,* 1940-1959.

Lilly, J., & Lilly, A. *The dyadic cyclone.* New York: Simon & Schuster, 1976.

Lipset, D. *Gregory Bateson: The legacy of a scientist.* Englewood Cliffs, N.J.: Prentice-Hall, 1980.

Lovelock, J. *Gaia: A new look at life on earth.* Oxford: Oxford University Press, 1979.

Lyons, L. Interview with Oscar Peterson. *Contemporary keyboard,* March 1978, pp. 30-33.

Madanes, C. *Strategic family therapy.* San Francisco: Jossey-Bass, 1981.

Maruyama, M. The second cybernetics: Deviation-amplifying mutual causal processes. In W. Buckley (Ed.), *Modern systems research for the behavioral scientist.* Chicago: Aldine, 1968.

Maslow, A. *The psychology of science.* Chicago: Henry Regnery, 1969.

Maslow, A. *Motivation and personality* (2nd ed.). New York: Harper & Row, 1970.

Maturana, H. Autopoiesis: Reproduction, heredity and evolution. In M. Zeleny (Ed.), *Autopoiesis, dissipative structures and spontaneous social orders.* Boulder, Colo.: Westview Press, 1980.

Maturana, H., & Varela, F. *Autopoiesis and cognition: The realization of the living.* Dordrecht, the Netherlands: D. Reidl, 1980.

May, R. Gregory Bateson and humanistic psychology. *Journal of Humanistic Psychology,* 1976, *16,* 33-51.

McCulloch, W. S. *Embodiments of mind.* Cambridge, Mass.: M.I.T. Press, 1965.

McCulloch, W. S. Lekton. In L. Thayer (Ed.), *Communication: Theory and research.* Springfield, Ill.: Charles C Thomas, 1967.

McCulloch, W. S., & Pitts, W. H. A logical calculus of the ideas immanent in nervous activity. *Bulletin of Mathematical Biophysics*, 1943, *5*, 115-133.

Mead, M. Cybernetics of cybernetics. In H. von Foerster, H. Peterson, J. White, & J. Russell (Eds.), *Purposive systems*. New York: Spartan Books, 1968.

Mihram, D., Mihram, G., & Nowakowska, M. The modern origins of the term "cybernetics." In *ACTES Proceedings of the 8th International Congress on Cybernetics*. Namur, Belgium: Association Internationale de Cybernétique, 1977.

Miller, G. A., Galanter, E., & Pribram, K. H. *Plans and the structure of behavior*. New York: Henry Holt, 1960.

Montalvo, B. Observations of two natural amnesias. *Family Process*, 1976, *15*, 333-342.

Neill, J., & Kniskern, D. (Eds.). *From psyche to system: The evolving therapy of Carl Whitaker*. New York: Guilford Press, 1982.

Noel, D. *Seeing Castaneda: Reactions to the "don Juan" writings of Carlos Castaneda*. New York: Capricorn, 1976.

Papert, S. Introduction. In W. S. McCulloch, *Embodiments of mind*. Cambridge, Mass.: M.I.T. Press, 1965.

Parsegian, V. *This cybernetic world of men, machines and earth systems*. New York: Anchor Books, 1973.

Pask, G. The meaning of cybernetics in the behavioral sciences. In J. Rose (Ed.), *Progress of cybernetics*. New York: Gordon & Breach, 1969.

Pask, G. *Conversation, cognition and learning*. Chicago: Aldine, 1973.

Pearce, J. *The crack in the cosmic egg: Challenging constructs of mind and reality*. New York: Pocket Books, 1974.

Perry, R. *The thought and character of William James*. Oxford: Oxford University Press, 1935.

Plato. The republic. In *The dialogues of Plato* (Vol. 1; B. Jowett, Trans.). New York: Random House, 1967.

Pritchard, R. Stabilized images on the retina. In R. Held & W. Richards (Eds.), *Perception: Mechanisms and models*. San Francisco: W. H. Freeman & Co., 1972.

Pryor, K. *Lads before the wind: Adventures in porpoise training*. New York: Harper & Row, 1975.

Puharich, A. *Beyond telepathy*. New York: Anchor, 1962.

Rabkin, R. *Strategic psychotherapy*. New York: Basic Books, 1977.

Rabkin, R. Who plays the pipes? *Family Process*, 1978, *17*, 485-488.

Rappaport, R. Sanctity and adaptation. *CoEvolution Quarterly*, 1974, *2*, 54-67.

Rosenblueth, A., Wiener, N., & Bigelow, J. Behavior, purpose and teleology. In W. Buckley (Ed.), *Modern systems research for the behavioral scientist*. Chicago: Aldine, 1968. (Originally published, 1943.)

Roszak, T. *Person/planet*. New York: Anchor Press, 1977.

Selvini-Palazzoli, M., Cecchin, G., Prata, G., & Boscolo, L. *Paradox and counterparadox*. New York: Jason Aronson, 1978.

Simon, H. In praise of muddleheaded anecdotalism. *Western Journal of Speech Communication*, 1978, *42*, 21-28.

Slater, P. *Earthwalk*. New York: Bantam Books, 1974.

Sluzki, C., & Beavin, J. Symmetry and complementarity: An operational definition and a typology of dyads. In P. Watzlawick & J. Weakland (Eds.), *The interactional view*. New York: W. W. Norton, 1977.

Snyder, G. Poetry, community and climax. *Field*, 1979, *20*, 21-36.

Spencer-Brown, G. *Probability and scientific inference*. London: Longmans, Green & Co., 1957.

Spencer-Brown, G. *Laws of form*. New York: Bantam, 1973.

Sullivan, H. S. *The interpersonal theory of psychiatry*. New York: W. W. Norton, 1953.

Szasz, T. *The myth of psychotherapy*. New York: Anchor Books, 1978.

Umpleby, S. *Some applications of cybernetics to social systems*. Unpublished doctoral dissertation, University of Illinois, 1975.

Varela, F. J. On observing natural systems. *CoEvolution Quarterly*, 1976, *10*, 26-31. (a)

Varela, F. J. Not one, not two. *CoEvolution Quarterly*, 1976, *11*, 62-67. (b)

Varela, F. J. On being autonomous: The lessons of natural history for systems theory. In G. J. Klir (Ed.), *Applied general systems research: Recent developments and trends*. New York: Plenum Press, 1978.

Varela, F. J. *Principles of biological autonomy*. New York: Elsevier North Holland, 1979.

Varela, F. J., & Maturana, H. R. Mechanism and biological explanation. *Philosophy of Science*, 1973, *39*, 378-382.

von Foerster, H. Logical structure of environment and its internal representation. In R. Eckerstrom (Ed.), *International design conference, Aspen 1962*. Zeeland, Mich.: Herman Miller, 1963.

von Foerster, H. Physics and anthropology. *Current Anthropology*, 1964, *5*, 330-331.

von Foerster, H. Review of *Embodiments of mind* by W. S. McCulloch. *Computer Studies in the Humanities and Verbal Behavior*, 1970, *3*, 111-116.

von Foerster, H. Computing in the semantic domain. *Annals of the New York Academy of Sciences*, 1971, *184*, 239-241.

von Foerster, H. Perception of the future and the future of perception. *Instructional Science*, 1972, *1*, 31-43.

von Foerster, H. Cybernetics of cybernetics (physiology of revolution). *The Cybernetician*, 1973, *3*, 30-32. (a)

von Foerster, H. On constructing a reality. In W. Preiser, *Environmental design research, II*. Stroudsburg, Pa.: Dowden, Hutchinson & Ross, 1973. (b)

von Foerster, H. *Ecological source book*. In K. Wilson (Ed.), *The collected works of the Biological Computer Laboratory*. Peoria, Ill.: Illinois Blueprint Corporation, 1976. (a)

von Foerster, H. An epistemology for living things. In K. Wilson (Ed.), *The collected works of the Biological Computer Laboratory*. Peoria, Ill.: Illinois Blueprint Corporation, 1976. (b)

von Foerster, H. The need of perception for the perception of needs. In K. Wilson (Ed.), *The collected works of the Biological Computer Laboratory*. Peoria,

Ill.: Illinois Blueprint Corporation, 1976. (c)

von Foerster, H. On where do we go from here? In K. Wilson (Ed.), *The collected works of the Biological Computer Laboratory.* Peoria, Ill.: Illinois Blueprint Corporation, 1976. (d)

von Foerster, H. *Self-fulfilling prophecies: Old and new.* Paper presented to the Third Annual Don D. Jackson Memorial Conference, San Francisco, 1978.

Von Neumann, J., & Morgenstern, O. *Theory of games and economic behavior.* Princeton: Princeton University Press, 1944.

Watts, A. *Psychotherapy east and west.* New York: Ballantine, 1961.

Watts, A. *Tao: The watercourse way.* New York: Pantheon, 1975.

Watzlawick, P. *How real is real?* New York: Random House, 1976.

Watzlawick, P., Beavin, J., & Jackson, D. *Pragmatics of human communication.* New York: W. W. Norton, 1967.

Watzlawick, P., & Coyne, J. Depression following stroke: Brief, problem-focused treatment. *Family Process,* 1980, *19,* 13-18.

Watzlawick, P., Weakland, J., & Fisch, R. *Change: Principles of problem formation and problem resolution.* New York: W. W. Norton, 1974.

Whitaker, C. Psychotherapy of the absurd. *Family Process,* 1975, *14,* 1-16.

Whitaker, C. On family therapy (Interview with Bruce Howe). *Pilgrimage: The Journal of Existential Psychology,* 1979, *7,* 107-114.

Whitehead, A. N. *Science and the modern world.* New York: Free Press, 1967. (Originally published, 1925.)

Whitehead, A. N., & Russell, B. *Principia mathematica.* Cambridge, England: Cambridge University Press, 1910.

Wiener, N. *The human use of human beings: Cybernetics and society* (2nd ed.). New York: Avon, 1967. (2nd edition originally published, 1954.)

Wiener, N. *Cybernetics: Or the control and communication in the animal and the machine* (2nd ed.). Cambridge, Mass.: M.I.T. Press, 1975. (2nd ed. originally published, 1954; 1st ed. originally published, 1948.)

Wilden, A., & Wilson, T. The double bind: Logic, magic and economics. In C. Sluzki & D. Ransom (Eds.), *Double bind: The foundation of the communicational approach to the family.* New York: Grune & Stratton, 1976.

Wilder-Mott, C., & Weakland, J. H. *Rigor and imagination.* New York: Praeger, 1981.

Wynne, L. C. On the anguish, and creative passions, of not escaping double binds. In C. Sluzki & D. Ransom (Eds.), *Double bind: The foundation of the communicational approach to the family.* New York: Grune & Stratton, 1976.

Wynne, L. C. *Structure and lineality in family therapy.* Unpublished manuscript, 1982.

Wynne, L. C., Ryckoff, I., Day, J., & Hirsch, S. Pseudo-mutuality in the family relations of schizophrenics. *Psychiatry,* 1958, *21,* 205-220.

Zieg, J. *A teaching seminar with Milton H. Erickson.* New York: Brunner/Mazel, 1980.

AUTHOR INDEX

SUBJECT INDEX